ANGEL
OF
DEATH
ROW

ANGEL OF DEATH ROW

MY LIFE AS A DEATH PENALTY
DEFENSE LAWYER

ANDREA D. LYON

PUBLISHING

New York

Angel of Death Row is based on true events; however, names, places, and other details have been changed for the sake of privacy.

Acknowledgments for photographs and illustrations: All photographs are from the author's personal collection. Court sketches of the author are used by kind permission of the artist, Andy Austin, and WLV-TV.

© 2010 Andrea D. Lyon
Published by Kaplan Publishing, a division of Kaplan, Inc.
1 Liberty Plaza, 24th Floor
New York, NY 10006

Library of Congress Cataloging-in-Publication Data
Lyon, Andrea D.
Angel of death row : my life as a death penalty defense lawyer / Andrea D. Lyon
; foreword by Alan M. Dershowitz.
  p. cm.
  ISBN 978-1-60714-434-2
1. Lyon, Andrea D. 2. Public defenders—Illinois—Chicago—Biography.
3. Capital punishment—Illinois. I. Title.
  KF373.L963A3 2009
  345.773'01--dc22
  [B]   2009023219

Printed in the United States of America

10 9 8 7 6 5 4 3 2 1

ISBN: 978-1-60714-434-2

Kaplan Publishing books are available at special quantity discounts to use for sales promotions, employee premiums, or educational purposes. For more information or to purchase books, please call the Simon & Schuster special sales department at 866-506-1949.

*To my family: my daughter, Samantha; my son, Will;
and my husband, Arnie. Also to my parents and siblings,
colleagues and friends.*

*But most of all, this book is for my clients,
who trusted me with their stories, and their lives.*

CONTENTS

FOREWORD

THERE IS CERTAINLY room for debate about whether nature or nurture plays a greater role in many aspects of human life, but it seems clear that zealous criminal defense attorneys are born to the task. Fighting the establishment is in their DNA. Defending the unpopular is inherent in their nature. It takes a certain amount of inborn contrariness to be the one person in the world whose job it is to stand up for those whom the vast majority of people want to see imprisoned or executed. It takes a firm resolve to join a profession where most of the time you lose, even when you put up a stronger case than your opponent. It takes an even rarer breed to be a death row lawyer in a nation, and at a time, when capital punishment is popular and death row lawyers are seen as obstructions to justice.

Andrea Lyon is truly of that rare breed. She was a defense attorney from birth, if not from within the womb. Her commitment to the downtrodden, to the abandoned, and to the despised, became evident at an early age. She was born to be an angel of death row, and a devil to those who see execution as a quick fix for the social ills of our age.

In fact, Lyon, the first woman to be lead counsel in a death penalty trial, has tried more than 130 murder cases, a third of which were potentially death cases. Of that number, 19 went to the penalty phase — where the jury or judge has to choose whether to put the defendant they have convicted to death — and she won all 19.

Lyon is also a storyteller par excellence. I can just imagine how compelling she must be in court, especially if she talks to her jurors and judges as she writes for her readers, with a high dose of common sense and a low tolerance for BS. Unlike some zealots of her radical generation, Lyon does not place cause over client. She believes that by defending her clients with zeal and professionalism, she is indeed serving the causes to which she has committed her life.

Despite the serious subject, Lyon has a sense of humor. She seems like she would be fun to be with (but not to argue against). She is confident but self-effacing. She takes her role, but not her persona, seriously. She is the kind of defense lawyer who makes those of us who teach young law students wish that more of them would devote at least a portion of their careers to defending those on death row or facing long imprisonment.

It is not an easy sell to the current generation of law students, who — even with the current recession — can expect to be paid multiples of what capital defenders and other public interest lawyers receive. The few Andrea Lyons out there, who are willing to sacrifice lifestyle in order to fulfill the mandate of the Sixth Amendment, cannot undo the scandal of how our society deliberately skews the criminal justice system against the indigent accused by underfunding defense lawyers, investigators, experts, and other resources essential to mounting an effective defense. Moreover, the civil practice is so much "cleaner" and "nicer" than the criminal practice. For today's crop of law students, it is far easier to explain to parents who have sunk their life savings into a legal education why you are representing a wealthy banker or corporation rather than an accused indigent rapist or murderer.

But as the accounts in this memoir show, there is no more exciting or rewarding (in the nonmaterial sense) practice of law than serving in the emergency ward of our justice system, where lives can be saved — or lost. I wish every student entering law school would read

Lyon's riveting stories, if for no other reason than to be exposed to alternate career choices than the standard corporate ones for which most automatically opt.

Lyon's story includes a groundbreaking moment that made national headlines. She writes of the decision by then Illinois governor George Ryan to free four innocent men and commute the death sentences for those remaining on death row in the state to life without parole. Critics of Governor Ryan's actions argued that it would have been enough simply to pardon those who were exonerated by newly discovered evidence. Why was it necessary to impose a moratorium on the execution of the guilty as well? This debate reminded me of a similar one about the famous biblical story of Abraham's argument with God concerning the sinners of Sodom, in which God agrees to save the entire city if a certain number of righteous people can be found in it.

God surely saw the flaw in Abraham's advocacy. He could have responded, "Look, Abraham. You accuse me of overgeneralizing — of sweeping away the righteous with the unrighteous. And you have a point. But you're guilty of the same thing: You are sweeping the wicked along with the righteous, and giving them a free ride. If I find fifty — or forty or even ten — righteous, I will spare them. You've convinced me of that. But why should I spare the wicked just because there happen to be fifty righteous people in their city?"

The answer lies in the fact that in the narrative, God is teaching Abraham how to create a legal system that strikes the appropriate balance between convicting too many innocent and acquitting too many guilty. Since human beings are never capable of distinguishing precisely between the guilty and the innocent, it would be unjust to destroy a group that might contain as many as fifty or even ten innocents. It might not be true of only one or two.

Since it is always possible that any substantial group of guilty people could include one or two innocents, selecting so low a number would make it impossible to construct a realistic system for convicting the guilty. But tolerating the conviction of as many as ten innocents would make any system of convicting the guilty unjust, or at least suspect. When the number of people on Illinois's death row who were freed because of their possible innocence reached double digits, the public began to express concern. Seemingly, the execution of one or two possibly innocent people was not sufficient to stimulate reconsideration of the death penalty, but once the number climbed beyond ten, even many death penalty advocates began to question whether the system was working fairly. The Anglo-American ratio — better ten guilty go free than even one innocent be wrongly convicted — is also somewhat arbitrary, but it, too, uses the number ten in attempting to strike the proper balance.

This biblical narrative has been particularly salient to criminal defense lawyers, like Lyon and me, who know that many of our clients are probably guilty of the crimes with which they are charged. We know this not because they tell us — very few confess to their lawyers. We know it as a statistical matter, since the vast majority of people charged with crime in America, and in other civilized countries, are guilty. Thank goodness for that! Imagine living in a country where the majority of people charged with crime were innocent! That might be true of Iraq, Iran, or China, but certainly not of the United States. So we can safely assume that our clients are no different from the statistical norm; a majority of them are probably guilty. (If anything, my appellate clients are more likely to be guilty than those of a typical trial lawyer, since my clients have already passed through the most significant check on prosecutorial error or abuse: the trial. And they have been found guilty. Some of them, of course, are innocent.)

But when private lawyers, unlike public defenders who do not have the luxury of choosing their clients, decide to take a case, we rarely know whether any particular client is among the guilty majority, the innocent minority, or somewhere in between. Were we to take the position, urged by many, that we represent only the innocent, we could probably take only a handful of cases. It is extremely rare to know for certain that a prospective client is innocent. We have our suspicions (which have turned out to be mistaken — both ways — on numerous occasions). But we do not have certainty.

We represent the guilty for several important reasons of principle. The first is that we cannot always distinguish between the guilty and the innocent. If it were the case that only those who appeared to be innocent could be represented by decent lawyers, many clients who were in fact innocent would remain unrepresented by competent lawyers with the ability to establish their innocence. We represent the "guilty," therefore, in order to prevent injustice to the innocent. This is in the tradition of the Sodom narrative, at least as I interpret it. It is analogous to the reason why God told Abraham that he would save the many guilty "for the sake" of the few innocents.

We also represent the guilty to ensure that the government is always challenged, that it never gets sloppy, lazy, or corrupt. If our legal system were ever permitted to act on the statistical assumption that the vast majority of defendants are guilty, prosecutors would grow less careful about whom they charged with crime, and the statistics might become reversed, as they have in some autocratic regimes.

It is always distressing when the guilty go free. But it is a price we must pay for ensuring that the innocent are only rarely convicted. That was one of the messages God was sending to Abraham when he agreed, as a matter of principle, that it is better for many guilty to go free (to be swept along with the few innocents) than for a significant number of innocents to be punished (to be swept along with the guilty). It is a difficult message that continues to confound, and to engender controversy, but it lies at the core of any civilized concept of justice.

Andrea Lyon and others who question authority and argue with the "gods" of our criminal justice system continue the great tradition of the biblical Abraham. Like Abraham, they often lose, but like Abraham, they provoke, challenge, confound — and keep the system honest. This conundrum existed in ancient times, and it exists now. Lyon's life — as a lawyer, a clinical professor, and a person — and her deep respect for her clients tell us why these questions continue to matter and, most important, why we should care about those whom society is all too ready to forget.

Alan M. Dershowitz

INTRODUCTION

My heart was about to pound right out of my chest. Walking up fourteen flights of stairs in the now-defunct Robert Taylor Homes on Chicago's South Side will do that to you, especially if you're wearing three-inch heels. But I knew the police eschewed the elevator, so I did, too. The stairwell was dark and smelled of urine, cigarettes, and something oddly, sickly sweet, but at least you could run up or down a stairway if you needed to get away from something or somebody. In an elevator, you are stuck.

I was in pursuit of a witness I had been chasing for months. His name was O.G., which stood for "Old Guy" but apparently had nothing to do with age, since this elusive witness couldn't have been more than twenty. My client's brother lived at the Taylor Homes, and I had told him to be on the lookout for O.G. I had already been to O.G.'s mother's house, his aunt's apartment, and his former workplace. I had left business cards and messages everywhere. O.G. was the one person who could corroborate my client's claim of self-defense. He had seen the events that led up to the shooting, and he knew my client had been backed into a corner. But O.G. was doing his damnedest to avoid me. He didn't want to testify. After all, the victim of the crime was a gangster disciple with a raft of brothers — of both the blood and gang variety.

My client's brother had called on a Friday afternoon after four o'clock.

"Miss Lyon?"

"Speaking."

"This here's Daron, Derrick's brother." He was talking softly, but I could understand him.

"Hi, Daron. You got news for me on o.g.?"

"Yup. He here at Taylor, seein' one of his girls. She live in fourteen-ten."

"Did you see him yourself?"

"Yup, he just went up there. He should be a while."

I nodded to myself. "Daron, good work. You go ahead and get out of there, so if I find him, he doesn't connect it with you. I'm on my way."

The problem was, late on a Friday afternoon, the Public Defender's Office had emptied out. Normally, we never interviewed a witness alone — partially because of the possibility of physical danger, but more important, in order to have someone to back up what the witness said if he later "remembered differently." But this time, I had no choice. If I didn't move quickly, o.g. might be long gone.

I grabbed my briefcase and dashed out to my vw, cursing my shoes as I went. I drove as fast as I dared to State Street and then south to the projects. After parking on the street, I handed a dollar to a big-eyed little boy to watch my car, promising him another two when I returned.

Finally, struggling to regain my breath after the climb, I stood in front of Apartment 1410. I knocked loudly. A tall, handsome, shirtless young man opened the door. He looked silently at me, and I knew he knew who I was.

"You best come in," he said, resigned. I walked into the front room.

"You just ain't gonna leave me alone, are you?" he asked.

"No," I said. "Derrick needs your evidence."

o.g. stepped back and looked at me appraisingly: a young white woman in a white cotton suit and purple blouse, with high heels on, clutching a briefcase and still breathless from a fourteen-floor hike up the stairs of an all-black housing project.

"You know why no one fucks with you here?" he asked, a hint of a smile on his lips. His girlfriend had slipped into the room and was staring at the two of us.

I smiled. I would bite. "No. Why?"

"'Cause they figure either you got a submachine gun in that case, or you crazy. An' they ain't interested in finding out which." I nodded appreciatively. I got my interview with O.G., and ultimately, Derrick was found not guilty.

FROM THE START of my career, I learned quickly that the facts don't arrive in three paragraphs at the start of a judicial opinion; you have to go find them. And if I had to do that alone, so be it.

When I became a member of Homicide Task Force in 1979, I became the first woman to serve as lead counsel on a death penalty case. In total, I have argued more than 130 homicide cases, all for clients who could not afford a lawyer. Many faced the possibility of execution. The greatest challenge an attorney can face is defending a convicted murderer against the death penalty. Nineteen times in my career, I have represented a client found guilty of capital murder. Nineteen times, I have argued for that individual's life to be spared. Nineteen times, I have succeeded.

The phrase "Angel of Death Row" was first applied to me in the headline of a *Chicago Tribune* feature in 1995. The reality is, I fear, that I am all too human. Rather than a benevolent apparition, I see myself as a sometimes cranky warrior standing at the intersection of life and death. My foe is a criminal justice system that, despite common belief, gives enormous advantage to the prosecution and stacks the cards according to wealth, race, and social status.

Nevertheless, some people will peg me as one of those slick defense attorneys who get killers "off" to roam the streets and kill again. That seems to be a popular conception of defense attorneys today. There used to be a place in mainstream American culture for the valiant defender: Perry Mason, E. G. Marshall's Lawrence Preston in *The Defenders*, Andy Griffith's *Matlock*, and, of course, the gentle and beloved Atticus Finch of *To Kill a Mockingbird*. These days, television is peopled with quirky homicide detectives, heroic prosecutors, and weasely defense lawyers. The criminal defender portrayed on today's crime shows is, at best, an anonymous, briefcase-toting suit who arrives in the interrogation room to whisk away the guilty client before he or she can confess. At worst, television defense attorneys ooze slime — educated, corrupt accomplices to those who prey on the innocent.

Yet here I am, proud to be a criminal defense attorney representing men and women accused of murder. I wrote this book to remind people of the essential importance of criminal defense in a free society. The work of defense needs doing, and it needs doing well. Someone has to stand up to the State and make it play by the rules, to assertively remind the State that the rules apply to it as well as to the rest of us.

I also want people to gain a better understanding of the death penalty: when it is sought, why it is sought, and why it is so difficult to defend against. The need for citizens to have an educated, nuanced view of capital punishment becomes increasingly urgent as a growing number of states choose to reexamine the death penalty at the same time that the practice continues unabated in other states. From April 2008, when the Supreme Court ruled that lethal injections were constitutional, to this writing, fifty-nine human beings have been executed in the United States.

My final reason for writing this book is to reveal the humanity that our criminal justice system so vigorously strives to deny. I have represented gang members, a serial rapist-murderer, a paranoid schizophrenic, battered and abused women, and battered and abused men. Some, indeed, committed the acts they were accused of, and some did not. But no matter what they did or did not do, I believe that every person I have defended is a human being of value. Some are terribly damaged; some lack even tenuous connections to reality. Each of their lives tells us about the ways in which individuals and institutions can go horribly astray, but they also reveal what remains human and noble in the midst of such waste. Even people facing the most horrendous prospects are still capable of caring about someone other than themselves. And even those who have demonstrated total indifference to the lives of others can change. Redemption is possible. As long as there is life, even if it is a life in prison with no chance of parole, there is hope for change. That's why I chose this career. That's why I'm still at it.

The stories in this book are true. The narrative has been derived from memory, trial notes, and in some cases, transcripts. I have used, with their gracious permission, the actual names of my family members, friends, and many of my colleagues. Nearly all names of clients, witnesses, judges, and prosecutors have been changed. I believed it important to protect the privacy of those individuals and their families as best I can, even though some readers, particularly those in the Chicago area, may recognize certain cases by their facts. Literary license has occasionally been applied. For example, if a conversation with a jail guard occurred during one case but applies equally to another, I have used the conversation where it furthers the narrative. I make no claim that any of these cases is "typical." They are the stories, among many others not included, that I feel driven to tell.

CHAPTER 1

Lyon for the Defense

THE CARPET WAS RED and the chairs were purple. The scanty shelves in my windowless office would never hold all my books. The warped metal desk drawers rarely opened without sticking. And the copy machine in the room next door wore an Out of Order sign, as it would regularly in the coming years. But as I lugged my cartons of books and files into the suite of shabby offices on that sweltering July day in 1979, my mind was focused on only one thing: I was in the Homicide Task Force. The twenty-six years of my life thus far had all been preparation for this moment.

I rarely had the time or inclination to turn on the television during that period. If I had, I might have caught *Charlie's Angels* jiggling as they chased down murderers, or *Police Woman* Angie Dickinson donning fishnet stockings in undercover pursuit of a perp. Even if one viewed these female characters generously as pioneers, they were not my role models. I wasn't planning on wearing bikinis or fishnet on the job, but that was the least of it. Angie and the Angels were in the business of putting people behind bars. I intended to devote myself to keeping them out. The Homicide Task Force that I was joining was part of the Public Defender's Office of Cook County, Illinois. What drove me was an unrelenting desire to champion the underdog.

My mother used to say she could tell that I had brought someone or something home with me by the particular tone in my voice when I called, "Mom?" upon entering the house. She would call back, "Four legs or two?" One day, I carried a raccoon in my arms, and on another day, a box of puppies.

"Andrea, how did this happen?"

"Mom, they followed me home."

"*Very* clever puppies," she said, shaking her head.

Once, I was accompanied by an old man I had found crying in the park.

"Honey, what were you thinking?"

"I was thinking he would like a peanut butter and jelly sandwich."

My grandmother regularly shook her head in dismay, doubting that I would ever become a lady. Of course, if being a lady meant eating corn on the cob kernel by kernel with a fork and knife, as Nana did, it wasn't high on my list of life goals.

Both my mother, Yolanda, and my father, Harvey, began their professional careers in academia, and taught at a number of colleges in several states. After I was born, my sisters, Rachel and Erica, followed, and then, when I was ten, my brother, Jon, was born. Dad found it difficult to support a growing family on a literature professor's salary, so he went into business, and we resettled in the Chicago area. My father made and lost two small fortunes as the head of his own companies, but then found his niche as a consultant on mergers and acquisitions. Mom remained a teacher, ultimately becoming chair of the Theatre Department at Roosevelt University.

We lived in a sprawling two-story house in Evanston, Illinois. The wood-frame house always needed a coat of paint, and in the winter, its noisy old radiators fluctuated between stone cold and suffocating heat. Nevertheless, trees, various dogs and cats, a porch swing, and a dinner bell, as well as plenty of children and laughter, made it a lovely place in which to grow up.

Typical of many well-educated, secular, liberal Jewish parents of the time, my mother and father naturally mixed their politics and philosophies into everyday life. We children were limited to three hours of television per week, and dinner table conversation was often dominated by discussion, and arguments, over local, national, and world events. The mealtime bans on singing and reading reflected our family's eccentricities. We sang all the time, especially on car trips, when we three sisters would fight over who got to sing soprano. And I read every minute I could, including walking to and from school. But we were not allowed those pleasures at the table. That left time for whining about the television rule or protesting a curfew or, later, pleading for use of the car, but there was room for real talk, too.

Despite the intellectual bent of my family life, like most kids, I wanted to be popular, sophisticated... *cool*. But I wasn't. Correcting my freshman English teacher's *Hamlet* quote on the first day of class was not a good way to start high school.

Then there was the matter of my size. At the age of ten, I began putting on extra weight. My great height came later, and suddenly. When I finished junior high, I was five foot four — nothing unusual. But by Christmas of my freshman year in high school, I had grown almost to my full height of six feet, nearly eight inches in six months, and had added the pounds to go with it. My size became a dominant fact of my life. Heavy kids get teased, isolated, and judged. They are subjected to fat-girl jokes. Their parents worry about them: "It's your *health* we're concerned about." True, perhaps, but not comforting. Being tall, as well — that makes it even worse. I was taller and smarter than most of the boys, hardly a formula for social success.

Those realities forced me to devise strategies to get by. I learned to make self-deprecating jokes about my size. I even used my writing skills to compensate. My P.E. teacher, who was working on a master's degree, was intelligent but a poor writer. I, on the other hand, couldn't seem to pass the mandatory fitness requirements. So we traded. I wrote papers from her research, and she coached, cajoled, and browbeat me into sitting up, pulling up, and climbing ropes. She earned her master's, and I passed gym.

Ultimately, the social stigma made me both tougher and more empathetic. I have been called many names, and I am not saying names don't smart. But I learned how to use that hurt to connect with the hurt that is in all of us, a capacity that has served me well with both clients and juries. One of my strongest skills as an advocate is the ability to listen to someone else and see into his world. To this day, my stature remains a key part of my identity. I was and am an outsider. Only now, I'm not *oh-poor-me*. I'm more *too-damn-bad-if-you-don't-like-it.*

But long before I learned to connect with homicide suspects, I found a way to feel a sense of belonging *as* an outsider: in political activism. Born in 1952, I came to consciousness during the civil rights era and came of age during the antiwar movement. I remember watching a television news report one day in which grainy black-and-white images showed young African-American men and women, carefully dressed in slacks, ties, and shirtwaists, marching in protest, and then helplessly fighting the spray of fire hoses turned on them. I didn't understand. Why should anyone have to take to the streets to say what I had been raised to believe: that we are all equal?

As I watched the televised mayhem, I reasoned it through. If the protesters believed they needed to march for equality, and if there were people who would hose down the marchers for speaking up, well, I had better speak up, too, because how else would I distinguish myself from the person wielding that hose? My desire to oppose injustice grew out of that news report. Thank goodness I hadn't already used up my television quota that week.

My high school years, from 1966 to 1970, were an opportune time to turn that abstract thinking into action. I joined in the political discussions that sprang up everywhere in those days, signed petitions, and eventually marched. I even joined a gospel music group called Spirit of Soul. I didn't mind singing Christian gospel songs. I was not a religious Jew, and I had always preferred Aretha Franklin to the Beatles. Spirit of Soul was intentionally racially diverse and performed concerts around the city wearing (*I am not kidding*) colorful dashikis.

My political companions became my friends, which gave me the confidence to socialize with others as well. My friends crossed all divisions of race, gender, religion... and rhythmic capability. When I refused to dance at a predominantly black party at the union hall, my friend Shirley dragged me to the bathroom, where a gaggle of laughing, fluid-hipped girls in miniskirts (which I wouldn't dare have worn) showed me how to move like they did. All my life, I have been grateful to those young ladies for teaching me to dance with a little bit of soul.

At Evanston Township High School, I led student protests over policies we thought racist, such as the academic tracking system that separated students too much by race, class, and even gender. One math teacher told me that girls didn't belong in honors math because we were "too emotional." Sometimes we radicalized students would simply walk out of class at a predetermined time to assemble on the grass outside, a sea of denim and T-shirts.

Once, my mother came to retrieve me after I had marshaled one such walkout and the school had called her in. She successfully talked the administration out of suspending me and smiled at everyone as we headed to the car, haranguing me *sotto voce* the whole time: "Must everything be a political statement with you, Andrea? Can't you just break curfew like a normal teenager?"

"*Mom*," I replied sanctimoniously, "all acts *are* political." Why she didn't kick me remains a mystery.

While finding my voice politically and my niche socially, I was formulating a grand plan for my future, which I announced at the dinner table when I was just fifteen. Over Caesar salad and meat loaf, I declared that I wanted to be a lawyer.

My dad looked up from his meat loaf. "A what?" he asked.

"A lawyer," I replied. "The only way to change this country is by reforming it from the inside." I wanted to help people stand up against the might of government, which I saw as corrupt and oppressive. I was serenely confident that I could change society for the better, apparently on my own.

"Oh, please!" my sister Erica interrupted. "You just want to show off."

Well, of course. Part of the law's appeal was its potential as a "bully pulpit," and I liked to speak in public.

My parents neither laughed nor attempted to discourage me, for which I give them credit. On the other hand, I don't think they realized how serious I was. They may have objected if they could have seen into the future: their bright, spunky Andrea traipsing up fourteen flights of stairs at the Robert Taylor Projects, in high heels, to investigate a murder.

But just as they might not have grasped the seriousness of my intent, I was clueless about the difficulty of my mission. I had no idea how few girls set their sights on the law. In 1967, fewer than 5 percent of American attorneys were women. Today, that figure exceeds 30 percent, and female students slightly outnumber male students in most law schools. One adult relative fondly chided me that I couldn't become a lawyer because "all women lawyers are dykes." I wasn't sure what a dyke was, but I wasn't going to let it stop me. Every major decision I have made since then has supported the life plan I began designing at the age of fifteen.

My father and mother had attended Harvard and Radcliff, respectively. I think it's safe to say they expected me to follow a similar path. After all, when a new sidewalk was installed in our backyard, someone playfully wrote, "Veritas — to hell with Yale" in the wet cement. But after my immersion in soul music and protest marches, the Ivy League did not entice me. In the fall of 1970, with my parents' disappointed acquiescence, I headed off to Livingston College at New Jersey's Rutgers University. Livingston had opened just a year earlier as an intentionally diverse, nontraditional residential college — Rutgers's response to the turmoil of the 1960s.

When I arrived that first September, Livingston was still "under construction." There were no grassy quads yet, but a lot of red mud to muck through between dormitory, classrooms, and cafeteria. The college was feeling its way politically, too. A group of radical black students, for example, declaring that integration was a trap, demanded their own dormitory — and got it. By then, I had found a tight circle of multiracial, multiethnic friends. We responded to the black separatists by asking for and receiving permission to set up our own, deliberately integrated dorm: the Martin Luther King House. King House was so successful that a second, similar residence choice was offered the following year.

Livingston offered plenty of opportunities to satisfy my thirst for political activity, although after National Guardsmen killed four students during a Kent State University demonstration in 1970, the antiwar activities at my college were more likely to feature panel discussions than street protests.

Almost everyone around me was drinking, smoking pot, and ingesting heavier stuff. I disdained the pressure to join in. Perhaps I was being oppositional, or I may have been afraid. There are addicts in my family. I did not want to become like them, of course, but I didn't consciously abstain for this reason. Refusing to do drugs was my way of defining myself. I could dance as wildly as the drunkest person, laugh as much as the ones passing the joint around…and I would remember it all the next day.

As for academics, I chose political science and economics for a double major, and then added minors in urban planning and philosophy, greedy to learn quickly as much as I could about the world, as I was in a hurry to save it. Ah, what hubris. By taking grueling course loads, I graduated in three years. My intention to go to law school had never wavered. Both Georgetown Law and the Antioch School of Law, also in Washington, D.C., offered me a place. Antioch, like Livingston College, was a new school, the brainchild of Yale graduates Jean and Edgar Cahn. The Cahns envisioned a different kind of law school, heavy on hands-on experience and committed to turning out public interest lawyers. I chose Antioch and never regretted it.

At the age of twenty, I was the youngest person there. Antioch attracted a more diverse student body than most law schools. Many of its students had worked at other professions before choosing law, and most had chosen it for political reasons. My fellow students were grown-ups; I was not. For example, I didn't know that toilet paper didn't come with an apartment. Making friends and adjusting to Washington therefore proved more difficult than the transition to Livingston had been. Nevertheless, those years, which saw the Watergate hearings and

President Nixon's resignation, were a heady time to be living in D.C. Despite our heavy workload, my classmates and I would often find ourselves glued to the televised proceedings of the Senate Watergate Committee and the House impeachment hearings. The arrogance of our so-called leaders amazed us, and we were eager to get out in the world and do something about it.

At Antioch, students were put to work in the legal clinic after only three months of classes. I represented low-income people in landlord-tenant disputes, worked on a gender discrimination suit, defended juveniles against criminal charges, and represented young people needing protection from their own parents. With those rich and varied experiences under my belt, I gained a solid idea of what I liked, what I was good at, and what, for the sake of all concerned, I should stay far away from out in the real world.

Yet, the experience that most shaped the lawyer I am today had nothing to do with a legal case. Antioch's deans reasoned that since students were serving a poor population, we should understand that community. They determined that each student should live with a poor family for two weeks. I was sent to live with Delores "Dee" Scales and her family. Dee was a widow with three sons and a daughter, who herself had two children. Dee's late husband, the father of two of her children, had killed himself in front of her — had just picked up a gun and put it to his head. Dee never explained why, and I did not ask. All three generations were crowded into a tiny house on 5th Street Northwest. Although there was hardly room for an extra person, Dee signed up for the program for the little money it provided, to supplement the Social Security checks her family lived on.

When I knocked on the door of the brick row house in the "wrong" part of Northwest D.C., Dee, a plump woman about forty years old, let me in. Although she was expecting me, her manner was reserved, bordering on suspicious. I was nervous, myself, but I knew the basics of being a good guest: you bring something to eat, and you help with the dishes. Dee and I made awkward conversation as I set down my bag of groceries in the kitchen.

I had noticed a stereo system as we walked through the living room, and since I had just that day bought a forty-five of the Isley Brothers' "That Lady," I asked if I could play my new record. Dee assented, but as she told me later, she mentally prepared herself for the rock music she expected a twenty-year-old white girl in 1973 to listen to. When the smooth tones of the Isley Brothers floated out of the speakers, Dee began to reconsider; maybe there was something to me beyond a stereotype.

But when I returned to the kitchen to unpack the groceries I had brought, her suspicions flared anew.

"Why did you bring food?" she asked. "Did you think I wouldn't have nothin' in my kitchen?"

"No, but you know, Mrs. Scales, I eat a lot, so thought I should contribute. Did I bring the wrong things?" Of course, the truth was, I had worried that there might not be enough. I emptied out bread and tuna, mayonnaise, lettuce, and tomatoes from the bag.

Dee harrumphed at me. "No, I like tuna." Then she smiled, dimples flashing, and I saw how pretty she was. "But I like Miracle Whip, not mayonnaise." I hate Miracle Whip.

"I'll remember next time."

"So, how come you in law school?" she asked. I tried to explain — about politics, and wanting to make the world a better place. God, I was so *earnest*. Dee looked at me with wariness, and perhaps a tinge of interest.

Yet when I finished my ingenuous recitation of my plans for improving society, she had only one question: "You got a boyfriend?"

Perfectly content to shift gears, I replied, "I did. But we broke up. Probably it's for the best." I had been seeing a guy in New Jersey who was charming and fun, but also manipulative and going exactly nowhere with his life. When law school intervened to whisk me away, I had heaved a big sigh of relief.

Now I asked Dee, "Why, are you trying to fix me up?"

Now Dee laughed easily. "Nope." She got up and began taking out things for dinner. "Here," she said, handing me an onion and a knife. "Chop this up. And I mean chop it *fine*."

We cooked and chatted and laughed the rest of the afternoon. One by one and two by two, the other six members of the household arrived, and I was introduced to them. We all sat down to a noisy dinner together, not unlike the ones I had grown up with in Evanston. Later, as I was going to sleep, I thought to myself, perhaps with some surprise, I am happy here.

As Dee explained later, I passed the test. She had determined that I was not looking down on her. I was accepting her family as it was, and trying to find my place within it. As for me, I felt lucky to know them. Maybe it was because they were so openly affectionate with one another, like my own family, yet so direct with one another when they had a beef, unlike my family. And there was so much laughter. Ten-year-old Mikey would make me laugh until I ached. He would laugh so hard himself that he would cry and his little round belly would shake.

I lived with Dee and her family for only two weeks, but really, I never completely left. During the rest of my time at Antioch, I drove to Dee's house once or twice a week to share a meal or go out with the family. I helped Mikey with homework and encouraged his older brother, Rusty, when he decided to join the Marines. To my pleasure, Dee began introducing me as her goddaughter. She had survived years of trying circumstances with a greatness of heart intact. Everyone's troubles were hers; every child who needed a meal or a bed ended up at her house. On the day that my mother called to tell me that she and my father were divorcing, it was to the house on 5th Street that I immediately headed, sobbing as I drove. I had known my parents' marriage was troubled. On some level, I had even known the split was coming. Nevertheless, the reality hit me hard, and it was to Dee that I brought my grief.

When I graduated from Antioch, Dee threw me a party, with basketsful of the Maryland blue crabs that I love. In an impromptu speech, punctuated with irreverent hooting from the audience and multiple toasts, I thanked Dee for her support during law school, and for the home away from home she had shared with me. I reminisced about her cooking, which was good for my soul if not my hips, and about the time she had embarrassed me by shouting across a store that she had found the "big butt" jeans I was looking for. I had turned bright red... but the jeans fit.

I left Washington soon after, but we stayed in touch. I felt the first flush of grown-up pride when I helped Dee with a HUD application and some of the down payment for a bigger and better house. But, sadly, Dee's vulnerability of heart was not just a metaphor for kindness. One day, five years after I left Washington, that big heart just stopped. I was scheduled to litigate a motion the following day. In shock and grief, I called my co-counsel, asking him to step in for me and get a continuance so I could leave immediately for D.C. I needed to thank Dee one last time.

In the summer of 1976, law school was behind me, but I had no job and no idea what to do about it. I considered staying in Washington and taking the D.C. bar exam, but I opted for the Illinois exam instead. Frankly, I was broke, so living with my mother in Evanston was an attractive option.

While preparing for the bar, though, I needed to begin my job search. Graduating from law school does not automatically hook one into the legal world. Many law students have family or friends well situated in the profession; I did not. My unconventional alma mater and my age, just twenty-three, added to the challenge. And, oh yes, there was the fact that I was female. Few women were established in the legal profession in 1976. Even fewer worked in criminal defense. At Antioch, I had found that I was best suited to civil rights and criminal defense. Both allowed me to help individuals and to protest against practices and institutions most in need of reform. That was what I *wanted*. But at that point, what I *needed* was simply a job.

The way opened up almost by accident. I decided to apply to the Cook County Public Defender's Office, which represents any indigent people in the county who are accused of a crime. Its lawyers are overburdened with cases, but their work is vital, both to the people they represent and to the system that requires checks on its excesses. In 1976, James Doherty was the Public Defender of Cook County, but his assistant vetted all applicants. From my point of view, I was smart, worked hard, had experience in a criminal defense clinic, and was sufficiently idealistic to accept the pittance the position was likely to pay. I should at least get an interview, right? Knowing what I know now, I laugh at my naïveté. Political patronage plays a substantial role in hiring for those positions. If my legal connections were paltry, my political connections were nonexistent.

Nevertheless, early one afternoon in August, I took the L downtown to the Richard J. Daley Center, résumé in hand. I was wearing my best job-hunting outfit, a green print sundress that I attempted to make more businesslike with an ill-matching green blazer. The day was hot, the L not air-conditioned, and I was nervous. I was directed to take my résumé to the assistant's office on the fourth floor.

"Can I help you?" a sprightly young lady at the reception desk asked.

"Um, hi. I'm here to apply for a job with the Public Defender's Office. I was told downstairs that my application should go to Mr. Doherty's first assistant?" The receptionist confirmed this, but told me that both the assistant and the secretary were out.

"Hmm," I said. "I really don't want to just leave this on someone's desk, you know what I mean?" The receptionist smiled and nodded. She knew that if I did, my labored-over résumé would likely end up in tomorrow's trash.

"Is there someone else I can speak with?"

"Mr. Doherty's secretary might be in. Miss Kelly. Maybe she could take care of it for you."

I made my way to Miss Kelly's office but she was out as well. I was standing there, not sure what to do, when a ruddy bear of a man emerged from the inner office: Jim Doherty himself.

"Can I help you?" he asked. I gulped. This was the interview I was trying to get. I knew I should jump at the opportunity.

"Mr. Doherty?" He nodded. "My name is Andrea Lyon, and I am applying to work in your office." I could feel the sweat running down my back, but I looked him right in the eyes, hoping my voice wasn't quavering. "I think it would be to your advantage to talk to me." That just popped out. I was standing there not knowing if I had sunk my own ship when I heard what would be the first of many irresistible belly laughs from Cook County's public defender.

"To my advantage, huh?" He stepped back into his office and gestured broadly. "Come on in."

In addition to the usual desk and bookshelves, the large office held a couch, two upholstered chairs, and a coffee table. On a separate table, with two chairs facing each other, was a chess set. Mr. Doherty gestured for me to sit, still chuckling at my temerity.

"So, why is it to my advantage to talk to you?" he asked. I told him that I was smart, organized, hardworking, and fiercely dedicated to clients and their constitutional rights. At the same time, I kept glancing at the chess set. One gamble had paid off; why not another one?

I pointed at the chess set. "So, Mr. Doherty, do you play, or is that for show?" My father had taught me chess, and he was so much better than I was that I had not been able to develop my offensive game. But I was a decent defensive player. I could hold my own, I thought, and I was trying so hard to make a good impression.

Doherty looked at me and smiled — a spider-to-the-fly kind of smile. Uh-oh. "Is that a challenge?" he asked.

"You bet," I replied. I didn't expect him to take time for a game, but I learned later that chess was his way of relaxing and transitioning from one piece of work to another. He loved it. So we played. Jim was an excellent, if undisciplined, player. For the only time in all the games we would play over the years, I beat him.

After the game, I thanked him for his time and prepared to leave. An Evanston neighbor had arranged for me to have an interview with a downtown law firm. I knew I had no chance of getting hired, since I hadn't gone to Harvard or Yale and was a woman besides, but I thought I should at least try. I explained to Mr. Doherty about the interview.

"Do you want to work for some big firm?" he asked, incredulous.

"Not really. I want to work for you. But I need a job, so I'm going to the interview." I must have sounded forlorn.

I left my résumé with him, and did my best at the law firm interview, which was clearly being conducted merely as a favor to our neighbor. Back home, sitting at the kitchen table, I was about to tell my mother about my day when the phone rang.

"May I speak to Andrea Lyon?"

"Speaking."

"This is Jim Doherty. You start Monday."

I called my father to give him the good news, and to thank him for teaching me chess.

My first assignment in the Public Defender's Office was to the Appeals Division. I was disappointed. I wanted to be trying cases, not writing about ones that had already been lost. The Appeals Division is a research and writing assignment: you get assigned the case of a client who lost at trial, you read the transcript and look for errors in the record that occurred at trial and research the law and statutes, and then write a brief to the higher court, usually arguing why the defendant should receive a new trial.

But Appeals turned out to be an unexpected gem of a job. I had to learn a lot of Illinois law fast, and I grew adept at spotting relevant legal issues. I gnawed over the many opportunities I perceived that the original trial lawyers had failed to take advantage of. The law doesn't let the defense raise an issue on appeal if the defense didn't raise the same issue during the original trial, giving the original trial court the opportunity to fix what was wrong. For example, if the defense doesn't object at trial to a piece of evidence improperly obtained, and then loses the case, no complaint about that evidence can be made to a higher court. There are a few exceptions, but believe me, they are rare. I vowed that I would never make that kind of mistake when my turn came as a trial lawyer. I would "dog the record," that is, file and fight for every appropriate motion and object on any plausible justification.

In other words, if there were grounds to object, I would, and even if the law wasn't where I thought it should be yet, I would object anyway, sometimes in a written motion, sometimes in open court. After all, someone has to be the first to say something. If I didn't succeed at trial, my client would then have the chance to raise those issues down the line. I am certain my experience in the Appeals Division made me a better trial lawyer. I am also sure that certain prosecutors and judges would say it made me a pain in the ass.

When I had been in the Appeals Division a little less than a year, I met Bill Murphy, an encounter that changed my life. My task at the time was to write the appeal in a notorious case that Murphy had tried. His co-counsel, referred to as the "second chair," had been a young attorney with a big swagger. The two defendants in the case were "generals" in the Chicago street gang called El Rukns. They had been acquitted of a grisly murder but convicted of a home invasion and rape. I was astounded at the extent of prosecutorial misconduct I saw in the record, but wondered if I might not be missing the larger context. For example, the prosecutor had referred to the defendants as "predatory apes," and to their lawyers as "slick dealers in deception."

So I called Bill Murphy to ask to meet with him about the case. Bill later told me that my phone call immediately tipped him off that I was "different." Most appellate lawyers simply work from the record. They don't go to the prison to see their clients, or talk to the trial attorneys, or spend time with their clients' families. I don't understand that. Why wouldn't an attorney want to know the person he or she is representing?

So one October day in 1977, I went to meet Bill at his office. Bill Murphy is a football-playing, tough-talking man's man. He emits a constant restless energy. But what I focused on that day was not his demeanor but the sign on the front door: Homicide Task Force. I had never heard of such a division within the Public Defender's Office, so I asked him what it was.

"It's where the best trial lawyers and the real troublemakers end up," he replied with a grin.

That got my attention.

"Well, you know that the Public Defender trial attorneys are assigned by courtroom, right?" he asked. I nodded. He continued: "So the defendant sees one lawyer for the preliminary hearing, another one at arraignment, then maybe two or more assigned to the felony court he ends up in."

I had known that, but had not considered how bad the system was for the accused. This meant that no one lawyer would get to know him or his case well. And being handed off over and over again couldn't possibly engender trust in each succeeding lawyer, no matter how good each one was. I said as much to Bill. He leaned forward, interest quickening on his face.

"No, it isn't good at all. So I decided to experiment with murder cases — death penalty and regular ones — to set up a unit that would take the case from the preliminary hearing on. Follow it the whole way through."

"How did you convince the powers that be to let you do it?" I asked.

"Well, number one, I'm a troublemaker. Number two, now that the death penalty is back, we have to look like we're doing something in response." Just months earlier, Illinois had reinstated its new, "improved" death penalty, five years after the u.s. Supreme Court had voided all the states' capital punishment laws. "So I made a deal," Bill continued. "In exchange for being able to organize and run this unit, I would stay out of the rest of the politics. Now other troublemakers — you know, such as appellate lawyers who don't think the trial lawyers are stupid, for instance, who come and talk to us — well, if they're good enough, they can end up here."

"No pussies, though," said a voice behind me.

Bill's assistant on the case I had come to talk about had just walked in. Mr. Second Chair was blond and good looking, although not as good looking as he thought. A smile accompanied his comment, but I got the impression he meant it.

"There are no women in the unit?" I asked Bill, not looking at the other attorney.

"Nope," Bill said. "We haven't found one good enough, tough enough, to handle it. We let one in, but she lasted only a couple of months, so we won't make that mistake again." This caught me off guard. I thought Bill had implied that I was the right sort of person for this unit, but now he appeared to be agreeing with his chauvinistic assistant.

"Right," the younger man said, smirking. He was still standing over me. "It's tough work. You gotta be able to handle the streets, the clients, the pressure. Most *guys* can't handle it, let alone a girl."

This was not a challenge I was going to let pass. I smiled sweetly at him and rose from the chair. My six-foot, more-than-two-hundred-pound frame forced the shorter attorney to back up a step. "Maybe you just picked the wrong 'girl.'" I let that sink in for a moment and then took my chair again and turned to Bill. "Mr. Murphy, can we talk about the case now? Or do I have to listen to more 'mine is bigger than yours' from your friend here?"

There was a silence, and then they both hooted with laughter. "Maybe we *did* pick the wrong girl," Bill said.

We spent the rest of the time discussing the case. But when I left, my mind was as unalterably made up as it had been when I decided at age fifteen to become a lawyer. My future was in the Homicide Task Force.

Not long after I made up my mind, the arrogant Mr. Second Chair went into private practice. He soon became addicted to the fast life, as well as to cocaine, and began to serve as something more than a lawyer for some of Chicago's infamous street gangs. He was indicted on federal racketeering charges and served prison time.

For almost two years, I badgered Bill about putting me on the task force. I offered to help with motions and to translate. My Spanish is nearly fluent, although I can use only two grammatical tenses. I worked as hard as I knew how at my job in Appeals and, later, in the preliminary hearing division and then the felony trial division. Even while yearning to get on the task force, I harbored some reservations about working homicides. I wasn't sure how I would react to blood spatter and autopsies and clients who had committed vile acts. What would it be like, looking at the families of their victims? I knew that representing those charged with murder would not make me popular. But I believed, and still believe, that every person amounts to more than the worst thing he or she has ever done. And I try, very hard, to presume innocence. I knew I would learn from the work, from judges, colleagues, and even from my opposition. What I didn't realize was how much I would learn from my clients.

Finally, Bill relented. In July 1979, I joined the twenty lawyers of the Cook County Public Defender's Homicide Task Force. As I unpacked boxes on top of my white metal desk in my new windowless office, I knew this was where I belonged, where I would fight, scream, curse, cry, and, I hoped, make a difference.

CHAPTER 2

Enough Pain to Go Around

M OST OF THE task force members had welcomed my arrival. Most, but not all. Some sneered at me for being anal-retentive. My files were organized and indexed, and I had hung pictures on the walls. Everything was just so. But most viewed the fact that I spoke Spanish and liked to write as plusses. I also think my plus *size* impressed them, as it had impressed Murphy's second chair. I looked like I could hold my own.

On the other hand, a few days after I began work with the task force, I returned from court to find someone had taped autopsy photographs of an obviously dead, naked woman to my office walls. I walked into the central area of our offices, where the secretaries sat, and loudly proclaimed, "Okay, someone has put pictures of *his girl-friend* up in my office. I am going to get some coffee and when I come back, I am sure whoever it was will have taken his pictures back." When I returned, the offensive photos were gone.

I wasn't easily deterred. I wanted to be Atticus Finch. I wanted to exonerate the innocent and expose corruption in the system to the fond applause of an admiring public. There was only one problem. The venerable attorney of *To Kill a Mockingbird* lost his famous case. Actually, that wasn't the only problem. I soon discovered that the cases I would try were rarely about absolute guilt versus absolute innocence. Most of the time, the question needing to be answered was not *"Did* the accused kill?" but *"Why* did the accused kill?" This was not the picture I had in mind in my original, romanticized view of the life of a public defender.

One of the first murder cases I tried, and the first in which I took the lead, was the defense of Charlotte Lyman. Charlotte was what we would now commonly refer to as a battered woman. This was 1979, though, a year before the concept was popularized in *The Burning Bed*, a nonfiction account of an abused Michigan housewife who set her husband's bed on fire while he was sleeping, and five years before the television movie version starring Farrah Fawcett.

I met Charlotte, who was charged with killing her husband, Mike, at the Preliminary Hearing Court after being assigned to her case with another, more senior attorney. Charlotte was small, with a chocolate complexion and dimples. I could tell she had been pretty when she was younger, before all the pain had settled on her face. After explaining what would happen in the hearing, I told her that I would come to the jail to see her within a few days. I never felt comfortable, I explained, trying to have a real conversation with someone in a court lockup, where privacy was nonexistent. I asked if she needed me to get in touch with family members. Perhaps they didn't know where she was? She shook her head sadly. Everyone knew where she was, she said.

Two days later, I picked up Charlotte's meager file, which contained only the arrest sheet and preliminary complaint, and headed over to the women's division of Cook County Jail. I was nervous — not about going to the jail, which I had been doing for three years by now, but because the senior attorney on this case had told me that I could be first chair. He figured this was an easy case: wife kills husband; he probably had it coming; plea it for a lesser offense; skip the trial. I wasn't totally naïve; I knew that I was going to do the lion's share of the work and that's why I was being allowed to take the lead. Still, it was an opportunity to show "the boys" at the task force that I was just as good and just as tough as they were, that it hadn't been a mistake to integrate the force with a "pussy." This was going to be the first task force case with a woman at the lead, so a lot was riding on it. Not just for my client, but for me, too.

As I walked over to the women's section of the jail, I admit, ignoble as it may have been, I wasn't really thinking about my client; I was thinking about myself. I have always found women's jails and prisons harder to visit than men's. I can more easily see myself in another woman, and under these circumstances, that's rarely comfortable. For women as desperate as these, the civilized veneer easily slides away, and what I find in their exposed faces shows me more than maybe I want to know. In my female chauvinism, I often assume that women are better than men. And of course, we aren't. That became evident as I learned more about, and from, Charlotte Lyman.

Division Three, the women's division of Cook County Jail, sits directly south of the courthouse at 26th Street and California Avenue, on the West Side of Chicago. The neighborhood is barren of anything but the criminal justice system: courthouse, administration building, and a slew of pretrial detention centers, otherwise known as jails. Every person you see on the street is part of the system or is involved in a case. Since that time, there have been attempts to pretty up the area: a fountain here, some plants there. Back then, no one was even pretending.

Inside Division Three, the linoleum floors yielded hints of an indeterminate design that had at one time contained the color yellow. I think. It smelled of Lysol, yet never quite clean. Behind the check-in desk, the guards sat on stools. On the desk were two phones, visitor sign-in books, and a layer of grime that no amount of cleaning — done by inmates — could combat. I quickly learned not to lean on the counter if I was wearing anything I cared about; it would end up with a greasy film hard to get out even if I was talented in the laundry room, which I wasn't.

A fog of indolence settles on places such as county jails. Formerly cordial, motivated people become sluggish, suspicious, and cynical. When you visit, you are disrupting the guard's attention. This is true even though it is the guard's job to handle inmate visits. This person will look for any reason not to let you in to see your client: he'll reject your identification or force you to walk back to your office to get rid of an offending pen (one day, "the pen *has* to be clear" and the next day, "your pen *can't* be clear"). Even if you call ahead for the commander to approve your visit, delay and dispute are inevitable.

You have to learn how to roll with it. First, it's important never to appear impatient. I always bring a file or the latest case law to read. Then, if I have downtime, such as while the jail guard is "looking me up in the system," which might happen at a maddeningly slow, one-fingered-typing rate, I am using my time and not getting worked up. Second, there is a certain banter that greases the way with some guards. It requires knowing something about sports (fortunately, not much), the local news, and, with women guards, fashion. As my friends will tell you, I am challenged in the fashion department, so instead of parading my savvy, I let myself be a target for guidance. Given my height and "curvy" stature, I prove something of a challenge. One female guard surveyed my outfit and tactfully inquired, "Don't you think that might be a lot of *red*?" Finally, it is important to remember that sometimes the officious junior-high-school hall monitor grows up and continues on that same career path — and there will be no pleasing him. So I show my ID as many times as I am asked, step out of my shoes, empty my pockets, and smile the whole time.

Having run the Division Three gauntlet that day, I arrived in the second-floor visiting room. The space was small and windowless, except for the wired-glass opening in the door. The table was metal, the chairs molded plastic, and the lighting fluorescent and unflattering. I read while I waited for the guard to bring in my new client, and looked up when I heard the door open. I stood and offered my hand.

"Ms. Lyman?"

"Yes." Her voice was soft, unobtrusive. She didn't take my hand, but sat as I turned the proffered handshake into a gesture to take a seat.

"We met for a brief moment in court the other day. I am the lawyer from the Public Defender's Office assigned to represent you." I had learned to say I was a lawyer right away. There is a widespread belief that public defenders aren't really lawyers.

"I remember."

"Well, I'm here to talk with you about your case, so I can start working for you." Charlotte smiled at that. It was a sad, I-don't-believe-you smile. I had seen it before; it was the smile that comes from having been lied to, consistently, by everyone with any power, all of your life. It was the smile of the poor. With a more street-tough client, I might have tried confronting that distrust, but Charlotte looked so vulnerable that I hesitated. That I was only twenty-seven (and looked even younger with my long hair hanging down my back), worked for the Public Defender's Office, and was female didn't help. None of this inspired confidence in someone caught in the system. And even though Charlotte had no criminal record, she would know to worry. Virtually any black person growing up in the United States believes that *justice* isn't a word that necessarily applies to him, and most African-American families have experience with a family member being "in the system," whether deserved or not.

"Does that sound so hard to believe: that I want to work for you?" I asked.

Charlotte had been looking at the table, shifting in the one-piece jail uniform that reminded me uncomfortably of a high-school gym suit. "Well, yeah. It does."

"I understand. After all, you don't know me. You didn't pick me. And I could be someone who means you some harm, right?" I was a new public defender, relatively speaking, but I knew how clients and their families viewed us: We were a part of the system. We didn't care. We just wanted to plead every case, and often the best advice *is* to take a plea. The same guy paying us was paying the prosecutor. You get what you pay for. All of these beliefs got in the way of our establishing relationships with clients. I had learned that my best bet was to speak to those beliefs directly and try to lay them to rest by my actions.

Her mouth twisted. She was trying not to shake. "It don't matter anyway."

"It does to me," I said.

"Why?"

I had thought a lot about that very question. Why did these cases, these clients, matter to me so much? They didn't pick me, and I sure didn't pick them. "I can't put my finger on it, Ms. Lyman," I replied. "I just know that it's true. I believe that people, whether they are charged with crimes or not, are human beings who deserve respect, and that the State, unchecked, will run rampant over everyone's individual rights. I think that what I do is important for my clients and for the good of the country." I looked at her and saw on her face the expression you see in high school students on Career Day, that "you've got to be kidding" look. "I can't really say anything that will convince you, I know. But I can *do* things that may. Just watch me work."

Charlotte looked at me. Then she sighed. "What do you want to know?" It wasn't trust, or even the hope of trust, speaking. She had merely arrived at resignation.

"In order to represent you, I am going to need to know all about what happened the day you were arrested, and an awful lot about you." I paused. "In other words, things that would otherwise be none of my business are my business now. Who you are, where you came from, all about your marriage, your home life. I need to know a lot to figure out what might help us, and what to go and investigate."

"Ain't nothin' to investigate. I stabbed Mike. He died. I'm guilty." She sounded matter-of-fact.

"How much do you know about the law?" I asked after a moment.

"Why?"

"Because the law makes distinctions among different kinds of homicides. There is first-degree murder, which usually means the person planned and did it intentionally, or killed someone during a robbery or something. There is second-degree murder, which is when a person was provoked — such as when a man finds his wife in bed with someone, or a person thinks they were acting in self-defense but went too far." I paused, looking to see if she was with me. She was nodding as though she was, but I knew I would need to come back to these concepts. "And then there is self-defense. A person has a right to use force, even deadly force, to protect him- or herself from death or great bodily harm." I waited another moment. "A person acting in self-defense, even if she stabbed and killed someone…well, that person isn't guilty of a crime at all."

"Oh." An uncomfortable silence grew. She was thinking and remembering and starting to shake again. I worried that she might run out of the room.

"Look, Ms. Lyman, we don't have to talk about the case today if you aren't ready to. We don't even have to talk about you, although we'll have to soon. We can just talk." We both took a deep breath at the same time, and then, startled at the synchronicity, both laughed. Just a bit, but it was an encouraging moment.

"Tell me about your children," I prompted. And she did, for quite a while. I learned that the eldest boy, Mike Jr., was tall and growing like crazy; Charlotte couldn't keep him in pants. The next, a girl, Kita, was shy, and Charlotte worried she would never learn to speak up for herself. The next two were boys only ten months apart, and they acted like twins. The baby girl — she was only three — was allergic to anything red: strawberries, tomatoes, red peppers. I found out that Mike Jr., mostly called Junior, looked just like his dad. When I later met Junior, I could see how a teenage Charlotte could have fallen for her husband. Junior was muscular, with mahogany skin and a big smile. It was impossible not to like him. Apparently, Mike Sr. could be just as charming.

Charlotte had been only fifteen when she married Mike, and he hadn't been much older. He hadn't gone past the sixth grade, and Charlotte had dropped out sooner than that. Shortly after they married, they moved to Chicago from the rural depressed South. Mike's brother worked in a factory in Chicago, and they came for the work. Not long after, Charlotte became pregnant with Mike Jr.

After we talked for a while, I told Charlotte I was going to send a subpoena to the Police Department for all of the police reports, and that I would file a motion for discovery and come to see her in a few days. I asked her if she wanted me to check on her kids, but she told me that might not be a good idea, since they were with Mike's mother. I told her I wasn't afraid of her mother-in-law. She smiled then and said, "But I am." I decided to wait on making that call.

A few days later, I went to see Charlotte again. I didn't have the police reports yet, but I felt I needed some direction from her. As a general matter, the defense has few advantages in the system. We are the reactors, not the actors. No one really presumes innocence, not even us, and everyone is afraid of crime. But we can gain some advantage if we move quickly to investigate, and that is what I wanted to do. I knew from the preliminary hearing that my client had made an admission (probably the same one she had made to me), that she had no criminal history, and that it was her husband she had killed. There had to be a reason why.

Entering the visiting room, Charlotte looked thinner than she had just a few days before. "Why aren't you eating?" I asked almost as soon as she sat down.

"Don't much feel like it."

"Look, we are going to have to start facing this. You are in serious trouble. If you want to be allowed to stay a mom to your children, we are going to have to work together." I cleared my throat. "You do want that, don't you?"

She sank lower in her chair, but said nothing. I waited a bit and asked her again in a stronger voice. Her eyelids fluttered. She seemed smaller somehow. "Yes, I do," she said softly, not looking at me.

I had to be careful; I could see that I easily frightened her. "Then you have to eat, even though the food is awful. You have to stay strong." After a pause, I said, "Ms. Lyman, can we talk about your marriage, please?"

She nodded. She told me about the young Mike, about the young Charlotte. About how they fell for each other, hard, "like a freight train goin' downhill." She talked about the move to Chicago, and the children and the apartment on the South Side and how things began to go bad when Mike got laid off. "He started really drinkin' then. He always liked a beer, but now it was hard stuff and early in the day, and I couldn't say nothin'." She had been looking down, but I guess she felt my eyes on her. "He started really hittin' me then." As opposed to fake hitting her, I wondered. I just nodded and put down my pen. "I couldn't do nothin' right. The food was too cooked or not cooked enough. He would knock me down. An' he started usin' his fist."

The room seemed to grow smaller. She was drawing breath through her mouth, almost gulping. "I would try, so hard, to be good. An' then he would be lovin' me again, tellin' me he was sorry. He *was* sorry, too."

Maybe he was. All I could hear, though, was that he was hitting her. As the afternoon wore on, she told me how at first he hid it from the children, from everyone, and then it didn't seem to matter who knew. He even hit her once in front of his mother. He would get a job, then lose it. It was always someone else's fault. He was angry all the time, except when he was sorry. And of course, she told me, she wasn't the perfect wife. She would provoke him by being sloppy or dressing wrong. Charlotte told me about getting a job at the local convenience mart, just part time, to help out, and that Mike came to her work, grabbed her, and dragged her out of the store. They fired her. She was too embarrassed to even shop there anymore. The words poured out of her. She had so much bottled up, and I was listening.

The police reports arrived a few weeks later. There weren't many, since Charlotte had been present when the police arrived and told them she did it. This was no whodunit. But the reports showed that there had been a fight before the stabbing. The police had talked to

Junior and to Mike Sr.'s brother, who had seen Mike knock down Charlotte just before they left the apartment. Neighbors who were canvassed indicated that Mike was loud and violent. Everyone knew he was beating Charlotte, even though she would explain the bruises as falls or accidents. I made notes as I read the reports. I would go to the scene, interview the neighbors myself, see if maybe Charlotte had gone to any of the local health clinics after the beatings. Perhaps someone at her children's schools had noticed something. I was sure that this was a case of self-defense. I still hadn't had a conversation with Charlotte about the specifics of the killing. We were inching our way there. Now a court date was nearing, so I went over to the jail to see her again.

"Hi, Charlotte." She had given me permission to call her by her first name, and I had done the same. She still tended to call me "Attorney Lyon" most of the time, though.

"I finally got the police reports." This case was pretty straightforward from the police and prosecution perspective. The police responded to a "man stabbed" call early Sunday evening at the Lymans' home. When they got there, Mike was lying dead in the kitchen with a serrated knife in his chest. Charlotte was standing in the corner crying. Mike's brother had called the police after Charlotte had phoned him to say that Mike was hurt.

According to the police summary, Charlotte didn't initially respond to questioning, but after a while, she began to talk. She told the police that she had been carving the ham for dinner, fixing Mike's plate. They had "argued" earlier. In fact, it had been far more than an argument. Mike's brother and Mike Jr. had been in the sitting room when Mike, hollering about his dinner not being ready yet, had dragged Charlotte in from the kitchen. When she protested, he had hit her on the side of her head with his fist, knocking her to the floor.

Mike's brother had remonstrated with him, but Mike didn't listen. Mike's brother and Junior left. The younger children were at Mike's mother's house. There was no one but Charlotte and Mike at home when the stabbing occurred.

The police account reported that after the "argument," Charlotte went into the kitchen and finished making dinner. While she was slicing the ham, her statement continued, Mike came up behind her and began choking her. She turned around and stabbed him with the knife she had been using to slice the ham. When Mike fell to the floor, she called his brother.

It sounded like self-defense to me. But the prosecution had chosen to charge her with murder. I believed that their decision made evident the core question we were going to have to confront: If Charlotte's life with Mike was so dangerous, why did she stay? And if it wasn't, why was she justified in stabbing him?

Armed with this knowledge, I began to talk with Charlotte about what had happened. Although Mike had hit her before and hurt her before, that day was different. "It was like he couldn't see me. I was just gone. An' there weren't no air." I nodded encouragingly. "I ain't never seen him look like that. In his eyes. Cold." She paused. "I stabbed him jus' to breathe." She recounted these details in a flat, emotionless voice. I decided to ask her a different kind of question.

"Charlotte, I know what you remember *happening* that day. What I want to know now is what you remember *feeling*." It was as if we had returned to the first time we talked. She closed in on herself. "What does that matter?" she asked, her mouth tight.

"The hardest thing for me to do in this case," I tried to explain, "isn't to defend what you did that day. What is going to be the hardest thing is to explain, so a jury or judge can understand, why you stayed with someone who was beating you."

I didn't really understand it, either, even though I had been read-ing about battered woman syndrome. I knew about the concept of "learned helplessness" and the cycle of violence. First, there would be a small act of violence or arguing, then a bigger act, and then there would be loving contrition afterward, often accompanied by gifts and sex and promises that it wouldn't happen again. And then the cycle would repeat itself. Absent some kind of help, the cycle would con-tinue to escalate until some major act of violence or police involve-ment brought it to a halt. I understood all of this intellectually, but it didn't make visceral sense. *How could she have stayed?*

My face must have betrayed my thoughts. "You don't understand," Charlotte said. "I love him. I do. I don't love all he do, but I love *him*." I noticed the present tense. She tried to explain to me how they were connected through history and children and crippling poverty. How she couldn't support herself, let alone her children, without him. Where would she go? How would she start over? And who would love her if she left Mike? I was young and single at that time and convinced I didn't want marriage or children. I would never have tolerated anyone hitting me. I had been raised to believe that a man should never hit a woman, no matter what. Charlotte and I were utterly different. Weren't we?

I identified and talked to people who had witnessed Mike and Charlotte's behavior, as well as to an expert on spousal abuse. I had started this case focused more on my own reputation in the task force; but now I was turning over every stone for Charlotte's sake. I found neighbors who frequently heard Charlotte being knocked around through their shared wall. I chatted up a school bus driver who picked up Charlotte and Mike's younger boys and would see her wearing sunglasses on cloudy days, with bruises on her arms.

"Honey," the bus driver told me, "my sister's ex used to beat her ass. I knowed that look anywhere."

I studied the autopsy report showing that Mike had a blood alcohol level of 0.18 milligrams per deciliter. Research revealed that this level of intoxication was not only more than twice the legal limit for driving, but was also well into the "combative" range. In addition, the reports showed there were traces of ham on the knife recovered from Mike's body. This supported Charlotte's statement that she was acting reflexively while being choked. She had the knife in her hand because she was slicing the ham, not for some more sinister reason.

The case was assigned to Judge Mitchell, a gruff but decent adjudicator. He was what we refer to as a "balls and strikes" kind of guy. Close calls would go to the prosecution, but if the law were clearly in my favor, he'd rule for the defense. Because we had to decide whether to try the case before the judge alone, which is called a bench trial, or before a jury, I carefully watched Judge Mitchell's reactions to Charlotte during the preliminary hearings. He was at least one generation older than I. Was he also of the mind-set that "some women just like to be beaten"? Sensitive judge-watching is part of what makes a good advocate. I looked to see how he responded to the prosecutor and to me, too. After all, a woman trying a murder case was still novel then.

I also wanted to see how Judge Mitchell reacted to seeing Mike's mother, who came faithfully to every court date. She was a plump and elegant presence, dressed as though she were attending church, in suits with matching hats or scarves. She gripped a large purse — what my grandmother would have called a pocketbook — and stood sadly each time the case was called. Judge Mitchell noticed, and once I saw him nod in her direction. That slight gesture told me that the judge saw the humanity in his courtroom.

Humanity is sometimes what turns out to be more important in a case than any amount of legal maneuvering. One day, after a status hearing on Charlotte's case, I stepped out of the courtroom and there was Mike's mother, standing in the hallway near the large window that overlooks the jail complex. It was an awkward moment; we were alone together, and we were supposed to be enemies. She frowned at me, but it didn't feel like hate, exactly. It flashed through my mind that under any other circumstances, I would have expressed my sympathy to her for the loss of her son.

These days, death penalty defense lawyers will tell you that it is a good idea to bridge the gulf between defendant and victim, when it can be done without giving offense, but at that time, no one talked about such things. Perhaps if there had been another woman in the Homicide Task Force, I could have followed her lead in a situation such as this. I had heard some of my colleagues make dismissive and even unkind remarks about victims. Or they simply avoided the subject altogether. Maybe it was too painful, or maybe they believed that tough criminal defense lawyers shouldn't feel anything but the desire for victory.

Well, I wasn't one of the boys, and I was getting sick of feeling as if I should act like them. This woman in front of me had lost her son, and whatever wrong he had done to Charlotte, she had to be hurting. I walked up to her and said, "I'm so sorry for your loss, Mrs. Lyman."

Surprise and puzzlement flashed across her face. "I appreciate you saying that," she said, "but you that woman's lawyer."

"Yes." I swallowed. I couldn't let that stand by itself. I knew from investigating this case that Mike's mother *had* to know something about what Mike had been doing. So I braced myself and said softly, "That woman is the mother of your grandchildren."

Mrs. Lyman looked startled. "And she killed their daddy."

I nodded. This was absolutely true. "She misses her kids. She worries about them, even though you are taking good care of them."

"How do you know that?"

"She told me." She had also told me that she was afraid she would never have their love again, but I didn't mention that.

"You said in there that you have an 'affirmative defense.' Did I hear that right?"

"Yes. We are defending this case based on self-defense."

She took a deep breath, and I thought she was going to light into me, at least verbally. Then she exhaled and looked, really *looked*, at me. "You believe that?"

"Yes." I was uncomfortable. I was saying that her son was violent, that he'd had it coming. But I couldn't soft-pedal this.

"I see." She looked down. Her face, lined from frowns and smiles, stilled. She was thinking, breathing slowly. She looked back up at me and endeavored not to cry. "He was hitting her, you know. It wasn't him, not really, it was the liquor an' everything."

"That's what Charlotte says. She still loves him." I may not have understood it, but I knew she wouldn't mind if I told his mother that.

Her eyes misted. "It ain't her fault." She shook her head and straightened her shoulders. "I said some things to her, about her, I'm 'shamed about. I know she didn't mean to kill him."

I was amazed at her seeing this, let alone saying so. I knew it, too, but I wasn't Mike's mother. "I don't know what to say."

"My boy, he wasn't himself. He was hittin' her, hurtin' her, and..." She stopped. I reached out my hand to her. How could I not? She was in so much pain. She took my right hand in her left and looked up at me. "You tell Charlotte, when it come time, I will tell what I know." She pulled her hand from mine and walked down the hall to the elevator.

There are times when I wonder at man's inhumanity to man, when sadness and despair take hold. And then someone like this, who has little or nothing but grief and pain, gives a gift of such nobility.

Charlotte was charged with first-degree murder, which wasn't an appropriate charge. Even from the prosecution's point of view, anyone could see that this wasn't planned or premeditated. But charging her with the highest level of offense was typical of most prosecutions: the more a defendant has to risk by going to trial, the more likely he or she will cut a deal. Plus, in Illinois, knowing your actions are likely to "cause great bodily harm or death" can form the basis of a first-degree murder charge, so technically they could do it.

At most, Charlotte should have been charged with second-degree murder. We could have decided to plea out the case for second-degree murder and the lighter jail sentence that such a crime would entail. Charlotte and I had talked about this, but Charlotte was concerned that any more jail time would be the end of her relationship with her children. Nevertheless, I would likely have recommended a plea to avoid the risk of a first-degree murder conviction, and I think she would have heeded my advice, but the prosecution refused to reduce the offense. They thought they had the horses, since Charlotte had been caught red-handed and had confessed. The prosecutors flat out told me that battered woman syndrome was "feminist bullshit."

"Good luck with that," they said. So it would be a trial.

My co-counsel and I decided a bench trial would be best. In Illinois, the defense has the unilateral right to waive jury and have the judge decide the case. In most other states, both sides have to agree, and they seldom do. If the defense wants a bench, the prosecution generally doesn't, and vice versa.

I had researched Judge Mitchell, and his recent rulings had reassured me. He also seemed to react well to our client and to me. He had granted the few motions we had filed. They were nothing earth-shattering, but it told me he was listening. We had a solid defense, there had been no publicity that would produce political backlash, and the judge wouldn't be shocked the way a jury always was by the sight of autopsy photos. Plus, the judge had just been reelected, and the next election was three years away. I felt ready. I knew the case, I knew my client, I had corroborating evidence for the battering, and I had researched the psychological literature. Still, I hadn't figured out how to answer the big underlying question: Why had she stayed? How could I explain that she couldn't leave, psychologically, that she was dependent on this man and loved him even while caught in a lethally dangerous trap?

About three weeks before the trial, a friend who was a counselor for a Chicago YWCA called to ask a favor. They ran a battered woman's shelter near Uptown. On Wednesday nights, they had informational meetings. Speakers came in and talked on such topics as how to get a GED or how to apply for health insurance. My friend wanted me to speak about the criminal justice system, to tell her clients how they could file for protective orders, for example, or what rights they had to keep the schools from giving out their addresses to their children's fathers. I said sure.

I had been representing Charlotte, a battered woman, for more than a year now, and I had learned all about the syndrome. I knew, intellectually, that this phenomenon crossed all lines — economic, cultural, and racial. But knowing it and *seeing* it are two different things.

When I walked into the room at the Y that night, I wasn't prepared for the nearly forty women there, of every background, ranging from a sixteen-year-old black girl with two children to a middle-aged Jewish woman from the affluent northern suburbs with diamonds on her fingers. The latter had finally left her husband when he plunged an ice pick into her shoulder.

What really surprised me was how many of them were educated and had good jobs. In our public lives, I know, we behave differently from the way we do in our intimate lives. At work, I was confident. I knew I was capable, hardworking, and committed. I would stand up for what I thought was right even when I had to take on older, more experienced, and often brilliant men, some of them my bosses. In my personal life, I wasn't so sure of myself. I describe myself as "handsome," but I know I am not beautiful or even pretty. With time, I've come to be glad about who I am because I think that pretty ages poorly, but handsome ages well. Still, how I felt about myself professionally and how I felt personally were significantly different. So I could understand logically that a woman might seem assertive and together in her public life, but still be vulnerable to abuse in an intimate setting.

Still, the violence didn't make visceral sense to me. I spent two hours with the women at the Y, answering questions, listening to their stories, and getting madder and madder at the men who'd abused them, at the system that hadn't helped them, and at the indifference of much of the world to their dilemma.

After the meeting, I walked out alone to the parking lot behind the building where my car was parked. Too agitated to drive, I walked around my Camaro, muttering to myself. "If any son-of-a-bitch even *looked* like he was going to hit me..." I was smoking mad. At first I found justification for my anger in the devastation I had encountered that night. But then I stopped pacing. The mental lightbulb lit up.

Leo. I had been dating a good-looking, magnetic man. Leo was an athlete with a golden voice and a smile... well, a smile that could melt your heart. It had certainly melted mine. And this charming guy would call and ask if he could come over for dinner around six o'clock on a Monday. I would say sure, and he would show up at six o'clock... on Wednesday. And I would let him. I wouldn't say, hey, this is the wrong night. Or that I was busy, or even that I was upset he was two days late. I would just open the door, scrounge something to cook, and fall into his arms. I kept hoping things would improve, just like these women, with their histories and their children and their economic dependence on their men, were hoping, too. It wasn't masochism that kept them from walking out the door; it was hope.

Now I knew how to talk about Charlotte's case. Almost everyone has had the experience of staying in a relationship longer than they should; I could make the judge understand Charlotte's hope if I worked hard enough to help him. I had learned how to listen to Charlotte's world, and I felt I could teach the judge to do it, too.

The trial got off to a good start. The police officers who testified were pretty straight. They talked about what they saw and what they heard, and they didn't try to shade things too much. One of them, Officer Durkin, even admitted on cross-examination that Charlotte had looked "shocked and scared." That must have worried the prosecutor. On his redirect questioning, he tried to get the officer to say he had no basis to draw such a conclusion, since he had never seen Charlotte Lyman before that day. Durkin admitted as much. So, on re-cross, I asked him a few more questions.

"Officer Durkin, you are a trained police officer, is that right?"

"Yes." He looked puzzled.

"And a part of your training is in Illinois criminal law."

"Yes, ma'am."

"You need to know something about that so you know who to arrest and for what, right?" The prosecuting attorney objected, but was quickly overruled.

"Of course," the officer answered.

I wasn't sure, but I thought I saw the faintest shadow of a smile on Durkin's face. Maybe he knew where I was going and wanted to help me get there.

"You know about the concept called self-defense?"

"I do."

"And that means that a person has a right to use force to defend themselves, even deadly force, if they are afraid of death or great bodily harm, and that fear is reasonable, correct?"

"Yes."

"So the fact that Charlotte seemed both shocked and scared within minutes of your arrival at the apartment, that has some legal significance, doesn't it?" Now the prosecutor jumped up from his chair, objecting and arguing that I had no right to treat the officer as some legal expert when clearly he was not. This observation, I noted, was not going over well with Officer Durkin. The judge overruled but added a "Move it along, Counsel," an admonition with which most trial lawyers are all too familiar.

"Officer, have you ever been called to a domestic disturbance before?"

"More times than I want to think about," he replied.

"And when you have responded to those calls, have you seen women who were regularly being beaten by their husbands?"

"Do you mean battered women?" I was surprised: a male police officer at that time who knew the concept.

"Yes."

"I have seen them, yes. And the men who beat them." It was clear what he thought of those men.

"Based on that experience, Officer, was there any reason that you felt and still feel comfortable drawing conclusions about Ms. Lyman's emotional state?" Now this was a risk, but not much of one. The officer had stood strong with his conclusions and seemed sympathetic.

"Yes." Durkin cleared his throat. "I know a battered woman when I see one. That's what she was. Is."

"No further questions." I sat down. One of the hardest lessons for a trial lawyer to learn is to quit while you're ahead, and I judged I was as ahead as I could get with this witness. Charlotte's statement was entered into evidence, as was the physical evidence, and the State rested.

We called as witnesses the neighbors who had heard the beatings, as well as the school bus driver. Then I called Mike's mother. The prosecutor looked at me as though I had just undressed in the middle of court. Sputtering, he tried to object, but he had listed her as a potential prosecution witness, so there was no basis for the objection. I established her relationship with her son and Charlotte, and the fact that her grandchildren were living with her since Mike's death and Charlotte's incarceration.

"Mrs. Lyman, did you ever see physical violence between Mike and Charlotte?"

"Yes." She was looking down and speaking in a low voice, but the courtroom was so quiet that none of us had trouble hearing her.

"Who hurt who? Tell us about it, would you please?"

She began to tell it all: how Mike became more violent as time went on and how he loved Charlotte, but would get frustrated and angry and would hit her. "At first he would try an' hide it," she said, "but after a while, he didn't care who saw." I didn't keep her on the stand long. She confirmed what we had told the judge about the case. The simple fact of her presence and her support for Charlotte was what was important. We recessed for the day.

Now we had to decide whether to call Charlotte to testify. I was leaning toward not calling her, but I wanted to talk to her one more time and make sure she was ready in case we decided differently. I went to the jail and we went over her testimony, and then she told me something no lawyer ever wants to hear in the middle of a trial.

"There is something important I haven't told you."

"What?" I asked, trying to stay calm.

"It's personal, and I, well, I didn't know how to tell you." I couldn't imagine what it could be; we had talked about everything.

"So tell me."

"I think it'd be better if I just showed you." That day, she was wearing one of the two-piece jail uniforms. She lifted up the top.

There were little round burn marks all over her chest. He had put *cigarettes* out on her, as if she were an ashtray. Before I could stop myself, I said, "You should have shot him in his sleep." And in that moment, I meant it. I oppose executing a person for any crime, but right then I felt that Mike Lyman hadn't deserved to live. How could anyone do that? I took a breath and asked her why she hadn't told me about this before.

"'Cause you would think I was a freak. That he was evil. And I ain't, an' he ain't." I shook my head.

"I'm your lawyer, Charlotte. Whatever the facts are, good, bad, or in the middle, I need to know them, so I can fight for you." I was shaken. She was right about me, I thought. If I had known of the deliberate, as well as the situational, violence, maybe I would have seen her differently. Maybe I would have seen her as more complicit, or maybe as someone who had a reason to plan a murder. I was sure she hadn't done that, but the disclosure gave me pause. I sat for a moment, thinking. This was a good reason *not* to call her. "Okay. I know now, Charlotte, and that's good enough."

On my way home that night, I thought about her revelation and wondered if, in the end, it made any difference. Those circular marks of cruelty were dramatic, but the fact that her helpless love and hope-filled heart had let her tolerate even this didn't change what happened when she stabbed him. She was acting in self-defense. I was comfortable that the judge understood why she had stayed with

Mike. I had watched him nod at Officer Durkin's conclusion. I had seen that he had been moved by Mike's mom's testimony. I saw no reason to tell him or her children about those burns. I did not call Charlotte to testify.

And after I called Junior to the stand, I felt even more comfortable with that decision. Junior had aged in the year since his father's death. He was a sullen tough-guy teen. I had called him to describe the "argument" that had taken place before he and his uncle left the apartment, to establish that Mike was combative and drinking that afternoon — the usual prelude to his violence. After Junior had covered that ground, something made me ask one more question.

"Junior, can you tell His Honor why you left when you did?"

Charlotte's son gave me a look. He didn't want to answer. "What?"

"Why did you leave that night?"

And suddenly this tough sixteen-year-old looked like someone's little boy. His voice cracked. "'Cause I couldn't stop him. He was too big and I couldn't stop him … and I couldn't watch."

I looked between Junior and his mom, at something happening that had nothing to do with the trial. A connection reformed itself between them, a tenderness that was wonderful and painful to see. I looked up at the judge and saw that he was moved, too. "The defense rests."

Judge Mitchell found Charlotte Lyman not guilty. Mike's mother and Charlotte's children let out a ragged cheer. Charlotte, tears on her face, thanked my co-counsel and hugged me. Junior and the whole family pressed close as Charlotte was led back to the lockup. I explained to them that their mother would be released from the jail, but it might take a few hours.

I don't know what happened to Charlotte and her family after that day. Most of the time, clients don't stay in touch, even if things turn out well. The association is too painful. I understand that. But

it was a great moment, standing there with Charlotte's mother-in-law
and the children. I looked down as the littlest one, whom Charlotte
called her baby, the one who was allergic to anything red, pulled on
my skirt.

"Yes?" I smiled.

"Mommy is coming home, right?" Her eyes were big.

"Yes, in just a little while." The child tugged on my skirt again and
lifted up her arms in the universal "pick me up" gesture. I reached down
and did just that. She snuggled her head on my shoulder and whispered
three of the sweetest words I ever heard, "Thank you, lady."

When I got home that night there was a message from Leo about
dinner. I didn't return the call.

CHAPTER 3

Fighting for a Client Bent on Losing

I PICKED UP A folder from my desktop and stared at it. There must be something I had intended to do with it. Read it? File it? I set down the folder and picked up another one, but I was no more productive with this one. My brain was not functioning. Two hours earlier I had finished making the case to a jury that they should spare the life of Lonnie Fields, a man who had himself taken two lives. Now I was waiting to find out what those twelve citizens would decide. And I was flat out terrified.

The trial of Lonnie Fields was my first death penalty case before a jury. My role was assistant counsel, in charge of the sentencing phase. A year earlier I had been assigned as second chair on a capital murder case that was tried before a judge. There had been less suspense that time. In the pretrial negotiations, the judge had indicated that he would not impose a death sentence.

This wait was excruciating. Conventional courtroom wisdom

holds that the longer a jury is out, the better for the defense. I should be hoping for a long deliberation. I just wasn't sure how I would get through it. Many attorneys hit the bar while they wait for a verdict, particularly on a death penalty case. But I didn't drink. And I had naïvely believed I could work in the meantime.

Then, the task force receptionist appeared at my office door. "Jury's ready," she said. For an instant, I couldn't comprehend her meaning. How could there be a verdict so soon? I swallowed, stood up, and headed to the courthouse.

LIKE MOST LIVES that hang on a thread held in the hands of twelve strangers, Lonnie Fields's was marked by poverty, racism, disease, poor choices, and bad luck. He had served in the army in the 1950s, not easy for a black man, despite the integration of the troops. After the army, Fields applied to be a Chicago police officer. The records show that he was accepted despite a police psychologist's suggestion that his volatile personality was unsuited to the job. Shortly after joining the force, he met and married his wife, Anna. They had four children.

Fields's police record read like two sides of a strange coin. A commendation for bravery would be followed by an accusation of brutality. The worst allegation, later dropped, claimed that Fields had thrown a brick at the head of one of the tenants of a building he owned. Not surprisingly, he never rose within the police ranks.

Near the end of the 1970s, Fields was shot in the neck, though not while on duty. Despite my later efforts to find out what had happened, no one in the family would talk about it. Had it been the result of a family dispute? Or perhaps a failed suicide attempt? I never found out. As a result of the injury, Fields developed a nervous-system disorder that simultaneously caused numbness in one part of his body and a burning sensation in another. His balance was affected, too; he could walk for a few steps, but would then topple over. After the injury, he used a wheelchair most of the time.

More sinister symptoms appeared soon after. Grandiosity, religiosity, explosiveness, paranoia — he exhibited them all. Whether Fields's mental illness predated the shooting injury or was somehow caused by it, I don't know. His paranoia focused on white people and two of the primary symbols of their power, the medical profession and the legal system. Because he believed that white doctors were conspiring to use birth control as a means to suppress the African-American population, he would not allow his wife, Anna, to use contraception or seek medical care. Fields treated her like chattel, humiliated her in public, and insisted that she go on having his children "until God decides different."

Eventually, Anna filed for divorce. Even worse, as far as Fields was concerned, she hired a white lawyer.

For a divorce court hearing in 1983, Fields arrived in his wheelchair, representing himself. When the judge entered the courtroom, Fields calmly took out a thirty-eight-caliber revolver he had concealed in his lap and fired it at his wife's attorney. He then turned the gun on the judge. All of this took place in front of twenty-seven eyewitnesses. Afterward, Fields simply sat in his wheelchair until he was arrested. Both men died of the gunshot wounds.

The horrifying event caused a media sensation. Story after story featured the judge, the attorney, their families, and spoke of the need for security at the Daley Center Courthouse. To no one's surprise, the prosecutors stated from the beginning that they would seek the death penalty. This case was tailor-made for capital punishment: a high-profile event involving victims of stature. The prosecutors' decision would likely have been the same even if the defendant had been a rich white man. But Lonnie Fields was, in fact, a poor black man, and that reality would gather invisible weight until it became the proverbial elephant in the courtroom.

The Cook County Court decided that since one of the victims came from their own ranks, a judge from neighboring Lake County should preside over Fields's trial. That judge appointed our Public Defender's Office to represent Fields, along with Jed Stone, a private practitioner from Lake County. Jamie Kunz, a highly experienced member of Homicide Task Force, was named lead counsel, and Jed and I were appointed to assist him. I had been in Task Force for several years by now, but this was the highest profile case I had worked on — and only the second in which the death penalty threatened.

By the time Fields came to trial in 1984, more than twenty Illinois defendants had been sentenced to death since the reinstatement of capital punishment seven years earlier, but no one had been executed yet. I had always opposed the death penalty, but in a somewhat offhand manner, intuitively rejecting the idea of killing a person as punishment *for* killing. Over the years, my opposition would grow stronger and more knowledgeable. I came to see that it isn't the worst among us who are executed, but rather, the poorest, the members of despised groups, and those least able to defend themselves. Nevertheless, for a criminal defense attorney, a capital murder trial is the equivalent of the Olympics, and I was pleased and excited to be on the team, while respectfully aware of the challenges.

A death penalty case is actually two trials. The first determines guilt or innocence; the second decides the punishment. If the defendant is convicted of first-degree murder, the prosecution can then ask for the death penalty if the case includes at least one "aggravating factor." Aggravating factors vary by state, but common ones are the killing of a police officer acting in the line of duty, the murder of a woman during a rape, or the killing of more than one person. The latter was the aggravating factor in Fields's case.

Once the prosecution has established both guilt and death penalty eligibility, the second trial begins, with the same jury. During this "penalty phase," the prosecution presents aggravating evidence, that is, reasons to execute the defendant. These might include prior violent acts or victim impact evidence. The defense presents "mitigating factors," reasons to punish with imprisonment rather than death. These can include family history, mental or physical health issues, or the impact the client's execution would have on his or her loved ones. Since most mitigating evidence involves extremes of poverty, family dysfunction, and child abuse, it is usually shameful to the client and his relatives, and therefore, difficult to obtain.

In the fall of 1983, our team began the formidable task of defending Lonnie Fields. First, we looked at the record. After his arrest, Fields had explained to the police why he had brought the gun to the courtroom and taken two lives with it, or at least what he claimed as his motive. Fields believed that by killing those two men, he would be sentenced to death, not an unreasonable assumption. He also believed that the Illinois Supreme Court would eventually have to hear his case, also a reasonable assumption, since any death sentence results in an automatic appeal to that court. At this point in the plan, however, his psychosis got the upper hand. Fields was convinced that his act of murder against these agents of divorce, as he saw them, would persuade the Supreme Court that divorce was against God's law and that he was a warrior acting on God's behalf. In his deluded fantasy, the Court would outlaw divorce and declare Lonnie Fields a hero. He recognized that he might nevertheless have to be executed, but only after divorce was declared illegal. Fields was willing to be a martyr to his cause.

When the time came to see the warrior martyr in person, Jamie Kunz and I made the trip to the hospital wing of the jail, where Fields was being held due to his physical disabilities. Jamie is tall, cherub-cheeked, and slow of speech. His frequent long hesitations cause prosecutors to underestimate his intellect and deep understanding of people and juries. But Jamie is a formidable advocate.

To get to the jail's hospital, we rode in a small and stuffy elevator with a large, red-faced corrections officer.

"This ain't gonna be one of those cases make you popular," the guard opined. It wasn't a question.

"No," I agreed. Already, a letter to the editor in a Chicago paper had questioned why a trial was necessary, since Fields had committed his crime in front of so many witnesses. Just take him out and shoot him was the implication. "But we'll do what we can for him."

"Maybe you will an' maybe you won't," the guard said. The elevator doors opened, but intrigued by his comment, I kept by the guard's side as we walked toward the nurse's station.

"What do you mean?" I asked. Jamie didn't appear to be paying attention, but I knew he was aware of everything that was being said. He might later jot the conversation on a piece of paper and file it. Of course, Jamie's idea of filing meant throwing everything into grocery store bags. I used three-ring binders complete with indexes.

The guard explained. "You won't get points for winning anythin' in this case, so maybe it's better you don't try too hard." He was more astute than I had given him credit for.

I smiled. "If I wanted to be popular, I would have been a prosecutor."

He guffawed as he turned us over to the nurses. "That's what I thought."

This wing of the jail looked and smelled like a hospital, but a peculiar one. Nurses and correction officers intermingled. Some patients were dressed in hospital gowns, some in jail uniforms. And some were handcuffed to their beds.

We found an emaciated Fields rocking back and forth in his wheelchair while staring intently out the wire mesh window near his bed. This fifty-year-old former soldier and police officer had once stood tall and straight, but injury and illness had curved his spine and rounded his shoulders. When he spoke, he moved his head out at an angle from his neck, like a turtle extending its head from a shell.

Jamie had met him briefly before, so Fields recognized him.

"What you want?" Fields demanded.

"Mr. Fields — " Jamie began, but Fields cut him off.

"Look, I don't want no lawyer talk here. I was doin' what the Lord said do, an' that's that."

Jamie and I exchanged looks. It's always a bad sign when your client is on a mission from God. We were going to need Fields's cooperation in order to save his life.

"Why don't you explain it to me, then?" Jamie said.

"Ain't nothin' to explain," Fields said dismissively. He nodded in my direction. "And who might this be? Your secret'ry?"

Jamie started to explain that I certainly was not his secretary, but Fields had stopped paying attention.

"Are you trying to start something?" I asked Fields. Although my tone was mild, I deliberately used provocative words. I had run into plenty of distrust and contempt from men and had learned the importance of not letting insults pass. I wouldn't start a fight, but I had to let the client or prosecutor or cop know that I wasn't afraid of one. "You think I haven't been called worse?"

"A woman's place is in the home. That's what God say." He seemed to enjoy pressing our buttons. Still, the flame of belief burned in his eyes, not just the light of mischief. He cocked his head and looked at me. "You ain't got no argument with God, do you?"

"No. But I have one with you, apparently."

Jamie looked back and forth between us, unsure what to do. I let him take the lead and gave up trying to talk to Fields. I had learned to find ways to connect with almost every client, even the crazy ones. But sometimes things outside my control got in the way. I worked hard not to take it personally, while still trying to figure out if there was something I could do differently.

Jamie was skilled with mentally ill clients, but even his patience and expertise could not penetrate Fields's delusions. When we left the jail, it was late on a Friday afternoon. We had the sidewalk on California Avenue virtually to ourselves as we headed back to the Public Defender's Office.

"We're going to have to try this case around our client," Jamie said.

"It looks like it." I paused. "Jamie, do you want to replace me with a guy? Do you think it might help? Maybe a black guy?"

A public defender learns early on that sometimes the package one comes in — your gender, race, or age — can get in the way of representation. One client I had been assigned couldn't tolerate a woman in a position of authority. Another thought I couldn't possibly be tough enough. Rather than fight it, I turned to our unofficial barter system and traded my case for another, likely awful, case that some other staff attorney didn't want. This way, my client would have a fighting chance.

Jamie smiled at my offer to give up such a big case.

"Andrea, I appreciate the offer, but I think it will help to have a woman on the team, even if Mr. Fields doesn't agree." I had heard *that* before. "Get Andrea to try the case with you" usually meant it was a sexual assault case, or there was a child or elderly woman to cross-examine. You know, woman's work. I made no response but stopped walking.

"You're tired of hearing that, aren't you?" he asked.

"Maybe." But now I had to be completely honest. "And maybe I'm not," I admitted. "It gets me some interesting cases." Jamie smiled wryly. "It's why you asked me onto this case, right?" I said. Any attorney in the task force would have wanted this assignment, attracted by the notoriety, the flash of local fame, and, in a weird way, the fact that this case couldn't possibly be won on the facts.

"That was part of it." Jamie motioned me to start walking again. "But, actually, Andrea, it's what everyone else has been giving you shit for. That's really why I wanted you."

My first thought was, who has been giving me shit? No one to my face, anyway.

"What are you talking about?" I asked.

"That big heart of yours."

Oh, *that.* "You're too emotional for this work." "It's just a case." "You have to be tough." Sure, I had heard all of that. Just days earlier, another friend in the task force, Brad, had sat me down for a talk. I let myself get too involved, he said. I should be "objective" about my clients. I thought about what he was saying. True, the stress of the job leaked out everywhere in the task force. There was too much drinking, philandering, even drug use. I knew Brad liked me and wanted me to succeed. But the fact is I had been winning like crazy, garnering either outright acquittals or lesser findings such as manslaughter. Yes, I sometimes cried in the office. But I was healthy, damn it. I looked penetratingly at my colleague.

"Brad," I said, "*I* do not have high blood pressure. *I* am not losing my hair. And *I* do not have an ulcer. Don't talk to *me* about being emotional!"

Brad looked taken aback, and I quickly softened my response. "I know you mean well. But I can't sell what I wouldn't buy."

In other words, how can I ask a jury to care about my client and his life if I don't? Sure, being human in this inhumane system comes with a cost. If you open yourself up to emotional involvement with your clients, the prospect of losing is frightening, and the reality of losing hurts like hell. But it's a price I am willing to pay. Or maybe it's a price I don't know how not to pay.

And now, walking down California Avenue with me, Jamie seemed to understand. "I'm starting to think you might be on to something," he said. "You do the best interviews I've seen, leaving aside the one we just left." We both laughed. "If there is any chance of finding a justification to save this guy's life, you'll find it. You'll sit in somebody's kitchen until the right person talks to you."

Oh, so he had heard the story. I had had a client whose mother refused to come to court, and who was blocking me from talking to other family members. Her son's case had come down to sentencing. I needed witnesses, stories, and evidence to explain his behavior, and she was keeping them from me. So, one day, I showed up at her house right after church. She couldn't disrespect me in front of the neighbors, so she let me in. I sat at her kitchen table all day. I drank instant coffee and watched her cook. Eventually, she let me peel potatoes. When she handed over the onions, we started to talk. After nearly ten hours in this woman's kitchen, I left with an understanding between us. We gained a decent outcome in the case, and the woman's relationship with her son improved. My co-counsel, who had given the case up for lost because the mother wouldn't talk to us, teased me about my "kitchen advocacy," and the story got around.

"Ah, so that's my purpose." I wasn't entirely displeased. Nabbing the critical interview might not be as much fun as taking down a cop on cross-examination, or as intellectually stimulating as figuring out a cause of death, but it could make all the difference in a case. And yet I had rarely seen defense attorneys put sufficient effort into getting the right person to talk.

"Yup. And, frankly, I don't think Mr. Fields cares whether his lawyers are male or female. As far as he's concerned, we're all part of the conspiracy to keep God's truth from the world."

True enough. We agreed that Jamie and Jed Stone would work primarily on the trial, and I would work on the sentencing phase. Jed was the Lake County lawyer also assigned to the case. At that time, many lawyers considered sentencing to be the "lesser" job — women's work, if you will — because it deals less with hard facts and more with feelings. Perhaps that's why the task force was losing left and right at sentencing. In my view, sentencing work was about nothing less than trying to save our client's life.

Of course, no one was suggesting that Fields be acquitted and put back out on the streets. He needed treatment. Given the circumstances of the crime and the reality of Fields's mental state, we decided to mount an insanity defense. Not guilty by reason of insanity is a plea that reeks of melodrama, of madly cackling killers or wily defendants who fake multiple personalities in order literally to get away with murder. Insanity pleas tend to attract attention and controversy, and because of that, people believe that the defense is used more often than it actually is. In fact, the insanity defense is attempted in less than 1 percent of all criminal cases, and it succeeds in only 25 percent of those.

Why does it so rarely work? Juries seem to feel that finding a defendant not guilty by reason of insanity is failing in their responsibility to society, letting a killer "get away with it." What people don't realize is that "insane" defendants, on average, spend more than double the time in a mental hospital lockup than they would have spent in jail had they simply pled guilty.

In my mission to gather mitigating evidence against executing Lonnie Fields, I had my work cut out for me. Maintaining a balance between respecting a client's privacy and obtaining the needed insight into his life can be challenging. What I usually try to do is create an environment in which the client will willingly share information. With clients as damaged and uncooperative as Fields, you can usually gather history from family. But Fields's family was traumatized and hostile. His relatives wanted nothing to do with him and were unwilling even to talk about him. Only his youngest child, seventeen-year-old Cherise, returned my phone calls.

One afternoon, Jamie, Jed, and I were talking about the case. We had the records to support the insanity defense. Psychiatrists who had diagnosed Fields as paranoid schizophrenic and actively psychotic would testify. The problem was Fields. He wanted the death penalty. In the months since I had first met him, I had tried repeatedly to talk to him — about politics, the army, anything. But he refused to make eye contact, let alone speak to me. As predicted, he believed that his lawyers wanted to save his life in order to thwart his mission to get the Illinois Supreme Court to declare divorce illegal. He referred to us as the A-Team. I refrained from asking which of us was Mr. T.

"What do we do with the fucking guy?" This was Jed. Jed was a big guy, bearded and blustery. He loved to fight and thus was popular with clients and much less so with prosecutors and judges.

Jamie had been working with Fields the most, and even his vaunted patience was at an end. When we appeared in court on pre-trial issues, Fields would talk directly to the judge, openly contradicting us. When he wasn't referring to us as the A-Team, he was calling us "Judas goats." He accused me, loudly, of having "sexual congress" with the prosecutor. We began to believe not only that an insanity defense was appropriate but also that Fields was not even fit for trial.

"We know he isn't fit for trial," I said. "But there is no way a judge is going to say so, right? It's an election year, and the guy *killed a judge*, for God's sake."

Something you won't find in the law books is the role of electoral politics in judicial decisions. When people ask me what motion I file first in a death penalty case, I say "motion to continue in an odd-numbered year." It might be a joke, but it's also true. I don't want my client's case to figure in any judge's reelection campaign.

"So, let's take a jury," Jamie said.

Jed and I looked at each other. A defendant has a right to a jury trial to determine if he was fit to stand trial, but I had never heard of anyone exercising that right. Generally, if one has a client who is disturbed enough to be considered unfit, a judge will say so. Unless, that is, the client shot a judge.

So we picked a jury and tried to persuade them that Fields was unfit to stand trial. We argued that his mental illness prevented him from understanding what was going on in any meaningful way and that he could not cooperate with counsel. In opposing us, our client and the prosecution were in perfect accord: both thought Lonnie Fields was fine. Throughout the two-day hearing, our client offered objections, spoke over witnesses, and walked around until he fell and had to be helped back into his wheelchair. He vigorously agreed with the State's expert, who said Fields knew what he was doing, and he scoffed at ours. The experience was not fun — except for one moment. After the State had done its first closing argument and Jamie had closed for the defense, one of the prosecutors was arguing the rebuttal. (The State is allowed two closing arguments.) The prosecutor said there was no evidence that Fields could not cooperate with counsel. Now, there was disputed evidence on that point, but not *no* evidence. Before we could object, Fields yelled what I have so often wanted to say in court, "OBJECTION! The prosecution has a strong enough case without lying about it!"

In short order, the jury announced their agreement with the prosecution and our client: Lonnie Fields was fit to stand trial. One juror looked at me sadly and shook her head. I think she pitied us.

An atmosphere of unrelenting pressure surrounded the ensuing trial. In Illinois, cameras are not allowed in the courtroom, but that doesn't keep them away from the courthouse. Reporters stuck microphones in our faces as we walked by, asking silly questions: *Is Fields sorry? Will he kill again?* For the first time, I saw my name in the newspaper. A certain ego boost comes with that, but it was also frightening, given the heated level of public feeling. I switched to an unlisted phone number. We all received letters about the case, but what particularly disturbed me was the fan mail, not for me, but for Lonnie Fields. Some "men's rights" groups believed that Mr. Fields was legitimately speaking out against the divorce system on behalf of downtrodden men. One of them sent me a bumper sticker with a picture of a gun and the message "Lonnie Fields Had a Point."

Trying a death penalty case is profoundly different from defending other kinds of cases. The length of time, the amount of work, the emotional toll — all are exponentially greater. A death penalty defense lawyer is representing a client who is charged with acts that are often sickening, is despised by the public, and is almost always presumed to be guilty. The judge is painfully aware of the visibility of the case and his or her resultant political vulnerability. The stakes, obviously, are as high as they get.

Worse yet, the jury is constructed to be biased in favor of death. There are two ways in which potential jurors can be struck, or eliminated. A "for cause" strike eliminates potential jurors who cannot be objective because, for instance, they know one of the parties to the case. In a capital case, jurors can be struck for cause because they oppose the death penalty. There is no limit to the number of for cause strikes. Jurors who do *not* oppose the death penalty are called "death-qualified."

Each side can also eliminate jurors simply because they think they would be bad for their case. Each side has a fixed number of these "peremptory" strikes. The prosecution can use its peremptory strikes to avoid seating potential jurors who may not oppose the death penalty but who show some reluctance to impose it. What one ends up with is a jury made up entirely of people who have no qualms about the death penalty. The research tells us that these "death-qualified juries" are overwhelmingly white, conservative, and don't hold much with the concept of insanity.

The courtroom in which Fields's trial was held was packed with spectators every day, particularly from law enforcement and the prosecutor's office. The families of the attorney and judge who had been killed were always present. The brother of the deceased attorney swore and made faces and sound effects whenever we objected or put on evidence. I understood the pain behind his behavior, but I admired the contrasting way the family of the judge handled their grief. They always spoke politely to the defense team, and most important, they were kind to Fields's daughter, Cherise, the only member of his family attending the trial. Once, I saw the judge's widow pass a Kleenex to her.

The evidence against Fields was incontrovertible. The only issue was his state of mind: Was he sane at the time of the killings? Jamie's opening was masterful. It lasted more than an hour, beginning with, "You may have thought that you would be hearing about the workings of a criminal mind. But you won't. You are going to hear about the breakdown of a mind."

Our two psychiatrists said that Fields, guided by delusions, was insane at the time of the crime. The prosecution presented two who said he was not. And then, of course, there was Fields. He wouldn't be quiet. He shook his head, objected, yelled, and threw papers on the floor, all of which, in my opinion, made him look even crazier.

But the prosecution had one salient commonsense argument: Lonnie Fields planned the crime. He hid the gun under a blanket in his lap and took careful aim. Once he had shot the two men, he let the gun drop into his lap, raised his hands, and waited to be arrested. For many, if not most, jurors, that is the same as sane. They cannot believe that an insane person can behave rationally in any way. Mental health professionals know this to be a fallacy. I believe most prosecutors do, too, but they also know this argument works.

And it worked in this case. As with the fitness verdict, the jury returned with an answer in less than two hours: guilty of both murders. Fields nodded and smiled; he was one step closer to his goal. No defense attorney ever likes to hear a guilty verdict, but Jamie, Jed, and I were not surprised. We knew that a death-qualified jury would be unwilling to decide "not guilty by reason of insanity." Fields would never get treatment for his mental illness; it was up to me now to keep him from the execution chamber.

Normally, I would use the bond I had forged with my client to connect him to the jury. Then, when I asked the jury to spare his life, they would be considering the life of someone they "knew." But since I had been unable to build a relationship with this client, I needed a stand-in. Fields's daughter, Cherise, was the only choice.

I took to meeting with Cherise at a McDonald's not far from her high school. I couldn't go to her home. The rest of the family was dead set against helping Fields. Besides, the girl really liked McDonald's fries.

As difficult as it might be to understand, Cherise loved Fields. She related wonderful "dad" stories about him — how he would read *Green Eggs and Ham* to her over and over again, how he walked her to church and school, and taught her to ride a bicycle. Her eyes filled with tears as she told me how Fields had helped her with math, and then the tears spilled as she described how she had witnessed the father she loved come apart, piece by piece.

I knew what that felt like, at least to some extent. When I was ten years old, my mother got "sick." That's all we children were told. No one used the words *mental illness*. All we could see was that she was sad and no longer did the things we were used to seeing her do. She didn't drag us to plays with her, or sing arias in the kitchen, or quote Shakespeare when we children needed chastising. Twice, she was hospitalized. The neighborhood children called my mother names, and some wouldn't play with us. A few of the parents remained kind, but many shunned us, as though her sickness were contagious. As the oldest child, I had to grow up fast, to help out the family in her absence. I was frightened, and I know the experience deeply affected me. I was lucky, though. My mother was, and still is, a strong woman; she found a way to get better. And once she recovered, she was there for me, doing all the things mothers do for their daughters through adolescence and beyond. Cherise's dad just kept getting worse.

Through our shared experiences and my reaching out to her, Cherise and I developed a relationship. She agreed to speak on her father's behalf, in spite of her family's angry disapproval. I hoped that would be enough.

The prosecution went first in the sentencing phase. They had little evidence outside the crime itself, not that the crime wasn't enough.

They presented the incident with the tenant and the brick, as well as transcripts from divorce court in which Fields sounded menacing. Their part of the sentencing trial took up barely the morning.

When the judge excused the jury for lunch, Jamie and Jed offered to get me food, but I didn't want any. I find it difficult to eat during a trial, partly due to nervous energy. I also half-believe that my "suffering"—not eating and not sleeping—is part of what I must do to win. Call it superstition or asceticism, but it's a feeling I can't completely shake.

After the recess, I began presenting my mitigating evidence with the physician who had treated Fields after he was shot. That was just a warm-up, though; my case rested primarily on Cherise and on Fields's long-time spiritual mentor, Pastor Henry. Strangely enough, given Fields's race-focused paranoia, the minister was white. His testimony breached, at least momentarily, the racial schism in the courtroom. No one spoke a word about race, but you couldn't avoid it. The judge, the prosecutors, and a gallery packed with the friends and co-workers of the victims were all white. The defendant on trial for his life was the lone dark face.

Pastor Henry supported the death penalty, and this made him an effective witness. He told the jury that he believed that the State needed the death penalty to protect itself, but it was not necessary in this case. Mr. Fields was a believer, he said, a good man with psychological problems, who would pose no danger to anyone in prison. That was an important point. The alternative to death in this case was life without parole. Those are the only two options when someone is convicted of multiple murders. That these are the only choices works to my advantage in avoiding a death sentence. Otherwise, a jury may fear the defendant's release on parole. Even though that is an improper consideration in terms of sentencing, it often plays a role in the decision.

After Pastor Henry testified, Fields took the stand to give a rambling statement to the jury. He had insisted on speaking, despite our advice that he not do so — or maybe because of it. He raved incoherently about white conspiracies and white doctors trying to stop the growth of the black race. He thundered about God's laws being more important than society's laws. Occasionally, he would stand and weave about at the front of the courtroom. The diatribe went on for the better part of an hour.

When it ended, the now-sixteen-year-old Cherise came to the stand as my final witness. She wore a girlish navy blue dress and flat black shoes. Her hair was straightened and neatly parted in the middle. Glasses dominated her face, magnifying her naturally large eyes. Sitting nervously on the stand, she looked young and alone. I prompted her to recount the stories she had told me about her father. For the first and only time during all the hearings and phases of his trial, Fields listened and remained absolutely quiet.

"Cherise," I said when she had finished her stories, "can you tell us what you hope to do with your life when you finish high school?"

"I want to go to college," she replied quietly.

"Do you know what you want to study?"

"Yes." She paused. "I want to be a police officer, like my dad was before..." Her voice cracked. I looked away from her. I wanted to keep my emotions under control.

"Before?"

"Before he started thinking that way and actin' so..." Cherise couldn't find the words, but it was her presence, her vulnerability, and her belief in her father that mattered.

"Cherise, you know this jury has a hard choice to make, right?" She nodded. "So is there anything you would like to tell them that might help them in choosing which punishment to give to your father?"

Cherise nodded and cleared her throat. I heard a muffled stirring behind me. The judge's widow was weeping and had turned her head into her son's shoulder.

"I love my dad. I know there ain't nothing, I mean, there is nothing can be done to bring them people back. But...I would like to be able to talk to him sometimes, you know, while I finish growing up."

I nodded at Cherise. "Thank you. Now the prosecutor might have some questions for you, so hold on and let's see if he does." I held up my hand to her and turned to the lead prosecutor, raising my eyebrow at him. He shook his head. Nothing would be gained by questioning Cherise, and he knew it. Closing arguments would follow the next day.

I had asked a friend if I could spend that night at her apartment. I had been living alone and loving it. But on this night, before my first death penalty closing in front of a jury, I needed emotional support. I could have turned to Jamie and Jed, but I hesitated to show them how frightened I was. These days, I no longer worry about showing fear to colleagues, but back then, I still felt I couldn't afford to look weak.

Colleen Grace, my friend and colleague at the Public Defender's Office, was the perfect confidante. Our clients mattered to her. Though she never tried a death case or even a murder, she would not make light of what I was going through. And she already knew Fields's case.

"Are you hungry?" Colleen asked as I walked through the door of her second-story walk-up, my ratty garment bag in tow.

"Not really," I said.

She grinned. "You must really be worried." A bad appetite wasn't usually one of my problems. I sat down on her dilapidated plaid couch.

Colleen tucked her long legs under her on a chair opposite me. She was an attractive redhead, with no trace of the hot-headed temperament that supposedly accompanies the hair color. Her calmness was already soothing me.

"Is there anything you should have done that you didn't do in this case?" she asked, knowing the answer. I shook my head.

"Is there anything you could have done to get your client to work with you that you didn't try?" I shook my head again.

I knew what Colleen was doing, and maybe I could have done it for myself. But the connection with my sister-in-arms was as important as the questions she was asking. Criminal defense, like combat, forms an intense bond between people. And working in the Homicide Task Force is a little like the work done on *M*A*S*H*. Only with your comrades can you tell autopsy jokes. As Colleen asked me a few more questions designed to show her confidence in me, I felt better. Still scared, but better.

"Did you say something about dinner?" I finally asked. We laughed and talked deep into the night. Friendship, not sleep, was what I needed.

The prosecution's second chair opened the closing arguments the next morning, laying out the facts with precision and great detail. He recounted, step by step, the premeditation that had gone into the crime. He reconstructed the fear and horror of those who had witnessed the killings. He spoke of the loss society had suffered with the death of these two men of stature and the even greater loss to their families. He stated simply that Mr. Fields had forfeited his right to live. He was really good.

And then it was my turn.

When I began trying cases, the theory was — and remains today — that juries have short attention spans, and attorneys should make their points as quickly as possible. I don't deny that Americans are impatient. I think we lawyers would be in a bunch of trouble if juries had a remote control they could use to switch away from us to something more entertaining. I understand the principle that a closing argument should be a half hour or less. I simply disagree with it. When a life is at stake, I think a jury forgives an attorney for taking more time. Besides, in Illinois a death sentence must be unanimous. One dissenter means life in prison instead of execution, and you never know what point might sway just one juror.

So, on this occasion, my first death penalty closing to a jury, with a gut feeling but no experience to back it up, I decided to take my time. A sensitive attorney can gauge the prevailing energy in a courtroom, and in this one, after the prosecutor's closing, the air was hostile to Lonnie Fields. I wanted to slow the pace, to allow the jurors time to think and feel about Mr. Fields, about his mental incapacities, and his innocent, lovely daughter.

I stood, took my notes and a flip chart, and walked to the lectern. I reviewed the evidence. And then, using the flip chart, I began to laboriously list and explain each aggravating factor on one side of the chart and each mitigating factor on the other. This is a risky tactic unless you are totally fair. You have to admit the damaging material and not sugarcoat it. For this defendant, the bad evidence was front and center: he had killed two people. Deliberately. In addition, he had sometimes acted with brutality in his police career. I could counter with the fact he had also at times acted with bravery, but the facts were what they were. Then I began to list the mitigating factors, taking my time, explaining each one. I could list more mitigating than aggravating factors, and I hoped the simple arithmetic would work to my advantage. I trusted that if I were clear and committed to what I was saying, the jury wouldn't mind if it took a while.

My mother was in the courtroom that day, offering moral support. She later told me that she had worried that I was taking too long with the list. But then she noticed various jurors fixing their eyes on the chart, and she began to appreciate its power.

When I had finished the lists, I ventured into another untested, and possibly more dangerous, tactic. I was determined to make the prosecution pay for its continual reiteration of the words *judge* and *attorney* when describing the victims.

"Ladies and gentleman, I feel obliged to comment on something. I don't know about you, but I am a bit offended by the prosecution's constant reference throughout this trial to the status of the two deceased gentlemen." The jurors looked at me in some surprise. "I know their jobs were important, but should it matter one little bit if Lonnie Fields killed a judge and a lawyer, or two factory workers, or two bums on the street, or two criminals? Isn't every life as important as every other one?" I saw one juror start to nod, and I homed in on him. "I'm not saying these men's lives don't matter. They do. But you can't think that Mr. Fields should be executed for these crimes because of the victims' class or..." I took a deep breath, ready to speak the unspeakable, "or because of their race."

Behind me, at the prosecution table and in the courtroom, people stirred. No one said things like that out loud. I had not cleared my intention to raise this point with my partners. I had been afraid that if I had, they would have told me to can it. They would have said that those issues should be discussed in the office or in the bar, not the courtroom. But I felt it was time to "name the dragon," a concept that comes from mythology: if you learn the true name of a dragon, you gain power over it and it can do you no harm. The dragon here was racism, and I was damned if I wasn't going to take away its power. It was the first time I called out the ugly beast that I have repeatedly confronted throughout my career.

"The judge is going to instruct you," I went on, "that a person's race or class or religion should have nothing to do with your decision in this case. But let's not kid ourselves. This case had gotten the attention that it has," I gestured at the packed courtroom, "because of who died. It is my fervent hope, ladies and gentlemen, that you will not kill Lonnie Fields because of it."

The State objected, claiming the point to be irrelevant, but the judge overruled the objection. I reminded the jury of the pastor's testimony and spoke tenderly of Cherise's view of her father. After maybe an hour and a half, I began to wind things up.

"I don't know what it is like to fall to pieces like my client did or become convinced that God is telling me to do something awful. But I do know what it is like to watch someone you love fall apart." I could see the light of recognition in some of the jurors' eyes, remembering a time they had watched helplessly as someone close to them had succumbed to illness. I hoped that my mother heard the love with which I said this.

"And I also know that life is precious and redemption always possible. So, as I close, asking you to spare Lonnie Fields's life, I want you to think about this. Do we exact revenge on a sick man, a damaged man, a man who is loved? Do we take him in our time? Or do we choose life in prison without parole, and let God decide when he should die?" I walked away from the lectern and looked at Fields, his daughter, and the full courtroom. "All I am asking is to let Cherise talk to him sometimes, while she finishes growing up."

I sat down, spent, barely hearing the prosecution's rebuttal. I hoped that my raising the status issue had gutted one of their central themes. The prosecutor would think twice now before saying the words *judge* and *attorney*. When the rebuttal ended, the judge gave the jury their instructions. Soberly, they filed into the deliberation room to decide if Lonnie Fields would live or die. Fields was taken to the holding cell, and Jamie, Jed, and I returned to the office — to work, I thought, but actually, just to wait.

That's why the news that the jury was finished stunned me. They had been deliberating less than two hours. The previous brief deliberations in this case had resulted in decisions that Fields was fit for trial and was guilty of two first-degree murders. Now, as I rushed back to the courthouse, my insides were cold with foreboding. How could I bear it if my client, the person I was responsible for defending, was sentenced to death?

I was spared finding out. The jury foreman read the verdict clearly: "Life in prison without parole."

Angry explosions came from Fields, but I ignored him. I turned immediately to find Cherise. The two of us shook with relief in each other's arms. When I bid goodbye to her, the joy of the verdict was shadowed with the knowledge that, for now, this brave young woman was an outcast in her own family. She and she alone had been willing to speak on his behalf. The rest of the family may have been relieved at the life verdict, but they would likely resent her helping that to happen, or even feel guilty about not having helped themselves. But if redemption for Lonnie Fields remained possible, I hoped that reconciliation within his family must also be.

Jamie and Jed talked to the press. I just couldn't. I went home and fell into bed.

CHAPTER 4

Judge Misogyny

THE WALK from the parking lot to the courthouse entrance at 26th Street was only a block, but this morning it felt like a mile. It was windy and raining, and I had underdressed for the weather. Beautifully impractical shoes threatened to send me crashing to the wet pavement at any moment. Arraignment court started precisely at nine, and I could not afford to miss my new client's case being called.

Lincoln Freeman was charged with first-degree murder. A gang scuffle on Chicago's West Side in March 1983 had left a young man dead. Lincoln had been fingered in a lineup as the shooter. The case was not complicated... except for the fact that Lincoln was likely the wrong guy. In the arraignment, he would be formally charged, enter a plea, and the presiding judge would assign the case to one of the judges within the system. There are more than thirty judges at 26th Street. Which of them got the case could have a profound effect on my ability to prove Lincoln's innocence.

Fortunately, in Illinois, when the charge is murder, a defendant can invoke up to two "SOJs," that is, substitution of judges. The defense is given ten days from the time of arraignment to file an SOJ, but it is much easier to make the motion in front of the presiding judge on the spot, and have him ask the computer for another name, than it is to go to the assigned judge and file the SOJ with him. If I didn't make it to the arraignment on time this morning, I might have to tell a judge to his face that I wanted somebody, anybody, other than him. That was why I was risking a broken ankle on the slippery courthouse steps.

I arrived in the courtroom just before the chief judge took the bench. Whew. I sat down and glanced at the call list. I needn't have rushed. Lincoln Freeman, my client, was about twenty-five cases down.

Nearby, other task force members were likely doing what I was doing: praying to the computer gods to save them from the most egregious judges. At that time, there were four of these supremely bad jurists in the system. The Hanging Judge was known to brag that he had sent more men to death row than most states had. The Corrupt Judge could be bribed. If he wasn't paid off, he came down like a hammer. The Vicious Judge was perpetually angry, an ex-prosecutor known for the particular delight he took in winning death sentences. The final member of this "worst of the worst" club was The Bigot. He was closed-minded, foul-tempered, and had earned a reputation as a tool of the State. If two of these names came up, I would have to use both of my SOJs, and I could still end up with one of the remaining ones.

Why, even in a jury trial, does the judge make such a difference? The judge rules on motions to let in or keep out evidence; he enforces, or doesn't enforce, the rules of discovery; and he determines whether you will get enough time to prepare properly for trial. The judge also decides how jury selection will be run; she or he rules on objections during trial, and determines what instructions the jury will get before deliberation.

Most important, the judge creates the courtroom atmosphere. Juries look to the judge for guidance, and if the judge dislikes you, the jurors can tell. If, when you get up to cross-examine a witness, the judge rolls his eyes, turns his chair around, and tosses his pen into the air — I am not making this up — the message to the jury is clear: don't listen. If the judge's behavior signals that the defendant and the defendant's lawyers are bad people, well, that makes it damn difficult for the defense counsel to reach the jury intellectually and emotionally.

At this hearing, my client would find out who was presiding over his trial and, thus, over his life. Even though his was not a death penalty case, the prison sentences available if he were convicted ranged from most-of-the-rest-of-his-life to all-the-rest-of-his-life.

But until his case was called, I had time to contemplate my life outside the courtroom. I was dating a sweet and bright man named Eric, who, to my deep satisfaction, liked to dance. Music is essential to me. Finding someone for whom it was equally important, and who actually enjoyed going dancing, I felt as if I'd struck gold. But the gold was showing some tarnish. Eric was beginning to complain about my work. Why did I have to interview witnesses on a Sunday? (Well, that's when they're at home.) Why couldn't I leave the office at five o'clock or five thirty, like most people? (Because the work isn't finished by then.) And why was I breaking my neck over this client who wasn't worth it? (Would you want someone who had your future in her hands thinking that way?) I sighed. A month-long trial had once cost me a boyfriend. Was there some way I could keep that from happening again? Eric was *such* a good dancer.

My reverie ended when Lincoln Freeman's name was called.

"Here," I said as I walked to the bench, joining my client, whom I had first met at a hearing three weeks earlier. Lincoln was a high-school dropout, but had earned a GED and was working part time at a little food market. He was nominally affiliated with the neighbor-hood gang, but possessed a geniality and optimism rare for the West Side of Chicago. Short and slight, Lincoln was just twenty but looked older. Perhaps it was his tendency to cock his head to the right as he listened to me. At first I thought he had a hearing problem, but it appeared to be just a habit.

"Good morning, Miss Lyon," the presiding judge greeted me. I smiled at him. He ran a tight ship, and while his background as a prosecutor sometimes showed through, he tried to call the balls and strikes fairly. I liked him.

"Good morning," I replied and then added, "I hope."

He understood. "Mary?" the judge said, prompting his clerk for a courtroom assignment.

The clerk called out the name of the Corrupt Judge. I stifled a moan and indicated that I wished to soJ this judge.

"And who else are you naming?" the judge asked. Damn. I was hoping to see which name came up next and use my second soJ only if I had to. But I was obliged to identify the second judge I would soJ if the presiding judge asked. I replied with the name of the Hanging Judge.

The presiding judge smiled. He could have guessed. The Hang-ing Judge and I had had a dust-up during the previous election, when the Women's Bar Association had found him unqualified for office. Because I was on the judicial evaluation committee, he blamed me. He didn't seem to understand that using the C-word to refer to a female appellate justice (who had reversed one of his decisions) in front of that justice's law clerk had caused most of his troubles. Who was right or wrong didn't matter, however; for my client's sake, I had to stay out of the Hanging Judge's courtroom.

The computerized "roulette wheel" of jurist selection landed on another name.

The clerk called out the name of the Bigot, who will hereafter be referred to as Judge Novak. I tried to look stoic.

I leaned over and told Lincoln I would meet him in Judge Novak's courtroom for the hearing that would follow. Damn, damn, damn.

I had never tried a case in front of Judge Novak, but I knew his reputation. He was a bully, and like other bullies, he preyed on the weak. In a courtroom, that means the defendant. Judge Novak was known to denigrate defendants and their lawyers in personal and often bigoted ways. And he nearly always did exactly what the prosecution wanted. Most judges do tend to "vote" with the prosecution; it is politically expedient to do so. The press will hound a judge who grants a motion letting a defendant go, but not for "throwing the book" at a defendant. And a lot of the judiciary are former prosecutors themselves. This is a typical route to the judiciary: a career as a prosecutor, preferably with a good high-profile win, and then politicking with the judiciary on the bench, who can vote you as an associate judge, making it easier to run later.

Nevertheless, most judges will give the defense the ruling if the law and the facts require them to do so. Ideologues on the bench, however, make rulings based merely on their own sympathies. There weren't many ideologues on the Cook County bench then, but Novak headed the list. If I nurtured any hopeful doubt about this judge's reputation as I walked into his crowded courtroom, the big mocking smile with which the prosecutor greeted me squelched it.

"So, Andrea, guess your luck wasn't so good," he smirked.

"Maybe not," I replied. "But don't start racking up that win just yet."

He was about to reply when the door to the judge's chambers opened and Judge Novak stepped out.

"Hear ye, hear ye," the nasal voice of the courtroom sheriff intoned. "This Honorable Court of the Circuit Court of Cook County is now in session, the Honorable Chester Novak presiding. Please be seated. No talking or reading while court is in session." These days, of course, the "turn off cell phones" admonition is included.

Judge Novak's clerk looked to him and said, "Judge, we have two cases off arraignment, one murder. Want me to call them first?"

That would be my case. I hadn't had a chance to see if Lincoln had arrived yet, so I began to walk to the left of the bench, toward the swinging leather-covered door, which led to the anteroom, to the jury room, and, back and to the left, to the lockup, where my client would be.

"Where are you going?" the judge boomed. I didn't immediately realize that he was talking to me, but the absolute silence that followed tipped me off. I stopped, turned, and met his glare. Even though he sat above me on the bench, I could tell I had half a foot or more in height on him. Great. Would I have "little man" stuff to deal with, too? Okay, maybe I'm guilty of stereotyping, but my experience has been that men in positions of power who are shorter than me feel compelled to let me know that they command the driver's seat. Some of my women friends say I imagine this. Maybe so, but none of those women are six feet tall. Judge Novak's hair had thinned above his round face. His light, nearly colorless eyes were fired up.

"I was going to see if my client had been brought up, Your Honor," I answered in an unexceptional tone.

"Your client?"

"Lincoln Freeman," I replied. "He was just sent here off arraignment, and I heard your clerk indicate you might wish to hear arraignments first, so I was going to see if the sheriffs had brought him up yet."

The courtroom experienced the unsettling silence that fills a crowded place when someone's private words are suddenly heard by everyone, or in that moment on the playground right before a fight starts. My heart rate accelerated, even though the words exchanged had contained no obvious threat. This was Judge Novak's courtroom, after all.

"You're a lawyer?" he asked, incredulous.

"Yes, Your Honor. I'm sorry, I should have introduced myself. My name is Andrea Lyon. I'm a member of the Public Defender's Office."

"Task Force?"

"Yes, sir."

"Well, well, well." The judge looked around to make sure he had the room's attention. "Why did they send you here? Don't you know that I don't like women lawyers?"

Really. What do I say to that? By this time, I was an old hand at dealing with sexism from clients and colleagues, but with judges, it was trickier. If I responded in kind — the possible replies were tantalizing! — he could take it out on my client, and it was my client who would have to do those extra years. On the other hand, if I didn't fight back, the judge might think he could walk all over us, and that could have equally bad consequences. The courtroom remained still while I considered my options.

I had encountered misogyny on the bench before. Early in my career, I had been assigned to the courtroom of a judge who referred to me as "that broad." He called me "Mr. Lyon" and "sir" in open court. To keep from losing my temper, I continually repeated a mantra to myself, "This is his problem, not yours. This is his problem, not yours..." By the second day of one trial, I could see the four women on the jury, as well as one of the men, crossing their arms, body language that I think communicated their disgust. Those sympathetic folks struck back: they refused to convict and hung the jury. That experience helped me to develop my Judo Theory of Advocacy: they come at you, you move, they fall.

That day in Judge Novak's courtroom, though, I sensed that saying nothing — the equivalent of moving out of the way — would not be effective. This judge was not just prejudiced. He was mean. I decided to stand up to him.

"Actually, Your Honor," I said, "I had heard that you don't care for my gender." I smiled disarmingly up at him. "Of course, I didn't know if that was just gossip or the truth. I guess I know now." I took another step toward the lockup and then turned. "As to why I'm here, well, I ran out of SOJ's." I thought I heard the clerk gasp.

As I passed the sheriff on my way to the lockup, he pretended to cough. His eyes met mine and he winked. Well, at least I had one friend in the room.

"Hey, Mr. Freeman," I said, as I walked toward the floor-to-ceiling bars in the lockup. In our initial meetings, Lincoln had calmly related to me the events on the afternoon of the murder just as he had to the police. Now apprehension, even fear, animated his face.

"This ain't good news, is it?" he asked.

"You mean being assigned to this judge?"

He nodded.

I could have tried to reassure him, but I wasn't in the mood for platitudes after the judge's performance out there, and besides, Lincoln already knew better.

"No, it isn't good news," I admitted.

Lincoln shook his head. "If it weren't for bad luck..."

"You'd have no luck at all," I finished for him. He looked up at me.

"You know that song?"

"Which version do you like best?" I asked. "Personally, I like Bobby 'Blue' Bland."

"That's too old school for me," he responded. I smiled. I wasn't that much older than him, but I was surprised he liked blues at all. Most younger folks don't.

"That's me: old school," I said mock-sternly.

"I didn't mean you was old or nothin'," he protested. Someone had told him never to imply that a woman was old.

I laughed. "Don't worry about it. At least, not about that." The reference to the situation at hand sobered us both. I stressed that I would need information from him, primarily the names of anyone who could confirm his statement. The two of us went into the courtroom to appear before Judge Novak. The case was ordered continued, which, perversely, means *not* to move forward until a later time. This was expected, because a case goes through a process — discovery is exchanged, investigation has to be done, motions have to be filed and then heard, and then you set a trial. It takes at least a year before a murder case goes to trial, and even longer before a death case. Now I had to put aside my worries about the judge's maliciousness and focus on Lincoln's case.

On the West Side of Chicago where Lincoln lived, two factions of one gang were locked in conflict: the regular Gangster Disciples (GDs) and the Conservative Gangster Disciples (CGDs). The dispute sounded bizarrely like a division between Goldwater Republicans and neocons, or Reform Jews and Orthodox. The conservative faction felt that the regular faction wasn't living up to the gang's "code." Lincoln belonged to the regular GDs; the victim of the fatal shooting had been a member of the CGDs.

The police report relayed the facts of the case. On a spring evening in 1983, Edward Healey, his cousin Floyd Healey, and a friend named Frankie — all "conservative" gang members — were walking north on Lavergne Street when a much larger group of young men from the GDs began chasing and taunting them. A fight broke out between Edward Healey and a member of the other group. A shot was fired. The bullet struck Floyd Healey in the chest. He died later that night. No gun was recovered.

In Edward Healey's statement to the police, he admitted that he had engaged in a shoving match with a member of the opposing faction. He also maintained that his friend Frankie had intervened and broken them up. When they began to disperse, he said, someone from the crowd of opposing gang members drew a gun and shot Floyd. From a lineup, Edward identified my client, Lincoln Freeman, as the shooter. Frankie made a similar statement to the police, although he could not identify the shooter.

The police also interviewed Lincoln. He acknowledged that he had been in the crowd but claimed that he had not joined in the fight, did not have a gun, and had not shot anyone. I believed him.

Does that sound naïve? I think it was less naïve, actually, than the police's assumption that he was guilty. Their conclusion was based on one witness's identification; there was no physical evidence and no real investigation. Lincoln's explanation felt honest to me. By this time, I had represented a lot of clients, and I had learned to rely on a combination of evidence and gut instinct. Some criminal defense lawyers will tell you that factual innocence doesn't matter to them; some actually instruct their clients not to tell them what really happened. The truth matters to me. I don't push a client to tell me what happened; I try to let the facts emerge naturally. In time, a client will usually reveal what he is responsible for and what he isn't. Sometimes I have had to confront a client I knew was lying to me. The lies can go either way; I have had clients say they were guilty when they weren't. But the truth makes a difference. If your client is guilty — of some- thing, anyway — you work to make his situation better and ensure that his rights are protected. If he is innocent, you do everything you can to exonerate him. The odds are, however, that he will be convicted anyway, especially if he is a member of a despised class. In this case, Lincoln was poor, black, and a gang member.

With their ID in hand, the police considered their investigation complete; now it was time for mine. The chronically underfunded Public Defender's Office had a few professional investigators, but for the most part, the attorneys did their own footwork. I didn't mind. To me, detective work is one of the best parts of the job, and I was getting better at it all the time. Many lawyers are too attached to words, particularly the written word. Many read a police report and think they know the case; worse, they assume that the report is true. It might be, but many times I have gone to the scene to check out the police version and found the facts to be more favorable to my client — or, sometimes, less. There is no substitute for visiting a crime scene, walking around it, testing what you can see from certain perspectives, and letting the ambience of the place sink in.

Beyond the crime scene particulars, the investigator's most important resource is people. Witnesses do not have to tell you anything. But I have found that if you go into a neighborhood and ask, politely, for information, most people will talk to you. Asking for information isn't enough, though. You also have to listen to, and hear, what's being said beneath the surface. I like to think I have learned that skill. Everywhere I go, people want to tell me their stories. In a restaurant, the maitre d' will sit down and tell me all about his divorce — or his new kitchen. The truth is, I want to hear it. I love learning about people's lives.

When interviewing witnesses, one attorney often pairs up with another. An investigator needs a "prover," someone who can attest to what the witness says, in case the witness later changes his story. In addition, prosecutors sometimes claim that we have misrepresented ourselves to witnesses as police or State's attorneys when we are gathering facts harmful to the prosecution's case. I always figured that witnesses should tell the truth no matter who interviews them. But those allegations could get us into trouble, so we have to clearly identify ourselves, and bring someone along to verify.

The insurmountable drawback to thorough investigative work is the time it consumes, as the annoyed great dancer Eric could attest to. Given that reality, I often used to declare that I would not marry or have children. In order to be great at criminal defense work — and I mean Clarence Darrow great, which is what I wanted to be — I believed I had to forego a normal family life. A woman had to make a choice: marry, have children, and raise them well, or give what an illustrious career demanded. I was accepting a double standard, perhaps, but that's how I felt. I would be content to remain single and be an outstanding lawyer. But that didn't mean I didn't want love and companionship.

When the time came to kick off the investigation into Lincoln's case, I asked my student intern, Steve, to come along as my "prover." Eager for experience in the real world, law students are generally happy to tag along to housing projects, oft-robbed convenience stores, or, in this case, K-Town, one of the roughest neighborhoods in the West Side. Steve was a congenial young white kid from suburban Arlington Heights. He was an earnest worker and a decent writer, but his pale complexion gave the impression that he didn't get out much. This was the first time I had invited him to go with me on an interview. I needed to talk to Edward Healey and his friend Frankie about the night Floyd Healey was murdered.

"Hey, Steve, ready to go?" I asked, packing police reports into my battered tan briefcase.

"Sure," Steve said, looking not at all ready. Uh-oh, I thought, someone had told him about K-Town.

"Remember, all you have to do is listen and follow my lead. If you think I've forgotten to ask something, tug on my coat. Of course, we represent the person charged with killing these guys' friend and cousin, so they might tell us to get lost."

Steve swallowed. "Sure." He paused. "Will it be dangerous?"

"Probably not," I said. "If it feels dangerous, I'll get us out of there right away. But it's the middle of the afternoon, so we should be fine."

"Do you...ummm," he hesitated.

"Yes?"

"Do you have a gun?"

This guy had been watching way too much TV.

"Steve, it's going to be fine. But if you don't want to do this, you don't have to. I can ask someone else." He looked crestfallen. "I'm not saying you shouldn't be concerned," I continued. "It's important to pay attention, but I don't think we'll be in any physical danger."

I decided not to mention a recent investigation at a bar not too far from K-Town where I had managed a feat that had eluded me through years of P.E. classes: a forward standing roll. While I was trying to chat up a patron, someone had come into the bar shooting. In heels and a pale blue brushed-cotton suit, I dived into a somersault to reach shelter under the bar. It turned out the gunman was just a drunk who felt like making noise.

"And to answer your question," I said, "no, I don't have a gun. I'm afraid of them."

That made him smile. "Really? But you try murder cases."

"Odd, I know. But there you have it."

Steve seemed reassured. We went out to my little red Volkswagen Rabbit convertible. For years now, I have owned only convertibles, even if living in Chicago means for many months in the year, the top never comes down.

We arrived at the Healeys' neighborhood a half hour later. Single-family residences and multifamily flats lined the block. Some were well maintained; many looked sad, even abused. Steve glanced around nervously as we walked toward the Healey home. He appeared, if possible, even paler than usual. We headed up the sagging porch steps and knocked on the door.

A fortyish woman appeared.

"Hello, ma'am," I said. "I'm a lawyer with the Public Defender's Office, and this is my law clerk. We were hoping to speak to Edward Healey. Is he around?"

"Maybe. What do you want?"

I explained that our business concerned the shooting of Floyd Healey, who was, as it turned out, her nephew.

"I don't see why Edward should help you," she said. By this time, other people in the house had crowded up behind her on the other side of the screen.

"To tell you the truth, Mrs. Healey," I responded, "I'm not sure that Edward will be helping us. What he has to say may be good from our point of view or bad. Either way, I want to be able to tell my client."

"Why?" She seemed genuinely curious.

"I'm supposed to give Mr. Freeman advice," I replied. "My advice might be, 'We have a good chance in this case, let's go for it,' or it might be, 'Hey, we should plead guilty and try to get the best sentence possible.'"

Just then a lanky young man elbowed his way forward. "That's okay, Mom," he said. "I can talk to them." He stepped outside onto the porch and down the front steps, gesturing for us to follow.

"Sorry about that," he said. He had the awkward walk of an

adolescent recently grown tall. "Who are you again?" he asked, and I explained. "I probably shouldn't be talking to you," he said.

I grinned. "I'm sure that's what the police told you, even though it's illegal for them to tell you that."

"What you mean?"

"See, I can't make you talk to me. If you tell me and my clerk here to take a hike, that's what we have to do, and that's what we will do." I paused. "But no one can make you *not* talk to us, either. It's one hundred percent your choice."

"You representin' that guy who shot my cousin." Now there was no question in his voice.

"I am representing the guy you picked out of a lineup, yeah," I replied. "What I don't know is if he shot anyone or was just in the crowd, or if, out of everyone in the lineup, he just looked the most like the shooter. I don't know anything, and so I don't know how to tell Mr. Freeman what he should do."

"You tryn' to make me out a liar?" Edward asked matter-of-factly.

Well, it might be that I would have to do that, I thought, but I didn't know yet. "Look," I said. "I can't give legal advice to my client based on what the police wrote down in a report. The report might be totally inaccurate." He was nodding now, and seemed in no hurry to get away. Often when I interview witnesses who have a close relationship with a murder victim, I run into anger or grief. I wondered why I wasn't seeing that in Edward, but I didn't think it appropriate to ask, so I just waited quietly. But apparently, he read my mind.

"You surprised I ain't mad at you?" he asked.

"Actually, I'm just surprised you're so calm. I don't think I would be, just a few weeks after something like this." I could feel Steve's eyes going back and forth between Edward and me.

"I can't afford it," Edward said.

"Can't afford what?"

"Can't afford to let nothin' show. Don't mean I ain't feelin' it."

I thought about that. "Sorry," I said. "I was assuming, and I *did* let that show, didn't I?"

The young man nodded solemnly and then told us about the night of Floyd's death. Most of what he said jibed with the police report, but he added a few facts that opened up the possibility that he was mistaken about who shot his cousin. He told us it was dark that night and that he was nearsighted but wasn't wearing glasses or contact lenses at the time of the shooting. Edward didn't say that he was *not* sure that Lincoln had been the man with the gun, but by the end of the conversation he sounded *less* sure.

When Steve and I interviewed Edward's friend Frankie, the other eyewitness, he told us he was stoned that night. He also told us that during the shooting, he was too busy fighting to see much and that he never saw Lincoln with a gun. Of the other young men present that night, no one else could make an identification either; they were drunk, high, distracted by the fight, or just not willing to talk to us or the police.

This was all helpful to us, but the one person I really needed I couldn't find. Lincoln had told me that a young man named George Pinckney had been with him in the crowd that night. Pinckney wasn't a gang member, Lincoln said. He had grown up in the neighborhood and was just visiting that evening. The bullet that killed Floyd Healey had come from behind and passed right between Lincoln and Pinckney. Find Pinckney and I could have corroboration for what Lincoln told the police. The fact that the shot came from behind the two would explain how Lincoln could have been mistaken for the shooter.

But where was Pinckney? I dragged poor Steve out onto the streets half a dozen times more before his semester ended, and then another hapless student after him. I could find relatives and acquaintances of the elusive Mr. Pinckney, but no one had his current address or would tell us if they did.

For months I told Judge Novak that we were still investigating the case, but I did not name Pinckney as a witness we were looking for. What if he didn't corroborate my client's story after all? I needed first to get to Pinckney myself, to find out what he would say. I looked for him for more than a year. All this time, Lincoln sat in jail, because like most of my clients, he couldn't make the half-million-dollar bail typically set for murder charges. Although I did not want to go to trial without Pinckney, eventually I had to inform my client that I wouldn't be able to avoid a trial date any longer.

The trial was set to begin on a Monday morning in early December 1985. I told Lincoln I would try one more time to find Pinckney over the weekend, but that we would most likely have to rely on Lincoln's statement to the police and my cross-examination of the other witnesses. He seemed resigned. I left at the prison office the dress pants, button-down shirt, and a sweater I had gotten at the thrift store for Lincoln to wear at trial. He was disappointed not to be wearing a suit, but I had learned that my more streetwise clients tended to look either uncomfortable or much too slick in business attire.

On Saturday morning, once again leaving a disgruntled Eric, I walked all over K-Town with handfuls of subpoenas for George Pinckney. I served one at every address he or a relative had lived in. It didn't qualify as "proper service," since I wasn't putting the subpoena directly into his hands, but I figured one of them might make its way to him, and he would at least call me.

Astonishingly, that's what happened. On Sunday morning, I got a message from George Pinckney. We met at a diner west of the Loop. Rarely are such meetings so gratifying. Not only did he confirm that the shooting had happened just as my client had said all along, but he told me why I hadn't been able to find him. He attended Lincoln College (college!) in Springfield, Illinois, hoped for a career in computers, and was serving in the Army Reserve. He seldom came home to the neighborhood, because "things is too bad around here," and he was trying to walk the straight and narrow out of that world. I had to restrain myself from hugging and kissing the guy. His testimony wasn't going to be good. It was going to be spectacular!

Monday morning I appeared in court and asked to file what's called an amended answer to discovery. In Illinois, as in most states, the prosecution and defense have to inform each other of who their potential witnesses are, so the other side has the opportunity to seek its own interviews. I had never listed Pinckney as a witness, in order to make sure that I got to him first. But now that I had him and knew what he would say, I wanted to name him.

The prosecutor, a freckled, stocky fellow, objected. "This case has been pending for a year, and it's set for trial, and *now* she wants to add a witness?" His tone was outraged.

"Your Honor," I explained, "I have been looking for this young man for the entire time this case has been pending. I didn't add his name because I hadn't yet located him and didn't know where he lived or even if he really was a witness to the crime."

Judge Novak cleared his throat and tugged at his collar. I tried to steel myself. "Is this the way you practice law, *Miss* Lyon? Trying to hide witnesses from the state?"

The prosecutor rocked back on his heels. He didn't need to do a thing; the judge would do it all for him.

I plunged in: "Your Honor, things happened exactly as I have told you. I realize that adding a witness at this late date puts the State at a disadvantage. And so, while I am prepared to go to trial today, I would have no objection if the court chose to continue the trial so that the state can get ready."

"This case has been on my call too long as it is," Judge Novak answered. "I think you're just trying to avoid going to trial." Damn. I couldn't win with this judge. If I wanted to start the trial as planned, I wasn't being fair to the prosecution. If I suggested putting it off, I was trying to avoid trial.

I took a deep breath and tried to stay calm. "Your Honor, I am here, ready for trial." In retrospect, this may have been a mistake. I should have written a formal motion for a continuance, taking the blame for not being ready, but ensuring that I kept my witness.

"So you say. State, you want a continuance?"

After a whispered huddle with his co-counsel, the prosecutor announced, "We're ready, too. We just ask that counsel make this witness available to us to interview." I said sure, I would have him come in early on the day he testified.

The trial began positively. Lincoln sat attentively beside me, drawing strength from the proximity of his mother and loyal girl-friend, sitting in the gallery. I sensed that the jury members, while abhorring gang violence, cared about determining who had actually shot Floyd Healey. My opening statement laid out my client's story. The statement he had given the police made sense. Furthermore, my cross-examination of the State's two eyewitnesses revealed the flaws in their testimony: one was fighting at the time of the shooting and not wearing his glasses, and the other was stoned.

Still, I knew that wasn't enough. We give reverent lip service in this country to the presumption of innocence. The state bears the burden of proof, we claim. But no matter what we say, presuming innocence is counterintuitive. People cannot believe that police would arrest some-one if there were not good reason. The jury understandably wants to take action when a violent crime has been committed, and they are reluctant to free someone they fear could be dangerous. Even if the prosecution's case is weak, the defense can win only if the jury feels comfortable voting not guilty. They need the defense to show how the crime couldn't have happened the way the prosecution said it did, or, even better, a compelling alternate theory. Otherwise, even if the jury admits the state's case is weak, they may convict anyway, or compromise with a lesser offense when an acquittal would be more appropriate.

In Lincoln's case, I wasn't able to demonstrate that my client could not have fired the gun. And I couldn't identify an alternate suspect. But I could offer an alternate explanation of events, a corroboration of Lincoln's statement by a clean-cut witness with no axe to grind: the college-attending, computer-career-planning Army Reservist George Pinckney, telling the unvarnished truth. With my hard-found wit-ness in hand, I might have had reason to feel fairly confident...if Judge Novak had not been sitting on the bench.

He was, though, and the trial turned into a nightmare. The "Hon-orable" Chester Novak rolled his eyes every time he looked my way and spoke disdainfully to me in front of the jury. The prosecution took every opportunity to ask the police officers if they had "even heard of one George Pinckney," laying the foundation to contend that Pinckney had conveniently just "appeared." I got lucky when one of the officers on the scene admitted that he had spoken to a young man who had said that a bullet had "whizzed by" him.

The biggest challenge was to avoid being sucked into a nasty fight with Novak and the prosecution and losing sight of what I was about, which was taking this jury with me to K-Town and showing them what had happened that night. It took all my self-control not to answer back, especially on the day I asked to move the bulletin board. This large claw-footed cork board, used for displaying the court calendar and the occasional trial exhibit, was placed so close to the defense table that I would nearly collide with it every time I pushed my chair back to stand up. So I asked the sheriff (my friend from the first court appearance) if I could move the board slightly so that I could get up more easily. He said he didn't mind, but that I had better clear it with Judge Novak. Not wanting to incur any disapproval from the judge, I knocked on his chambers door just before court on the second day of trial. After being invited in, I respectfully explained to the judge, seated at his desk, about the placement of the bulletin board and asked permission to move it.

"I guess so, as long as you put it back," he replied. I nodded and was turning to go when he added, "If you lost some weight, this wouldn't be a problem." Then he laughed — so help me, the same laugh I remember from countless episodes of unkind teasing in the schoolyard. I wish I could tell you that it didn't bother me, because after all, this man was a bigot and a bully. But that would be a lie. He hit my vulnerable spot, something bullies can sense a mile away, and it hurt. I couldn't let him see that he had scored, though, so I simply stared at him until he broke the gaze by looking down at the papers on his desk. I turned on my heel and went out to the courtroom, where the sheriff helped me move the troublesome board. I think he had heard what the judge said, but to my deep appreciation, he merely told me that the board looked better in its new position.

Later that afternoon, the state rested its case; we would begin the defense the next day. I told the prosecution I would produce Mr. Pinckney shortly before 9:00 a.m., so they could interview him. The only other witnesses I planned to call were my student intern, Steve (who was getting paler at the thought, I was sure), a police officer who would clarify some testimony about the crime scene, and a task force investigator who had taken some photos I had used in cross-examining the State's witnesses. We had decided not to put Lincoln on the stand, since he would have little to add to his police statement, and the risks were too great. Lincoln was making a positive impression in court, though. He stood when I got up to cross-examine, and held my chair out for me when I returned. His mother and his girlfriend attended every day.

The next morning, I brought Pinckney to court with me, having already asked him to give an interview to the prosecution. He went into the anteroom outside the judge's chambers with a young prosecutor from their team and investigators for both sides as witnesses. I retreated to the defense table to chat with my co-counsel, Alex. Alex was the public defender assigned to Judge Novak's courtroom. Because he was new to felonies, his role in the trial was a minor one, but he was smart and observant.

Fifteen minutes later, the young prosecutor walked out of the antechamber and rushed over to his two superiors. Alex and I exchanged glances.

"Those guys look worried," Alex said. I glanced over at the huddle and grinned.

"Maybe they figured out what a great witness Pinckney is, and it's occurring to them they might lose," I said.

"Yeah, I think that's it. What worries me is what they're going to do about it."

"What can they do?" I asked innocently.

Alex knew better. "Andrea, this is Novak's courtroom. I'm here every day. If they can think of a way to stop you from winning, they have an ally on the bench." I realized he was right, but I couldn't imagine what they could do.

A few minutes after the judge took the bench and before the jury was brought in, I found out. The prosecution asked to make an objection on the record.

"Your Honor, we want to renew our objection to the defense calling this witness. We believe now, based on our interview with him this morning, that defense counsel has known about him for months and deliberately sandbagged the court. We ask that you bar his testimony."

What? This was outrageous. Hadn't we been through this already, when I added his name? I reminded the judge that I had told him and the prosecution that I had known of Pinckney's existence but had been unable to find him until right before trial. I also reminded the judge that I had offered to agree to a continuance, had given the prosecution all the information I had on the witness, and that they had said they wanted to proceed to trial. I should have saved my breath.

"Counsel," Judge Novak said, drawing out the word into three syllables. "I told you my view of your behavior. I agree that you deliberately sandbagged the State. I am inclined to grant their motion to keep this witness off the stand."

"Based on what evidence?" I asked. I was angry now and past caring if it showed. "Based on the fact that the prosecution has figured out that they might lose this case, because this college student, with no criminal record, is a terrific witness who corroborates what Mr. Freeman told the police?" I saw Novak's face and neck grow red, and he was tugging at his collar again.

"Just exactly what are you saying to this court?" he boomed.

"I am saying that there is absolutely no evidence to this assertion, and that it appears to me that your rulings are based more on who makes the request than what the law says." You could have heard the proverbial pin drop. I felt my knees weakening. Television lawyers may routinely talk back in the courtroom, but this was real life, where attorneys are deferential to judges, no matter what the provocation. I knew better than to do this, but my anger had gotten the upper hand. Beating up on me throughout the trial was bad enough, but denying an essential witness who could testify to my client's innocence? That was more than I could stand. And, yeah, I was probably still mad about the weight comment.

"Young lady, you are close to contempt." I knew it already. "I am granting the State's motion. Now sit down. We are bringing out the jury." He looked right at me, triumphant. No, I wasn't going down that easily.

"No, sir, I will not sit down until I make an offer of proof." An offer of proof is what you do if you are trying to put in some evidence or ask a question on cross, and the judge stops you. It is a way to tell a higher court what the witness would have said, a way for me to tell an appellate court how important the witness Pinckney would have been. Although I would keep on trying, I knew now I was going to lose this trial, and I had to lay the groundwork for appeal.

Judge Novak had no choice. Not allowing me to make an offer of proof would virtually guarantee a new trial, so he let me put on the record Pinckney's sterling background and his firm assertion that the bullet that had killed Mr. Healey had come from behind and between Lincoln and himself.

The rest of the trial passed in a blur. I put on my remaining witnesses and argued the case the best I could, trying hard to make eye contact with the jury, willing them to see how unfair the trial had been.

The jury was out overnight, but the next day they convicted Lincoln Freeman of first-degree murder. After the judge had kept Pinckney off the stand, I had warned Lincoln what to expect. Nevertheless, a murder conviction is a hard and frightening reality. His mother wept; his girlfriend was distraught. I told Lincoln that I would handle his appeal myself. It would add to my already crushing caseload of twenty-five murder cases, but I would find the time. The bailiffs led him out of the courtroom.

I stayed behind while the courtroom emptied. In Illinois, attorneys are allowed to talk to juries after a trial if the jury members agree. I always elect to talk to the jury — win, lose, or hung — because I always learn from them. Only they can tell me what mattered to them, what opportunities I missed, and what critical factors decided the case for them.

But first, Judge Novak, per custom, went into the jury room to thank the members for their service and to answer questions. I waited for my turn. From the jury room, the sound of raised voices emanated. Never before (or since) had I heard anything like that during a judge's visit to the jury. I never found out what passed there, but when Judge Novak returned to the courtroom, he had clearly decided to be "nice" to me.

"You shouldn't feel bad," he said. "These gangbangers are just bad guys. You did a good job." I wanted to hit the bastard. It wouldn't have been fair, though, since I was so much bigger. Instead, I met his phony paternalism with contempt.

"Judge Novak," I began, "don't blow smoke up my ass." I could hardly believe what I was saying, but I wasn't going to stop now. For maybe the first time in my career, I felt complete, unswerving confidence that I was right. "I have two promises to make you right here and now. I am going to write this appeal myself, and I guarantee you this case will be reversed and back in the trial court in eighteen months. Second, I am going to do my level best to see to it that you are not retained in the next election."

I kept my word on both counts. My confidence in the righteousness of my causes — both Lincoln's innocence and Judge Novak's unfitness for the bench — gave me the gumption to fight for them. Lincoln's conviction was overturned. The court ordered him a new trial, but when the prosecution offered him time served on a lesser count, he took the deal and went home. And after like-minded colleagues and I launched an almost unprecedented campaign against a sitting jurist, the citizens of Cook County voted no on returning Judge Novak to the bench.

Eric voted no also, on continuing our relationship. I began to wonder if even a satisfying dance partner could coexist with the fight for righteous causes.

CHAPTER 5

Differences That Divide

W E SYMBOLIZE our system of justice with a blindfolded lady. And yet, within that system, the human tendency to make judgments based on superficial differences among us is repeatedly laid bare. To lesser or greater degrees, prejudice has played a role in practically every case I have ever tried, but two stand out, for different reasons.

Isaac Douglas was an acquaintance of mine, a blues guitarist I knew from my frequent visits to Chicago's live music clubs. When he was a child, his birth family gave him up, and no one else ever offered him a permanent home. Isaac struggled, but combining day jobs with studio and club work, he managed to make a life for himself. And then he became obsessed with Renee, a woman he loved who left him without warning or explanation. Isaac repeatedly phoned her and tried to see her. She obtained restraining orders against him, and still he called. Eventually, misdemeanor charges worked their way up to felonies. By the time mutual friends contacted me, Isaac had been charged with illegal communication with a witness and intimidation of a witness. Renee was considered a "witness" for the earlier restraint violation charges.

I had seen enough abused women to know that stalking was an offense to be taken seriously. This case had a twist, though. Isaac played for me the taunting phone messages Renee had left for him: "You can't call me, Isaac, but I can call you. Do you still love me, Isaac, do you still love me?" She was intentionally driving a depressed, deluded, and pathetic man crazy. Now Isaac was looking at up to seven years in prison for making a phone call he shouldn't have.

I told the prosecutor's office about the recorded phone messages, expecting, or at least hoping, they would drop the charges. But they refused. Could their response have anything to do with the fact that Isaac was black and Renee was white? By this time I had experienced hundreds of prosecutors' decisions. Too many were influenced by mindless double standards. I had no doubt that if Isaac had been white or Renee black, this case would have gone away.

I prepared a defense based on Isaac's distressed mental state and on character witnesses who could testify that they had never seen Isaac behave in an intimidating or violent manner.

As the trial began, I felt the presence of that "dragon" that needed to be named in order to be defeated. Race was guiding the prosecutor's choice of jurors. At that time, each side could use ten peremptory challenges to excuse potential jurors. Prosecutors have long used peremptory challenges to rid juries of African-Americans, acting from the belief that black people are more sympathetic to black defendants than white people. The Supreme Court has declared that using peremptory challenges to exclude jurors based on race is illegal. But it's darn tricky to prove. This prosecutor used all ten of his peremptory strikes to dismiss jurors of color. Fortunately, increases in minority voter registration meant that there were more than ten

African-Americans in this jury pool. We ended up with a panel of nine whites and three blacks.

Then, during his questioning of witnesses, the prosecutor repeatedly asked if the witnesses found Isaac "intimidating," or if Isaac carried himself like he was "from the streets." There was a fine line here, admittedly, because the charges related to intimidation, but especially in his closing, I thought the prosecutor's argument went right up to, and maybe even crossed, that line. Consciously or unconsciously, he was appealing to racism in the jury.

To make that accusation without sounding "politically correct" or confrontational is difficult. But the prosecution had let the dragon in the door, and I needed to challenge it. In Lonnie Fields's case, I had called out the prosecutor for exploiting the victims' status and race, but I intended to go further this time. When I got to my closing, I reminded the jury of the lack of evidence that Isaac intended to intimidate or harm Renee. I spoke of his being depressed rather than violent. Then I took a deep breath and broached the still-taboo subject.

"Before I finish, ladies and gentleman, there's an issue in this case that hasn't been spoken about directly, and it needs to be. That issue is race." I gulped more air, frightened, but believing in what I was about to say. "It is the defense position that no crime was committed here, and that if Renee were a black woman or if Isaac were a white man, we wouldn't be here." Immediately, the prosecutor stood, shouting objections to relevance. The judge responded with what's called a "non-ruling" and told me to continue.

"If you have any doubt about it," I went on, "please remember back to jury selection when this prosecutor excused every black juror he could." I looked at the three African-American jurors sitting in the front row. "*You* are here because he ran out of challenges."

The prosecutor jumped to his feet again, and this time, the judge sustained. I turned to the prosecutor and said quietly, but in a voice audible to the jury, "Look me in the eye, then, and say it isn't true." Directly addressing opposing counsel in that way is patently improper. I admit now I shouldn't have. But my anger had built up for years — anger for every client who had been treated more harshly because he "looked dangerous," for every man stopped by police because he didn't "belong" in a neighborhood, and for all the capable people of color who were unfairly excused from juries. I calmed myself, accepted the objection, and continued with my argument. Nevertheless, I hoped the jury had noticed the prosecutor blush when I threw the challenge at him.

When the jury retired to deliberate, I walked with a colleague to Jean's, a nearby bar that was the favored hangout of the courthouse set. Prosecutors occupied one half of the long and dingy space, and defenders the other. It wasn't as if the two sides didn't speak to each other. But drink together? Uh-uh. My entrance prompted a few sarcastic comments on my recent closing. Word had gotten around fast. I ordered my usual grapefruit juice and sat at a table of co-workers. The telephone behind the bar rang regularly. Before cell phones, secretaries knew to call Jean's when verdicts came in. Sometimes juries had questions during deliberations; more than once, I had to rush back to the courtroom as the only sober lawyer in the bunch.

I had barely settled down with my juice when the bartender called out, "Lawyers on the Douglas case; you've got a verdict."

The jury acquitted Isaac. When I spoke with them afterward, the white foreman said that the jury members appreciated my having broached the subject of race. "You gave us permission to talk about it," he said. Bringing up race is often castigated as "playing the race card." But defending a person's life or freedom in the courtroom is no game. And when race is used against a defendant, that "card" needs to be turned up where everyone can see it.

RACE, OF COURSE, isn't the only difference you might confront in the courthouse. And sometimes the result is not what you expect.

Russell Leland was a round-faced, bright-eyed young man. At the age of five, already a victim of sexual abuse, he had been removed from his home. Like Isaac Douglas, he had spent most of his childhood in the Cook County foster care system. Continually uprooted from one foster home to another, Russell was denied the most basic belief that he was wanted by anyone. When I met him, he was nineteen, of average height and build, with a medium-brown complexion. What was most noticeable about Russell was the innocence that clung to him despite where he had been and what he had become. Russell was a prostitute. And he was accused of first-degree murder.

Russell lived in a rooming house on the near South Side of Chicago, not far from the high-rise projects that then oppressed the area. Originally a single-family home, the building had been cut up into tiny hot-plate-equipped bedrooms, let by the week and euphemistically referred to as "apartments." The renters shared a bathroom at the end of the hall and a sitting room with a refrigerator. Each bedroom door bore a padlock on the outside that the occupant could lock when leaving the house. Most of the residents did not have telephones or receive mail. Many were desperately poor and addicts as well, a combination that did not make for a secure environment.

Russell worked occasionally doing manual labor through a temporary employment agency. After the agency deducted its fee, his take-home dipped below minimum wage. The jobs strained his body and numbed his mind. When I got to know Russell better, I speculated that he had resorted to turning tricks, not just for the money, but because he was bored. Sadly, he got far more excitement than he had bargained for.

The victim in this crime had been a client of Russell's. One of the primary factors that erodes the "justice" in our criminal justice system is the unequal impact of the victim's identity. This was true with Isaac's Renee, and it's especially true in murder cases.

Race dominates these distinctions, but socioeconomic status matters, too. A dead businessman is perceived as more important than a dead homeless person. That's why the Lonnie Fields case had been particularly tough; the victims were not only white, but also men of stature. When an "important" person is killed, the efforts to find the killer and the impetus toward a harsh punishment are greater. Conversely, if the victim belongs to a category of people over whom the police, prosecutors, and jurors can shrug their shoulders, it just makes my job easier, sad to say. These perceptions are not necessarily conscious, but they are real.

In Russell Leland's case, the victim was African-American, but educated, married, and middle class. He was, in fact, an assistant principal at a Chicago public high school. That profile, I anticipated, would present a challenge.

This fifty-year-old educator had kept his desire for young men a secret — at least, from his wife, according to what she told the police. I cannot imagine what it must have been like for that woman to find out, first, that her husband had been killed, and second, that the suspect was a teenage male prostitute. I sympathized with her, but considered the victim a creep — for cheating on her, denying his sexuality, and exploiting adolescent prostitutes.

The school administrator had found Russell in one of the shady haunts that cruising men are attracted to and had hired him for sex. The deal included various entertainments with ropes and other restraints. Russell agreed, but the sex play turned more violent than he had anticipated. While Russell was gagged and restrained, the older man brought out a knife. I don't know that the victim planned on using the weapon, but Russell felt threatened. He managed to knock over the chair to which he was tied. The chair broke, allowing him to get free. He grabbed the knife and stabbed the assistant principal. Several times.

After vomiting repeatedly, Russell ran out of the apartment that his client had rented for these purposes. He wandered aimlessly until he spotted a Catholic church. He went in, found a priest, and promptly confessed to the killing. The priest recommended the young man turn himself in, but Russell was afraid. He returned to his rooming house and was still there, shivering on his bed, when the police arrived a day later. Investigators had tracked the deceased's phone records and found Russell easily: the teenager had given the man the number of the pay phone in the rooming house hallway.

Russell told the police everything. The detective's report noted that he spoke in a flat tone and stared at the floor. He behaved similarly when I went to the jail to see him for the first time.

"Mr. Leland?" I stood as he entered the visiting room in Division Six of the Cook County Jail. This visiting room was a little nicer than some of the others. As usual, the walls were of dull jail-green cinderblock, but at least the cubicle we were in offered a substantial table and two chairs. I put my hand out to shake his, but Russell didn't see it. He was staring down at the floor.

I had been worrying about him ever since I read the police reports. I knew gay men fared poorly in jail. They were abused and often raped. Sometimes prison officials isolated a gay man for his own safety, but I didn't know if Russell had wanted to be alone.

"Mr. Leland?" I repeated. I ducked down into his line of sight. "Won't you sit down?" I gestured at the chair, and he slid into it, very carefully, as if he hurt. Uh-oh, I thought.

"Mr. Leland, my name is Andrea Lyon. I'm a lawyer from the Public Defender's Office. I'm *your* lawyer." He wasn't reacting. His slow breaths made me think he was ill or crying, or both. "Are you feeling all right?" I asked.

"I guess." He had a surprisingly baritone voice for his size and age. He still wasn't looking at me.

"Look, Mr. Leland — "

"Don't call me that," he interrupted.

"Okay. Why not?"

"I ain't no 'Mr. Leland' to nobody," he said. "I ain't no 'mister' at all." The words were hostile, but the tone was defeated. I didn't know how to respond. Reassuring him, telling him everything was going to be all right, would have been ludicrous. He had confessed to killing his john, after all. I didn't want to insist that he was "Mr." to me, because that would have rung false. I had just met him. Lastly, I didn't have the least idea how to begin talking about whether he was being assaulted in jail.

So, when in doubt, tell the truth. "I don't know how to respond," I said. "I would like to say you don't need to worry, but that would be a lie." I sensed he was listening. "I could tell you that you deserve to be called 'mister,' but, after all, I've just met you, so that wouldn't sound honest, even though it is what I think." I took a breath. "And I don't have the least idea how to broach the subject of what is happening to you in here." For the first time, he looked up, his eyes startled. I held up my hand. "You don't have to tell me, Mr. Leland, you really don't. But I can't help without information."

I let my hand drop and just sat there. I didn't see what more I could say. It was up to him now, and I was prepared to wait. After what felt like a long time, he spoke again.

"What you say your name was?"

"Andrea Lyon."

"You a lawyer?"

"Yes."

"You gonna help me." I couldn't tell if it was a question.

"Yes. I have to do a bunch of work before I will know what I can accomplish for you, but, yes, I will help you."

"It your job." His voice was flat, carefully controlled. As I found out later, his life had been defined by authority figures who lied to him. They said he would be safe in foster homes, but he wasn't safe. They said he would be adopted, but he wasn't. He never got to finish high school; they kept sending him from place to place. Why should he believe me?

"You aren't a job, Mr. Leland. You're a person." He looked up, and I smiled. He nodded, a "we will see" kind of nod.

When I represented Russell in the mid-1980s, I knew gay people. But the gay people I knew were middle class. Sarah, a close friend from my early days in the Public Defender's Office, was a lesbian. I had met my friend David when I was in law school. He could always be counted on for an enthusiastic response to any invitation to an outing for which I wanted to bring, but didn't have, a date. After I returned to Chicago, he would visit, and we would dance our way across the city.

Russell Leland lived in a different kind of world. Maybe poverty or lack of education made the difference. Or maybe it was because his early life had taught him, over and over again, that no one would love him for the person he was. In my work, I have seen too many adults who had been lost in the labyrinth of the child welfare system.

Sometimes, they managed adequately, eventually making it through school, getting a job, and maybe finding a way to have love in their lives and families of their own. But many of them grew up to become criminal offenders or victims, drug sellers or users, members of the sad congregation of those chronically in trouble. Sometimes an individual not only is a product of the child welfare system but carries an additional stigma: being gay, for instance. With both strikes against him, Russell's chances of attaining a legal, productive, and loving life were that much slimmer.

For months, I worked on his case, learning more than I had ever wanted to know about the grim ways in which he survived. His was a world in which older, ostensibly respectable men routinely paid young, living-on-the-edge male prostitutes for sex.

By gathering information from other rooming house residents, I was able to locate and interview another young man who had been hired by the man Russell had killed. His encounter with the assistant principal had grown violent as well. This was good evidence for Russell's self-defense claim.

Learning about Russell's world was depressing; discovering more about Russell himself was a pleasure. Underneath his painful self-loathing, the young man was smart and imaginative. One day, while I was visiting him in jail, he opened up a little about his slide into prostitution. There was no glamour in selling sex, he told me.

"It's nothin' like in them movies," he said.

"No hookers with a heart?" I teased.

Russell smiled. By now, he was comfortable with me, knowing I wasn't offended by his sexuality. "Not a one. I kept thinking, you know, that if I could just turn a few more tricks, just get ahead a little bit, I could..."

"What?"

"It's so gay." His smile was wry.

"What is?"

"I wanted to go to the Chicago Design School. I can draw, and I know how to make a place look good."

I thought about the photos I had seen of his little room. Posters decorated two walls, and a swath of bright cloth covered another.

"I could see that," I said.

"Maybe." So much hope and despair in that one word.

"Maybe you'll have the chance." As I left the jail that afternoon, I was heartened by how far Russell had progressed from the first time I met him. Now I just had to find a way to ensure that he'd have a future in which to keep on growing.

Once I felt prepared to try the case, we still had to decide whether to choose a bench or jury trial. Russell's case had been assigned to Judge McCarthy, who had a good reputation with the defense bar; trying the case to him alone instead of a jury was worth considering. On the other hand, he was viewed as a little behind the times. How would this lurid tale play with him? I hesitated to make a recommendation to Russell without more information. I decided to ask for a conference in chambers.

In many judges' courtrooms, much of the decision-making goes on in chambers. Judges assist with plea negotiations, the parties involved discuss relevant legal issues, and cases are "pre-tried." Because judges prefer to limit the number of jury trials, which require more time, effort, and expense than bench trials, a judge may listen to both sides in a conference and tell them what he or she would do if there were a bench trial. If a defense attorney would like to reduce the seriousness of the charge, and the prosecutor won't do it for a plea, the defense attorney will ask to "conference" the case in hopes that the judge will indicate that he'd go for a lesser charge. The judge may even indicate what kind of sentence he'd hand out. In a busy judicial system like Chicago's criminal courts, conferencing helps move cases along and has the added benefit of helping the defense determine whether to go with a bench or jury.

We were scheduled to conference Russell's case on a breezy morning in April. As I battled the Chicago winds that whistled in force down the gap between the courthouse and the administrative building, my mind worked and reworked a plan for handling the meeting. I always prepared ahead for court appearances. Still, the drive to 26th Street and the walk from my car afforded a last-minute opportunity to rethink. The challenge with this conference was that I could not anticipate how crusty, old-fashioned Judge McCarthy was going to react to the sordid story I was about to tell him.

The appropriate resolution of this case, in my opinion, would be a finding on the lesser offense of voluntary manslaughter. I was sure that Russell had acted out of fear, but reasonable minds could disagree about whether his fear was warranted. If he had planned to kill the john — in retaliation for humiliating him, for instance — then he was guilty of first-degree murder. If he feared that he was in danger of death or great bodily harm, and that fear was reasonable, then he had a right to use deadly force and was guilty of no crime at all. But if he had "an unreasonable belief" that he needed to use deadly force — in other words, if he overreacted — then he would be guilty of voluntary manslaughter, a term Illinois later changed to second-degree murder.

While I believed Russell had been terrified, I knew a jury might hold against him, first, his "career," and second, his consent to the potentially rowdy sex game. Frankly, they might simply hate him for being a homosexual. I hoped Judge McCarthy would find the scenario less shocking than a panel of twelve average citizens would.

He had been in the criminal courts a long time. The judge would be able to see the merits of the homicide case apart from the provocative context. At least, I hoped he would.

Judge McCarthy started court at ten in the morning, in one of the newer courtrooms. Our conference would have to wait until after the judge had completed administrative business. At that point, we would go back in chambers. John, the prosecuting attorney, wasn't keen on participating in this conference. He feared exactly what I was hoping for: that the judge would lower the offense. John could have refused to conference, but he also knew that making a fuss might be counterproductive for him in the long run.

"Good morning," I greeted John as he walked into the courtroom.

"Hi, Andrea." John had what I call Prosecutor Swagger. It's similar to Police Swagger. I noticed that men who have power in the criminal justice system tend to walk dick first. Really. Check it out sometime. John had been athletic in his youth, but now a beer belly protruded from his suit coat. It was only ten in the morning, but his beard was already overcoming the morning's shave.

"The clerk tells me the judge has a couple of bond hearings," I said. "Other than that, he's pretty free today, so we should get in the back soon."

"Yeah. Then you can tell him your homosexual tale of woe." His voice dripped with sarcasm.

"John, if you were being honest, you would just reduce the damn case to voluntary and we would plead." I said this without rancor. Prosecutorial politics were at work, I was convinced. The DA would have willingly dropped the charge to voluntary manslaughter if the victim had not been a person of substance in the community. Although, so far, the case had generated little press, we all knew that it could blow up at any time.

John merely shrugged; he was saving his fire for the conference. Just then Judge McCarthy ordered a break in the courtroom proceedings and gestured us to come back to chambers.

In these new courtrooms, *chambers* was a grander word than the judges' suite deserved. Each consisted of a small windowless cave of an office, with the requisite private bathroom, of course. Judge McCarthy removed his robe, wiped his face with his hand, and ran his fingers through his hair. He took justifiable pride in his wavy, silver gray locks and wore them a bit longer than most judges would. He motioned to John and me to sit, and took the court file from his clerk. I sat quietly, letting him absorb the scant information in the file.

"Okay." His gravelly voice, signaling his readiness to listen, was directed at the prosecutor. "State, tell me about this case."

John was opening his mouth to speak when I cut in. "Your Honor, John can correct me if I'm wrong," I said, "but since I asked for the conference, would it be all right if I started?"

The judge's glance moved between us. "Hmmm," he said. "State, do you object to this conference?" I held my breath. Judge McCarthy could throw us out if he wanted, if John said he objected to the conference and the judge felt he was being imposed on. Damn it, I thought, why did I have to open my dumb mouth?

I looked over at John. I wasn't sure he'd heard the question as I had. "Sure, let her talk first," he said, affecting nonchalance. I scrutinized him more closely. Was he hung over? Whatever the reason for his laid-back attitude, I was ready to take advantage of it. I jumped right in as I had planned: start with the crime, describe the events objectively, and let the facts persuade Judge McCarthy to reduce the offense.

"Your Honor, my client was hired by the deceased. The deceased was an assistant principal of a high school here in Chicago." McCarthy nodded. I hadn't yet said what he had been hired for. "My client,

Mr. Leland, is nineteen years old and has been making his living mostly as a male prostitute. On the night in question — "

"Wait a minute," McCarthy interrupted me. "Are you telling me the vic was a faggot?" The judge paused, looking back at the file. "Shit," he said. "Well, that makes one less faggot in the world." Quiet hung in the room. Then the judge looked up at me again. "What's your guy's background?" he asked me.

In that moment, I experienced a phenomenon similar to seeing one's life flashing before one's eyes in a near-death event. But in this case, what blazed through my mind was a review of the moral principles and legal ethics I had accumulated in my lifetime. Without realizing it, I had asked to conference a case involving gay men with a homophobic judge. Should I say something? Should I let him know how deeply offensive I found his comment? John was snickering behind his hand.

I wondered how my friend Sarah would respond if she were Russell's lawyer. Would she say something? What if the judge had made a racist remark? Would I let that pass? As a moral matter, remaining silent was the same as agreeing with his bigotry, wasn't it? But that was not how I had always lived my life. I had fought righteously against the prejudices that had put Isaac Douglas and Lonnie Fields at a disadvantage.

Then I remembered: I was not here to talk about my political views of the world. Nor was I here to fight for gay rights, or anything else — except Russell's life, as much of it as I could save. So I swallowed and simply answered his question.

"Your Honor, Russell has been arrested but never convicted of anything."

"What's the bottom amount of time I can give on a voluntary?"

"Three years," I answered.

"That's what I'd do then. How much time does he have in?" At that time, an offense like this allowed for day-for-day good time. This meant that for every day a defendant spent in jail without disobeying the prison rules, an extra day would get knocked off his sentence. He would also get credit for the pretrial time he had spent locked up.

"It's been about eight months, Your Honor," I answered. With a three-year sentence, as long as Russell behaved in prison, he would have to serve only one and a half years total—and he had already served nearly eight months in county jail. "Okay, will your guy take it?"

"He'd better," I said. Then I corrected myself. "Yes, Your Honor, we've talked about this. He will take it. We can do the bench trial whenever you want."

With my head still spinning, the three of us set a day two weeks later to "try" the case in front of Judge McCarthy. The state would bring in a couple of witnesses, I would cross-examine, but essentially, we had already had the trial, sitting there in the judge's chambers. I had allowed blatant, hateful prejudice against the victim to work in my, and my client's, favor. Because the judge did not value the life of the man who died, he gave my client a minimum sentence. The result was a fair compromise, given that the killing could have been seen as pure self-defense. The manslaughter sentence was a reasonable price to pay to avoid the risk of a murder conviction.

I knew I had done well for my client. Nevertheless, I went home and took a long, hot shower.

CHAPTER 6

I Didn't Know I Couldn't Do That

T HE NIGHT PRECEDING my first argument before the Illinois
Supreme Court in Springfield, I talked one of the building
guards into letting me in to look around. I had never before visited
the magnificent courtroom. Its high ceilings were decorated with
frescoes of symbolic figures framed in gold leaf. Ornate sconces held
glowing glass globes. The dark cherry wood bench for the seven justices was carved and luscious looking. Large tables accommodated
the legal teams. Behind them, the seating for visitors was spacious
and comfortable.

I knew that this august institution was ruled by a set of legal and
social conventions. I was well aware, for instance, that one argued
only legal issues here, not the facts of a particular case. I was less
familiar, perhaps, with some of the other court practices. But I never
suspected, as I took in the room's grandeur, that on the following day
I would stand before that elegant bench and defy one after another of
those conventions — and risk looking like a fool. What else could I
have done? I was determined to salvage the dream of Jose Medrano.

The Supreme Court has no monopoly on standards of law and decorum, of course. Courtrooms everywhere are among the last remaining places in today's anything-goes culture in which every participant is expected to behave in a carefully prescribed manner. I have no argument with the conventions that lend order, efficiency, and fairness to legal proceedings. But more subtle constraints are rooted in a mind-set I don't share: the denial of emotion and the need to appear superior. We are taught in law school, for example, that rationality is the Holy Grail, and that feelings have no place in the law. Too many attorneys ignore emotions and then get righteously angry when juries don't. Pretending that a judge or jury isn't going to react to the extralegal subtext of a trial is wishful thinking, and not preparing that part of the case is to invite losing. The very thing that some of my colleagues and most of my opponents patronized me for — being a woman and therefore "emotional" — I believe has made me a better advocate.

I learned the power of being human (as opposed to a legal automaton) early in my career, quite by accident, when I forgot one of the most important words in a trial attorney's vocabulary. I was trying a misdemeanor bad-check case. We weren't denying that my client had written the check that bounced. The question was whether she had intended to defraud Toys-R-Us or had simply made a mistake. During the trial, the prosecutor asked the cashier who had taken the check if he could "tell" my client was writing a bad check. A completely unfair question! The issue of intent was one for the jury to decide, not the Toys-R-Us cashier. The clerk had nodded and was about to launch into his conclusion when I stood furiously to object. The problem was the word *objection* had completely fled my brain. I mentally flailed, angry and now panicked. In desperation, I shouted, "Oh no, you don't!"

Until that moment, I had never raised my voice in court. Everyone looked at me in astonishment. Then the judge began to laugh.

"Are you objecting, Miss Lyon?" he asked, chuckling.

"That's what I am doing, Your Honor! I am objecting!" I said in relief.

Still laughing and shaking his head, the judge ruled, "Sustained." The jury acquitted.

Now, maybe they would have acquitted even if I had remembered the word. What I learned, though, was that the earth did not swallow me up because I let the jury see I was humanly fallible, and emotional to boot. What the jury took away was that I was like every one of them. I didn't need to worry about *looking* like a lawyer. I *was* a lawyer. All I needed to "look like" was committed to my client and her cause.

Lawyers slip into a variety of habits that come out of the super-rational approach, including an overreliance on words. I try to think a little differently. There is a reason why many of us can still remember show-and-tell in kindergarten, and a reason why elementary school teachers still practice this ritual. Showing is as important, if not more important, than telling.

Showing became a key element in my defense of Randy, a client who had been charged in a shooting. He denied having participated in the incident, despite being told by police that he had been identified in a lineup (the truth) and that his fingerprints had been found on the gun (a lie — something that police may legally tell in order to get a suspect to confess). For twenty-six hours, police interrogators questioned Randy at the Area 3 Violent Crimes Police headquarters.

Randy was seated in an armless metal chair and handcuffed to a ring on the wall about four feet off the floor. No one hit him or threatened to hit him. They just pummeled him with questions, over and over again, for more than a day. Fresh teams of officers relieved the interrogators when they tired. And all the while, Randy sat handcuffed to the wall, with little or no opportunity to sleep. Despite all this, he kept insisting that he had not shot anyone. Finally, the police gave up and charged him without a confession.

When the time came for his trial, I wanted to convey how much pressure had been put on Randy to confess. The context added weight to his denials. But merely relating the circumstances in words would not adequately communicate the level of discomfort. When the lead police interrogator testified, I began my cross with a description of the room.

"The interrogation room is about ten feet by twelve feet, correct?"

"About that," Detective O'Shaughnessy stated. He was a big guy who looked uncomfortable in his shirt and tie.

"The walls are made of cinderblock?"

"Yes."

"They're painted a sort of light green?" O'Shaughnessy looked at me with care, realizing I could know this only from having been there.

"I guess you could call it that."

"There is a table in the room?"

"Yes, ma'am."

"And two chairs?"

"Yes, ma'am."

"The chairs are metal, too?"

"Yes, ma'am."

"Straight-back chairs?"

"Yes, ma'am."

"They don't have armrests, do they?"

"No, ma'am." He was trying to loosen his collar.

"And there is a ring in the wall?"

"Yes, ma'am."

"A ring about four feet from the ground?"

"Yes, ma'am."

"And you can handcuff a suspect to this ring, correct?"

He adjusted his collar again and said, "Yes, sir." I laughed to myself. So often, when I get under the skin of a police officer, I morph from "ma'am" to "sir."

"As you did Randy in this case, right?" That had already been established at a pretrial motion.

"Yes."

I walked away from the podium and pulled a straight-back wooden chair into the well of the courtroom. I had already tipped off the courtroom sheriffs that I planned to do this, since I didn't want them to freak out. The jury members watched with curiosity.

"Would you agree that the chairs in the interrogation room were like this one, other than being metal rather than wood?"

"Yes, ma'am." Now O'Shaughnessy looked curious, too.

"Okay, let's move this chair over near the podium and treat the podium as a wall, okay?"

"Sure." He shrugged, looking around as if to say, "What's with her?"

I took out a measuring tape and a roll of masking tape. "Okay, let's see where four feet hits on our 'wall' here," I said. I measured it and put a piece of masking tape at the right spot. "Agreed?" I asked the detective.

"Yes, ma'am."

I then opened a file where I had secreted a pair of handcuffs and a key. I taped the handcuffs securely to the podium at the four-foot mark I had just made.

"Detective, would you please come and handcuff me like Randy was?" O'Shaughnessy cocked his head at the prosecution. Surprisingly, they didn't object. One of them later told me that they had wanted to handcuff me for years. The detective left the stand, came down, and put the handcuff on my right hand — a bit tighter than necessary, I thought.

When O'Shaughnessy had returned to the stand, I continued.

"Would you agree that I am seated in more or less the position that Randy was for twenty-six hours while you interrogated him?"

"Well, he got to use the washroom a few times."

"Other than those times?"

"Yes, ma'am."

"Thank you." I proceeded with my cross-examination of the detective. About fifteen minutes into it, my right arm began to tremble. I controlled it, but fifteen minutes after that, my arm began to shake. I kept going, but I could see concern in the jury's eyes. After about forty-five minutes, I was sweating from the exertion of holding my arm in that position and trying to finish the questioning.

The detective couldn't help but notice. "Do you want me to unhandcuff you?" he finally asked.

"Actually, I would," I replied with a tired smile. "Would it be fair to assume you didn't make Randy the same offer, even after twenty or more hours had passed?"

O'Shaughnessy remained silent. He got the point.

You might expect that I'm now going to tell you Randy was acquitted, but he wasn't. No matter how solid or imaginative the defense techniques, acquittals in the courtroom are damn hard to get. The jury convicted Randy, although the conviction was later overthrown on a point having nothing to do with his interrogation. I still believe my handcuff demonstration was a good approach, and I would use it again.

For Jose Medrano, I took show-and-tell to that grand chamber in Springfield. The case began, as many of my cases have, in the pressure cooker of a neighborhood gang. Jose had grown up struggling against the pull exerted on younger siblings of gang members. His two older brothers belonged to the Latin Eagles; the boys' uncle had also been a member. But Jose was resisting. He was different from his brothers. He loved to cook and wanted to be a "homebody," he told me. He was eighteen and only a junior in high school, but doing reasonably well there, when Sebastian Vargas was killed.

On a November night in the early 1980s, Sebastian drove to his mother's home in Logan Square. The North Side Chicago neighborhood, which later became a favorite of artsy types, was then the epicenter of a raging battle between the Latin Eagles and the Satan Disciples. Like Jose, Sebastian's brothers were also gang members — in his case, Satan Disciples. That night, the curbs were lined with cars, so Sebastian double-parked and ran in to tell his mother that he would go find a parking spot and be right back. Apparently Mrs. Vargas was a stickler for punctuality. She accompanied her son to the door of the building and stood in the vestibule watching while Sebastian walked to the driver's side of his car. Just as he was about to get in, two men ran out of the alley across the street from the apartment building. They both opened fire on Sebastian, hitting him thirteen times. Then they ran back the way they had come. Mrs. Vargas saw her son riddled with bullets but couldn't see the men who shot him. She collapsed in the foyer.

When the police arrived, a large crowd of people had gathered. Unlike many cases, this one was lousy with eyewitnesses — or, at least, people claiming to be. One was a confidential informant, or CI, known to a tactical officer named Shalenski. A tactical officer is not a detective but a plainclothes officer who is assigned to a special beat and who develops information through informants. It's a controversial practice, open to plenty of abuse, but Shalenski was a rare breed: an idealistic cop. His informant on the street that night told him that the two guys who shot Vargas were Satan Disciples named Duran and Delgado. Why they would have hit the brother of fellow gang members, I don't know. Gang intrigue is as complicated as any political or corporate machinations. Shalenski arrested the two that night.

Also at the scene of the killing was Detective Murray, who found his own witnesses. Billy Vanek was a Satan Disciple from whom Murray had gotten information in the past. Vanek told him he recognized the shooters: two Latin Eagle enemies of his. (Right away, I'm suspicious when a witness fingers his sworn enemies.) One shooter, Vanek said, was Chico Hernandez. The other he referred to as "Bear" or "Little Bear" Medrano. Jose's brothers' nicknames were Bear and Little Bear. Jose was called Baby Bear, which he hated. The police picked up Hernandez right away. Detective Murray ran into a problem with Bear or Little Bear, though. Both of those Medrano brothers were in jail — the only alibi I trust, by the way. The only "Bear" left was Jose.

Detective Murray's second eyewitness was a thirteen-year-old named Mario Cortez. Cortez had been walking home on the opposite side of the street from the Vargas home when he heard the shots. He dropped down behind a parked car and looked through the window of the car toward the shooting. The boy reported that he saw only a profile of one of the shooters, and only for a few seconds. Murray kept Cortez's contact information in case he needed him.

After the detective learned that the two older Medrano brothers had been locked up at the time of the shooting, he picked up eighteen-year-old Jose. Relay teams of police officers questioned Jose, as they had my client Randy, but Jose's interrogation lasted three days. He wasn't allowed to make a phone call, and he wasn't given food regularly. Yet he kept telling them the same thing: he didn't shoot anyone, didn't know who did, wasn't a gang member, and had been drinking beer with a friend that night.

Now, what happened to Duran and Delgado, the two who had been ID'd by Officer Shalenski's confidential informant? This is where police politics comes in. Detective Murray outranked Shalenski. Murray dutifully included in his report what the CI had told Shalenski, but he pursued only his own leads. Duran and Delgado were released.

When it became clear that Jose wasn't going to confess, a police car picked up the Satan Disciple Billy Vanek and the young Mario Cortez to bring them to the station to view a lineup. In the car on the way, the officers gave them photographs of potential suspects to pass around and talk about. Jose's picture was included. Vanek went right to it, boasting about how he had recognized one of the shooters as a Medrano and telling the younger boy about Jose's supposed gang membership. At the lineup, Vanek identified Jose as the shooter. When it was his turn, Cortez did the same. Big surprise. Jose was charged with first-degree murder.

Wrongful identification is one of the great dangers in a criminal prosecution. Cortez's ID of Jose was completely corrupted by the ride in the squad car. But even when the police play fair, a person's natural eagerness to solve a crime can result in a tragic mistake. There's a belief that startling and disturbing events "burn" themselves into a person's mind. Science has learned that the opposite is true. The adrenalin produced during an intense experience, such as watching someone get shot, compromises the witness's ability to accurately recall what happened.

For a jury, though, few things are more powerful than an eyewitness pointing at a defendant and saying, "That's the man." The jury believes that if the witness is confident on the stand, he or she must be right. But again, research shows there is no relationship between confidence and accuracy. I have asked many times to present the results of these studies to a jury, but the prosecution's motion to preclude them has always prevailed.

When I agreed to assist my office mate, Michael Morrissey, on on Jose's case, I quickly sized up the players. Jose struck me as a sweet boy, earnest in his desire to stay out of the gang. Billy Vanek, whose eyes never met mine, was probably a liar. Mario Cortez was young and impressionable. The unknown factor was Officer Shalenski's CI, who had fingered Duran and Delgado as the shooters.

We filed a motion to suppress Vanek's and Cortez's lineup IDs of Jose based on the impropriety of showing photographs to multiple witnesses and letting them discuss them. As courts so often do in these cases, though, the judge found a sufficient "independent basis" for the identifications and allowed these witnesses.

We could balance their testimony with an alternate theory of the crime if we could only get to Shalenski's CI. For obvious reasons, an informant's identity is generally protected, but not if he or she is an eyewitness to a crime. On that basis, we presented repeated requests to discover him, as it's called, but the judge refused to order the police to give me his name.

By this time, I was no longer an outsider on the Homicide Task Force. Mike and I had become the de facto leaders among the lawyers on staff. Bill Murphy, the founder of the task force, was long gone; and the current boss lacked Murphy's ability to command and inspire. I was organized, had written motions others on staff could use, was willing to help co-workers, and had grown adept at combining an "emotional" approach with a willingness to kick butt. Mike was the Jimmy Stewart of the task force: tall, straight, and imperturbable, the epitome of integrity.

My father, right, with my Uncle Elliot and Aunt Miriam on the night of their wedding. My arms are wrapped around my uncle's neck. I was the flower girl.

My mother and me when I was a baby

At eight

Delores "Dee" Scales

*In my mid-twenties, when I was
new to Homicide Task Force*

*With Samantha, who
really wanted to play the
guitar with me*

With my brother Jon and sisters Rachel and Erica at his college graduation, 1986

With Samantha at two

Arnie and me on our wedding day, May 18, 1996

Cutting the cake

With Melody Bather-Gardner, one of my "best women" on my wedding day

Will, Samantha, and my goddaughter Mahalia Abeo Tibbs at our wedding

Samantha, Will, Arnie, and me celebrating the fifth anniversary of the Center for Justice in Capital Cases at DePaul University College of Law, Chicago

With Sister Helen Prejean, the keynote speaker at the fifth anniversary of the Center for Justice in Capital Cases at DePaul University College of Law.

With Samantha on the day of her high school graduation

The whole family on the day of Will's college graduation

Colleen Grace (center), with her husband Tom Herlihy (left), and Jamie Kunz

Mike and Nancy Morrissey

Chandra and Mort Smith, my crack investigator, and Ray and Shelby Prusak.

Courtroom sketch

Courtroom sketch

Angel of Death Row

For Illinois prisoners
facing execution, Andrea Lyon
is the last line of defense

By Cheryl Lavin
TRIBUNE STAFF WRITER

he only thing standing between more than 100 convicted murderers and a John Wayne Gacy cocktail is Andrea Lyon, who runs the Capital Resource Center for the State of Illinois. After Death Row inmates have exhausted their direct appeals, she's all they've got.

The feature article in which the Chicago Tribune *called me "Angel of Death Row," when I was running the Illinois Capital Resource Center*

Homecoming day: With Deidre and Bridget McCormack on September 2, 2008, the day Deidre was finally released

With Governor George Ryan and Madison Hobley

Mike and I tried many cases together. He was a devout Catholic who cared deeply about his clients and our work. He still does; he was later named head of the Chicago division of the Public Defender's Office. It took Mike a while to be comfortable with me, as I was loud, Jewish, and often profane. Yet, where it counted, we were kindred spirits. And where our differences complemented, we put them to work. He would often slow me down, help me to see the political side of our work. On the other hand, I goaded him to try new things and to express his creativity.

Shortly after we became office partners, he married Nancy, a teacher in the Chicago public schools and a beautiful woman. I worried when I first met her that she wouldn't like me — and I badly wanted her to — or worse, that there would be weird tension between us because Mike and I worked so closely together. For many years, I was the only female attorney in that office; sometimes, my co-workers' wives and girlfriends would be suspicious and uncomfortable around me. It wasn't me they needed to be suspicious of. I was merely the unwilling recipient of my colleagues' gossip and boasting about their sexual conquests. The stories I heard in the task force contributed to my conviction never to marry. But Nancy wasn't jealous and didn't need to be. Mike was the one guy I was certain didn't cheat.

As Jose's trial drew near, Mike and I were sitting in our shared office reviewing our options. We'd already lost on throwing out the lineup IDs and on forcing the police to turn over the CI. That left Jose's alibi on the night of Sebastian's murder. The friend Jose said he was drinking with was called "Wacko." Just in case Wacko ever forgot his nickname, it was tattooed across his knuckles. He was not a witness I wanted to call to the stand, even though he corroborated Jose's story. Mike was questioning my reluctance to put forward the alibi.

"Andrea, I'm worried that if we don't put Jose on the stand with the alibi, the jury will wonder why," he said. He was in typical discussion mode, swiveled around to face me, tilting back precariously in his desk chair, his long legs filling the space between us.

"I know," I replied, "but if we do, then we have to put Wacko on the stand to corroborate, and he has a record." The credibility of a witness can be challenged by a criminal record if he has a felony within the last ten years or any conviction for a crime of dishonesty. Wacko had two misdemeanor thefts. Those convictions, not to mention the darned tattoo, would damage his credibility.

Mike caught me looking at my knuckles and laughed. But then he countered my argument. "When we say Jose didn't do it, the jury wants us to show who did, or prove Jose was somewhere else, or both. At the very least, they want to hear him say he didn't do it."

He was right, especially on the last point. Juries really like to see the defendant testify. They think, if it were me and I were innocent, I would get up on that stand; I would prove where I was; heck, I would solve the crime myself. Hardly realistic, of course. If the defendant does get on the stand, the jury will decide the case based on whether they like him and believe him, not whether the evidence against him is any good. It's a serious conundrum for the defense.

"I know," I said, "but by pleading not guilty, isn't he *saying* it's not him?"

Mike knew it wasn't the same, but he also understood the risks of putting Jose on the stand. In addition to the Wacko problem, the innocent quality that had endeared Jose to Mike and me would make him easy prey for the prosecution. We finally agreed that it was too risky to let our client testify.

"So, how do we get across how innocent he is?" Mike wondered. "I mean, he withstood three days in the tender loving care of Area Three detectives."

Most people confess under that kind of pressure, some truthfully, some falsely. The first time Mike and I had interviewed Jose, Mike asked the young man why he hadn't confessed to the police. Jose opened his deep eyes in surprise and said, "Because I didn't do it." His boyish face and sweetness of manner made him seem younger than his eighteen years.

"I know," Mike said, "but sometimes, even innocent people confess — when police are as tough on them as they were on you."

Jose had looked pained at the memory. "Yeah, by that last day, I kind of wanted to give in and tell them anything. I just wanted to sleep. But I kept thinking about my dream. And then it was okay." He was utterly earnest.

I smiled and asked him, "What's your dream, Jose?"

The young man's grin transformed his face. "No way, I can't tell you. It won't come true if I do."

Since then, Jose's dream had become a source of curiosity and amusement with Mike and me. "Maybe if we knew what the dream was," I began.

Mike chuckled. "Whatever it is, it must be one strong dream. Damn, I hate innocent clients."

I knew what he meant. Since most trials end in convictions, losing is a reality of the defense attorney's life. When you represent an innocent person, the burden of doing right by them can be painful.

And then the burden got even heavier.

A young woman came to see us, the girlfriend of Duran, the Satan Disciple who had been named by the CI but released by Detective Murray. She said she knew that Duran had killed Sebastian Vargas. He had bragged about it; she even had a photo of him posing with the gun. But she would testify, she said, only if we promised to relocate her and protect her identity. If only we could, but the prosecution alone can protect witnesses. We explained this and urged her to go to the police or the District Attorney's office. But she just looked at us as if we were imbeciles, and said if she set foot in either of those places, she was dead. And if we tried to call her without protection, she would have "forgotten" everything she had said that day. With that, she walked out of the office.

Could this case get any more headache-inducing? Here was a witness who could go a long way toward freeing our client. But if we subpoenaed her, she would deny it all. And if we told the police about her, she might end up dead. We couldn't take the chance. Duran and Delgado, who most likely gunned down the young Sebastian Vargas, would never be held accountable. That's a fact of life in the criminal justice system, as incomprehensible as that may be to Mrs. Vargas.

And so we went to trial, without Shalenski's CI, without Duran's girlfriend, without Wacko, and without Jose's own testimony. We did enter into the record Duran and Delgado's arrest on the night of the killing. We weren't worried about the witness Vanek; he was so obviously lying. Our biggest challenge was the fresh-faced Cortez, who sincerely believed he had picked the right person. We planned to undercut him with evidence that contradicted his ability to see clearly that night. Photos taken at the crime scene on the same day a year later demonstrated how dark the street was, including a photograph shot through the window of a car parked where Cortez had crouched down. Still, we were worried.

The other side, it turned out, was worried, too. The amount of prosecutorial misconduct they committed was a dead giveaway. During the trial, the prosecutor made personal comments about Mike and me, and referred to Jose as a gang member even though there was no evidence to back up such a claim. He even told the jury that all the people in the courtroom were part of the gang. The prosecutor's dramatic sweep of his arm included Jose's father, his mother, with her hair coiled in a classic bun at the nape of her neck, his grandfather in a suit with shiny knees, and various cousins, neighbors, and friends. Our objections to these statements were mostly overruled.

But the worst transgression came during the closing. The prosecutor walked up to the witness stand and said, "Last week, the defense lawyer said that Jose Medrano is telling you that he is not guilty when he pleads 'not guilty.'" He let that sink in and then pointed to the empty witness chair. "Well, you didn't hear it from him."

This was misconduct of the highest degree. The Fifth Amendment of the Constitution states that no one "shall be compelled in any criminal case to be a witness against himself." The fact that a defendant does not testify cannot be held against him. The judge sustained our objection but denied our motion for a mistrial. He instructed the jury and sent them out.

While we waited for the verdict, I asked the prosecutor why he had made that closing argument — pointing to the witness stand, for God's sake! He must have known he was risking a reversal from a higher court. He told me that we had been getting too close to making our case. And if an appellate court reversed a conviction — well, he would have kept a bad guy off the street for a few years, anyway. I looked at him silently. A lot of lawyers, prosecution and defense, operate with a game-playing mentality, but his casual explanation staggered me. This prosecutor had deliberately planned an assault on a defendant's rights, one that the U.S. Supreme Court and thirty years of precedent had expressly forbade. This prosecutor, by the way, later became a judge.

No wonder the jury was confused. Their decision was a split verdict. They found Jose not guilty of the murder charge, but guilty of the lesser charge of armed violence, which was based on the murder they had acquitted him of. No, it doesn't make logical sense, but it is sometimes what juries do when they cannot agree. Wanting to avoid a hung jury, they "compromise" in this manner. Given the verdict's inherent contradiction, the judge should have set it aside and called it an acquittal. But he didn't. He accepted the armed violence conviction and sentenced Jose to fifteen years, a stinging loss.

We were sure we had more than enough grounds for appeal, however. I decided to write the appeal myself. The appellate court agreed to release Jose on bond, which is very unusual. Unfortunately, the percentage that had to be posted for the bond came to thousands of dollars, which his family didn't have.

From jail, the irrepressible Jose wrote a letter to Mike and me that we kept on our bulletin board for years. He thanked us for our work and expressed hope about the appeal. Then he wrote, "You know some of these guys they say, man you got a public defender? Ain't nothing going to happen good from that. They's paid by the state, they ain't no good. I tell them they don't know what they talk about. I told them you do this from your hearts and you gonna get me outta here. In the meantime, I finish my high school here, and help some guys that don't speak English too good. So I can go for my dream later. I can wait." It was signed, "Your friend Jose."

We won in the appellate court: an outright reversal of the conviction based on the inconsistent verdict. The state decided to appeal to the Illinois Supreme Court, a move that kept Jose in jail unless he could make bond. I asked for and got a lower bond, but, still, it was more than the Medrano family could afford.

When the time came for our appearance on Jose's behalf in the majestic court in Springfield, nearly four years after the crime, I invited his family to attend. I didn't realize this was one of those things that "wasn't done." Only lawyers and occasionally a party to the case are present. The jail would not be bringing Jose; a prisoner has no right to be present at an appellate argument. But Jose's family had believed in him and stuck by him. I thought they should be there, so they rented a van and drove to Springfield. My mother and stepfather were also going to be present.

Two death penalty cases would be argued before our case. We were third and last on the day's agenda, and I would be the final lawyer to speak. I was handling this myself; Mike was not there, and I was very nervous.

While observing the arguments during the two death cases, my keen interest turned to unhappy amazement. The justices, all white men at that time, appeared to be paying little or no attention. At intervals, one at a time, they got up and went back into chambers — to use the bathroom, perhaps. Who knew? They seemed to have decided ahead of time who would be "in charge" of each case, because only one justice asked the bulk of the questions. The others didn't seem interested. I got angrier and angrier. I was not going to let these men get up and go to the bathroom during my argument. No damn way. I decided to treat the justices like a jury. I would show them as well as tell them, not only that the verdict was legally inconsistent, but that the trial itself had been unfair and that they had the wrong man. I would get them to care, "conventions" be damned. I could hear Mike's voice cautioning me toward temperance, but then, just as clearly, I heard him say, "Andrea, trust your instincts."

Our case was called. The prosecutor dryly and precisely argued why the court should overturn the appellate court and restore Jose's conviction. Then it was my turn. I walked to the podium and began, "On a dark night in November, Sebastian Vargas made the ghastly mistake of double-parking his car in front of his mother's house. After he ran in to assure her he was there, his mother walked to the foyer and watched with horrified eyes as two men ran out of the alley and shot her son to death. He was shot thirteen times." Wham! Wham! Wham! With the flat of my hand I banged out thirteen shots on the podium. It took a long time. "The two men ran away," I continued, "and Justices of the Supreme Court, they are still running."

I went on to relate the circumstances of the murder. When I came to the faulty identifications, I ducked down on my hands and knees and acted out the bad view Mario Cortez had had through the car window. As I described the improper photo procedure in the police car, I sat at the defense table and pretended to be the driving policeman. When I spoke about the prosecutorial misconduct in falsely claiming that Jose and all his family were gang members, I asked the family to stand and introduced them to the court. I was on fire. Throughout my argument, not one of the justices left the room, not one of them looked anywhere but at me.

When it was over, an attorney from one of the earlier cases came up to me and said with a mixture of astonishment and disdain, "Don't you know you aren't supposed to do that in an appellate court? This is supposed to be an argument on the issues, not a jury closing." I nodded. I knew that, but I wanted the court to do more than think. I wanted them to feel what an unfair conviction this was. I hoped I had accomplished that.

Apparently, I had. We won another outright reversal, which amounts to an acquittal, seven–zip. Would I have won without my show-and-tell? Without taking the chance that I would look like a buffoon? Maybe. Would I do it all over again? Absolutely. Am I glad that in my subsequent appearances before Illinois's highest court I have never felt the need to do it again? You bet.

Jose would be freed. But the maddening bureaucracy of the court system would take forty days to turn the order into a mandate to release him. And it was two weeks before Christmas. So Mike and

I went to the original trial judge and asked him to grant a personal recognizance bond in the meantime. After all, Jose had been acquitted. To the judge's credit, he admitted that ten appellate judges had now said he was wrong, and he signed the order. Mike and I jumped into the car and raced to Stateville to get our client out.

As we drove a happy Jose back to Chicago, he asked us teasingly, "So, you wanna know my dream?"

Mike glanced my way. We sure did, he said.

"I wanna open a store. A little grocery store, with stools where people can sit and talk, an' I'll have Mexican food an' Mexican music. I wanna marry a nice soft girl with — excuse me — with big, you knows. An' have babies an' live on top of the store." He smiled. "That's my dream."

Jose went to work as a carpet installer. He saved his money. He married his girl. He opened his store.

CHAPTER 7

A Mother Accused

ONE DAY AFTER a trial, I returned to find a file on my desk that had been assigned to me from the preliminary hearing court. I flipped through it. Damn. A dead-baby case. I had been dreading the inevitable day when one of these would land in my lap. I am a committed defender of accused killers. But sometimes even I have to struggle to overcome my revulsion in the face of certain crimes.

During law school, I spent a clinical rotation in child advocacy. We represented children who were the subject of neglect or abuse petitions. The work was important and compelling, and I hated it. Satisfying resolutions were rare. Children who were abused, neglected, dirty, and hungry — even these children loved their moms and dads. They didn't want to leave their homes, no matter how miserable those homes were. So, when should the State step in? What, ultimately, is in the best interest of children? The ambiguity of the job was too painful. I intended to stay far away from work involving abused children.

Now, a decade later, I had to defend a woman who had killed her child. Annette Gaines was charged with murdering her twenty-two-month-old daughter Shania. She had admitted to hitting the little girl in the stomach. The blow had been so hard that the duodenum that separates the stomach from the intestines had burst. The toddler's own body had fatally poisoned her. The file told me little else.

On the evening before my visit to the jail to meet Ms. Gaines, I was going to have dinner with my friend Melody. While I drove to Peter Lo's Chinese restaurant on Howard Street, just over the Chicago line, in Evanston, I could think only of the next day's appointment. I wasn't sure I could handle it. Instead of running through potential legal strategies, I obsessed over my own negative reaction. I might not be planning on having any children myself, but I knew what a good parent was, and I had a pretty good idea how parents felt about their children, how deeply they loved and tried to protect them. What kind of a mother would hit her baby hard enough to break the wall of her stomach? The image wouldn't leave my mind.

"Hey, Melody," I said to my old friend as I walked into the restaurant. She smiled and hugged me. We chatted and ordered the dishes on the menu that are so spicy they make you sweat. Melody and I had been friends since I was sixteen. She and her sister, who was my classmate, had come to Chicago from Jamaica. Even though Melody was older and prettier than me, we quickly bonded. It was likely a case of simple empathy: at six foot one, Melody was even taller than me. She was also whip-smart. She had worked her way up from receptionist to vice-president at a black-owned Chicago advertising agency.

After sharing stories about our families, she asked me about work. When I answered vaguely, she shook her head. "You are not fooling me," she said in her Caribbean lilt. "What's wrong?"

I told her about the murdered child. While I talked, I realized why the prospect of this case was causing me so much anguish. I wasn't sure if that realization brought joy or terror.

"Melody," I said tentatively, "you know how I've always said that I couldn't imagine being married, that..."

"That career comes first," she interrupted, "that the last ting you want to be is someone's wife." Melody had trouble with the *th* sound in some words, but she was on a roll now. "That you can't see yourself tied down in a suburb somewhere."

"Right." I laughed a little at myself. "But I've been thinking lately that maybe I would like to have a child." I stopped, wondering if I should be saying this to Melody, who couldn't have children. "I'm sorry."

"Andrea, we been friends too long that you cannot tell me these tings." She waited for me to go on.

"I don't know why I feel like this now. There's no one I would consider marrying. I don't have anyone at all right now." I was in my early thirties. Was this the effect of the "biological clock" everyone talked about? I still loved music and dancing and hanging out in jazz and blues clubs, but lately I seemed to want more. The smooth, handsome guys still exerted their pull on me, but a small voice inside was asking, "What's the point?" Scariest of all, I was beginning to think I might like being a mother.

The possibility of a single woman intentionally setting out to have a baby by herself was just beginning to surface in 1986. I floated the audacious thought to my friend. "But nothing says I couldn't be a mom even if I couldn't find someone I wanted to marry...right?" Left unsaid was my fear that I wouldn't find someone who wanted to marry *me*: a big, opinionated, driven woman.

Melody was pragmatic. "Look, you're getting older. If you're going to do this, you'll have to do it soon, right?"

"I still have some time. But, yeah, once I get past thirty-six or thirty-seven, getting pregnant might be complicated."

"So, what are you going to do about it?" she wanted to know.

I didn't have an answer, but I thought about the question long after we had finished eating and said our goodbyes. The next morning, the question was still churning in the back of my mind as I went to see my new client...the one who had killed her baby.

A first meeting with a client is a delicate dance, and I liked to think I had learned the steps pretty well. As a homicide public defender, I always knew two things about a new client: he or she is in serious trouble, and poor. It's not a good combination. And it makes for a lopsided balance of power between client and attorney.

That lesson had come home to me when I picked up my first death penalty case. At arraignments, the judge appointed me to defend Burton Campbell. I followed my new client into the lockup to give him my card, present a quick overview of what had just occurred, and to let him know that I would come to the jail to talk to him in private within a few days. The lockup was noisy, crowded, and stank of sweat and urine. I handed my card to Mr. Campbell and, while writing notes on my pad, began my spiel. I thought it was a pretty good spiel. I knew the ropes and how to describe them clearly and succinctly. While I was talking, writing on my pad, figuring out which day I could make it to the jail — and frankly, not looking at my client — I got the sense that my words were not reaching their target. I raised my head to look at Mr. Campbell. His face was bathed in silent tears. Every part of him radiated anguish and fear. And all the time, I had been blabbing away. I had forgotten that while this was just another day at work for me, my client was standing at the rim of the abyss, staring into the blackness.

I try to remember that moment every time I meet a new client. But with this case, my own judgments were getting in the way. I attempted to keep those feelings from my face as Annette Gaines walked into the interview room at the women's jail. I was expecting a slovenly woman with a mean gaze, or an emaciated, pasty-faced junkie. Instead, Annette was a small, slender African-American woman with delicate features and big eyes that looked utterly lost. But I knew that appearances could deceive.

"Miss Gaines?" I stood and offered my hand. I might not like this case, but I would be professional. She looked around as if she wasn't sure to whom I was talking. She awkwardly put her hand toward mine, then withdrew it and put it behind her back, where it joined her other hand, the customary stance of a prisoner.

"Please sit down," I said. "My name is Andrea Lyon. I'm a lawyer with the Public Defender's Office, and I've been assigned to represent you."

Without a word, she sat on the edge of a chair and looked around, waiting. While I explained the first stages of the process, she sat impassively, reacting to nothing. "Miss Gaines," I said, "do you have any questions about this so far?"

She spoke for the first time, in a voice quiet but urgent. "Is it safe to talk to you?"

"What do you mean?"

"Will I get in trouble?" She was looking at the floor. Of course: she wanted to know if this was confidential. Sometimes clients confessed to me. Occasionally, it spilled out in an emotional rush, but often only after a careful explanation of the absolute rules of confidentiality. I am not allowed to disclose anything told to me in confidence without my client's permission. The only exception is if the client says that he or she intends to commit a crime and, by warning someone, I can prevent it. Even then, I must have solid grounds to believe the threat is credible.

This is how serious attorney-client privilege is. Many years ago, two colleagues of mine were representing a man who had confessed (truthfully) to shooting two police officers. He avoided the death penalty but would spend the rest of his life in prison. I had helped with the investigation and in writing motions. At one point, the client confided to his two lawyers that he had committed an additional murder for which another man was on trial. Because he could face execution for that killing, he refused to let them tell anyone. The innocent man was convicted and sentenced to life in prison. Hoping the guilty man would eventually release his lawyers to reveal the truth, we drafted an affidavit to record the date and contents of the confession. I notarized the affidavit, and one of the lawyers hid it in a lockbox. But their client never relented. My colleagues consulted legal experts, seeking some exception to privilege. The universal answer was no, there was none. Their obligation lay with their client. Finally, the guilty man died, and they were free to come forward with the truth. The innocent man, who was soon released, had spent twenty-six years in prison for a crime he didn't commit. The morality of the system may be debatable, but the law and legal ethics are clear.

In Annette's case, I figured she would tell me that the baby wouldn't stop crying, or perhaps that she was high that night. She would tell me that she was disciplining little Shania; that was all. She would say that she had no idea that the toddler was really hurt, and that is why she didn't take her to the doctor until the next day. Or maybe she would tell me that her boyfriend, who might or might not be the poor child's father, had hit Shania, and that she had taken the weight for him because she loves him. She might even cry. Mentally, I rolled my eyes. I was prepared to dislike her and to disbelieve her. But I dutifully went through my spiel on the sacred nature of privilege between client and attorney.

As I finished, Annette Gaines looked at me for the first time.

Her face was immobile, except for her slightly trembling bottom lip. I watched her draw in a deep breath to still it before she spoke.

"I just want to know what you need me to say. My baby's funeral…" She choked and couldn't go on.

"I'm sorry?"

"I want to go to my baby's funeral," she said. "The officers, they told me what to say so I could go. And then they brought in that other lawyer, the black one, and I said it again. Then the officers left for a minute, so I asked that other lawyer if I could go to the funeral now that I said what they wanted."

Hold on. If I was hearing her correctly, this client was telling me that she had been the victim of exquisitely effective police coercion. They had not handcuffed her to a wall or barely fed her for thirty-six hours or laid a finger on her. They had merely dangled in front of her the promise of letting her attend her child's funeral. She would likely have said anything, even if she was innocent, a possibility that had not occurred to me until now. I needed to confirm my suspicions. "Once you told that other lawyer that you had just said what the officers wanted you to say, what happened?"

"He went out of the room, and he was yelling out there," Annette explained. "The officers were yelling, too. Then the lawyer came back in and said he would straighten all this out, that he would write it down. I thought I could go to the funeral, but instead they brought me here."

I was thinking furiously now, my mind running down a track I hadn't expected to travel. The police officers had used Annette's emotional vulnerability to get her to confess. The "other lawyer" at the police station would have been the felony review assistant from the prosecutor's office. In Chicago, before felony charges are filed, a prosecutor who is specially trained and presumably more objective than the police comes in to review the strength of the evidence and the appropriateness of the charge. It's a good idea, but it doesn't always work well. The pressure to go along with the police is difficult for a young prosecutor to resist.

Annette had told this prosecutor that she had falsely confessed to the police. I wondered if the guy actually recorded her recantation, and if he noted the reason why she had given the original statement. Any defendant can say at trial that his confession was coerced and false; but if the defendant told the prosecutor the same thing at the police station, it's far more credible. Whatever I had previously been feeling about this crime was pushed to the back of my mind while my lawyer's instincts took over.

"Look, Miss Gaines," I began, "I am going to need to know a lot about what happened in order to represent you. But first, let me tell you about the system here and what you are facing." I began to explain about arraignment, bail hearing, investigation, and discovery. As I shed my judgmental demeanor, she relaxed into the back of the chair and listened intently. At some point, she began to understand the impact of what I was saying on the only thing that mattered to her.

"Wait," she interrupted. "This doesn't sound like it happens fast."

I had been leading her through the process just so she could understand that horrible, immutable fact. I could file a request for the sheriffs to take her before the chief judge, I could get a hearing on her request, but there was almost no chance it would be granted. The sheriffs would complain about security and manpower issues, and she was, after all, charged with killing the child whose burial she wanted to attend. I knew there was virtually no possibility that she could be present when they laid her baby to rest.

"No, it doesn't happen fast," I said. "And I'm sure I'll be filing a motion to throw out whatever you said to the police, and that will take time, too."

She hung her head, no longer able to look at me. Her shoulders shook as she struggled not to let me see that she was crying. One by one, I was discarding all my assumptions about this woman. She wasn't trying to manipulate me or to excuse her behavior. She just wanted to say goodbye to her little girl. And I wasn't going to be able to help her do that. I turned my head to conceal the tears filling my own eyes. We sat there for a long while, neither of us looking at the other. Later that day, I filed the motion, which was refused, and sent a flower arrangement to the funeral home.

Annette was charged with first-degree murder. The prosecution could ask for the death penalty. The law considered the killing of a child in a manner that was "heinous, atrocious, and cruel" to be an aggravating factor. They would not likely make that choice unless they discovered she had habitually abused this or any other child.

To my grateful surprise, I learned that the felony review prosecutor had done what he had told Annette he would. In his report, he had written down her recantation and the reason for the false confession. I hoped his statement would persuade the judge to grant a motion to suppress Annette's confession — that is, not allow it to be used at trial.

The constitutional protection against a person being compelled to testify against himself doesn't only mean that a defendant need not take the stand in court. It also means that a confession that isn't voluntary cannot be used. Physical coercion, obviously, can invalidate a confession. Psychological coercion, such as threats or promises to free the suspect if he confesses, can also overcome the will of the person detained. Sometimes, with gang members, police threaten to "let the street know" that the suspect is talking when he isn't. That can be tantamount to a death threat. Interrogators might also suggest that they will call Children and Family Services to take a suspect's children if she doesn't cooperate. Or promise to allow a grieving mother the chance to go to her daughter's funeral. Methods like these should invalidate any statements police obtain. A civil society should not tolerate police behavior of this kind. And a confession obtained by these means is notoriously unreliable — as likely to be false as true.

But in reality, elected judges don't want to appear "soft on crime" or be targeted by an irritated Fraternal Order of Police. And understandably, it is psychologically difficult to throw out a confession to a murder. In this case, the police would deny having made any promises to Annette, and the judge would likely be reluctant to suppress the statement of a "baby killer." Instead, we would have to attack her confession's reliability — the fact it was coerced *and* false — at trial.

The police report stated that Annette admitted she had hit her daughter the night before her death and that she knew that she was hitting her too hard. Her statement said that she was angry with Shania for crying and messing her diaper. She spanked her, she said, but that didn't stop her crying, so she punched her — in the stomach. The next day, her statement went on, she took her to the doctor, but it was too late. Her retraction to the prosecutor was also contained in the police reports, but came across as inconsequential, something like buyer's remorse: *Gee, I wish I hadn't said that.* Then, according to the police, she reaffirmed her original confession after the prosecutor left.

"That's a lie," Annette told me. "I said what they wanted me to at first, but I never said it after talking to that lawyer. I never did."

I was at the jail reviewing the police reports with Annette. I also had the autopsy report and the hospital records. Sometimes I think of myself as an archaeologist of social despair, unearthing, layer by layer, my clients' descent into criminal jeopardy. The innocent are often drawn into a vulnerable position by the same destructive forces. This investigation was leading, as so many of my cases did, to the critical intersection of poverty and health. Mental illness, child abuse, environmental toxins — all are damaging enough on their own. When they are intertwined with poverty, the result is often a hopeless downward spiral. I didn't yet know how and why this innocent little girl had died, but I had begun to suspect the cause was something more complicated than one moment of parental rage.

It was time for Annette to tell me what had happened to her daughter. "You need to tell me everything," I told her firmly, "not just what happened at the police station, but everything."

She nodded. "Have you talked to Jimmy?" she asked. Jimmy was her boyfriend and Shania's father.

"Yes, I have, Annette, but I want to hear from you what happened, including whatever he doesn't know about."

Annette nodded again and started to talk. She and Jimmy had gone out the night before Shania died. They didn't go out often; money was tight. Jimmy worked two jobs, one as a night security guard and the other stocking groceries during the day. Annette was taking secretarial courses. She couldn't afford more than one class at a time, so it was slow going. She worked part time as a convenience store cashier. They lived in a three-story walk-up that chronically needed repair. The front steps had crumbled to pieces, the stairwell had no banister, and the plumbing was erratic.

On that evening, Annette and Jimmy both had the night off, so they decided to splurge, hire a baby-sitter, and go to dinner and a movie. They left Shania with Brandy, the thirteen-year-old daughter of a neighborhood woman Annette knew from the convenience store.

Brandy had baby-sat Shania before. They returned around 11:00 p.m. Brandy told them that Shania had not wanted her dinner and had been restless since Brandy had put her to bed. When Annette checked on the toddler, she felt warm and was sleeping fitfully. Thinking she had a cold or virus, they gave her some baby aspirin and decided to take her to the clinic in the morning if she wasn't better.

The next morning, their normally bouncy toddler was listless, still feverish, and wouldn't eat. Middle-class parents in this situation would likely have called their child's pediatrician. Jimmy worked up to sixty hours a week, but both his jobs were considered part time; therefore, no health insurance. Medicaid covered Annette and Shania. Like most poor people with no health insurance, they didn't have a personal physician. The neighborhood health clinic, which charged little or nothing, was their best alternative.

So Jimmy and Annette, with Shania in her stroller, walked the six blocks to the clinic. The intake clerk told them that the wait was likely four to five hours. Jimmy had to work that afternoon, so they got on a bus and went to the nearest hospital emergency room, the other doctor's office for the poor. This ER was overwhelmed by the victims of a multi-vehicle traffic accident, so they boarded a second bus to get to another hospital. Here, only a few people were waiting to be seen, so they checked in with their Medicaid card. By this time, Jimmy had to leave for work. Annette sat in a waiting room chair holding Shania, who was breathing with increasing difficulty. The hospital supposedly had a triage system in place, through which they determined which patients were most urgently in need of care. The triage nurse on duty, who later refused to talk with me, never even looked at Shania.

A man who had suffered a seizure was called out of the waiting room to be treated. Shania grew even more listless in Annette's arms. After a while, Annette questioned the receptionist, only to discover that their paperwork had disappeared. The increasingly worried mother filled out the forms again and sat down to wait once more. The remaining patient ahead of them, a teenager with severe acne, was called.

A woman who had accompanied a relative to the emergency room noticed Annette and Shania. The woman was herself a nurse. On the pretext of admiring the pretty toddler, the woman walked over to the mother and child. As this woman later told me, her actual reason for approaching them was because she was concerned that Shania wasn't moving. Once she looked closely at Shania's head on Annette's shoulder, the nurse shouted out, "Oh, my God, this child's in cardiac arrest!" Suddenly, everything around Annette began to move. Orderlies and nurses appeared. Shania was taken from Annette's arms and whisked away. The woman who had set off the alarm told me that she watched a hospital staff person begin CPR on the child. The problem is, she explained, they administered the CPR with a full hand. Toddlers or babies should never have their small and vulnerable chests compressed with full hands — only with two fingers or the heel of a hand at the most.

Annette never saw Shania alive again. The child was rushed into emergency surgery but did not survive.

Much of this story was troubling, but for now, the pressing question was, how did Shania become injured in the first place?

"I don't know," Annette answered me.

"Well, I need to know, Annette." This child had suffered a blow sufficient to rupture her duodenum. I had to be able to provide an answer as to how that had happened, or my case and my client were done for. I wasn't sure what to believe. I had stopped seeing this young woman as an abuser, but that didn't mean she wasn't an enabler. "Did you hit her, Annette? Did Jimmy?"

She immediately started to crumble. "I knew you wouldn't believe me."

"I'm not saying I don't, but I have to know." I tried a less direct approach. "Parents hit children sometimes," I said. "And sometimes women cover for their men."

"I didn't hit her. Not ever." Her little chin was defiant. "My momma used to tell me I spoiled her because I wouldn't."

"And Jimmy?" I prodded. The young man had seemed caring and cooperative, but since when did that mean anything?

"I never saw Jimmy hit her," Annette declared emphatically. "He might smack her hand when she reached for something she shouldn't, but that's all."

I had known these would be Annette's likely answers, and I was no closer to finding an explanation. Annette was puzzled, too, and worried about her fate. I told her I would continue with my investigation, including talking to the baby-sitter and to the pathologist who had examined Shania.

Scientific detective work was an aspect of my job I had unexpectedly come to enjoy. High-school biology had been a nightmare for me, and I had convinced myself that I had no aptitude for the subject. When I tested out of the science requirements in college, I breathed a sigh of relief and never took another science course.

Once I was on the job, however, science became a tool for winning. If I needed to understand a point about chemistry or fingerprint analysis to help my client, then I would sit with a science textbook or an academic treatise until I had mastered the relevant information. Since I had chosen to specialize in homicides, I had thrown myself into learning forensic pathology, the science that addresses the questions surrounding a death by the examination of the body.

I studied the autopsy report on Shania. Peritonitis, an inflammation of the abdominal lining, in this case caused by the rupture of the duodenum, had killed the little girl. Medical examiner Herbert Bannerman had conducted the postmortem examination.

Dr. Bannerman had a reputation as an examiner who leaned toward the prosecution, but he knew his field thoroughly. This was my first case with him. In almost all my cases, I talked to the pathologist responsible for the autopsy, even if there were no questions regarding cause or manner of death. I always learned something. And every once in a while, the examiner would convey a piece of information that turned out to be helpful to my client in a way I could never have anticipated.

I called Dr. Bannerman and we arranged to meet several days later — at 7:30 a.m., as I had anticipated. I am not at my best that early in the morning, but for some reason, that's when pathologists always want to meet.

First, I needed to talk to Brandy Jones, the baby-sitter, and take a look at Annette and Jimmy's apartment. Maybe I would find something that would explain Shania's injury. When I arrived at the apartment, Jimmy looked even thinner and sadder than the last time I had seen him. Together, we walked carefully around the little apartment, but there were no obvious sources of danger. The student intern who was with me was furiously taking notes. I had tried unsuccessfully to break her of the habit. I have learned to delay writing things down until I return to my car. Note-taking impedes conversation and observation, and that's what investigation is about.

Jimmy walked us to a building two doors down to introduce us to Brandy and her mother, and then left for work. Mrs. Jones invited us to sit down on a plastic-covered sofa. I explained why I was there and that I wanted to ask Brandy a few questions. I said I was trying to solve the mystery of Shania's death.

Mrs. Jones nodded emphatically. "Ain't no way Annette hit that child. My girl will hep' you any way she can. Right, Brandy?" She turned to her daughter. I had not been watching Brandy, as I was focused on obtaining the mother's permission.

Now I saw that the girl was visibly agitated, more than the prospect of an interview should have made her.

"What's wrong wit' you, child?" her mother asked, concern wrinkling her forehead.

Brandy started to cry. My insides clenched. I can't say whether I was excited to be finally getting somewhere in this investigation or dreading what I might be about to hear from this girl barely in her teens.

I got up off the couch and went over to Brandy's chair. Her face still had baby-round cheeks and an undefined chin. I knelt down and looked up at her, catching her eyes. "Brandy, just tell me what happened," I said in a gentle voice. "Whatever it is, we'll figure it out, your mom and I will." I glanced over at the mother to see if this proximity with her daughter was acceptable. She nodded.

"It's all my fault," Brandy sobbed.

"What's your fault?"

"That Shania is dead." Oh, God. Had she hit her? I had to take this slowly.

"Tell me what you mean."

"I ain't supposed to leave they apartment when I take care of her," she began. I nodded encouragingly, staying at her feet. "But I wanted to go over my friend's house, just for a little while." She glanced up at her mother. "My friend Jamika."

To my surprise, my note-taking intern appeared at my side with a Kleenex. I handed it to Brandy, who wiped her eyes. "So I took Shania wit' me, and on the way back, she fell. Down them stairs." I pictured

Shania plunging down the stairs, the stairs with no railings, the rough, splintered, nail-embedded wooden steps. If she had hit her stomach on one of those corners, that might account for her injury. Brandy went on to explain that Shania had landed on her front and had cried hard but then seemed okay. "But then she wouldn't eat or nothin.' I knowed I shoulda told Annette and Jimmy, but I — I just…"

"You felt bad for disobeying the rules," I finished for her. She nodded. I asked if she would come to the walk-up with me and show me what had happened. The intern brought one of the disposable cameras I kept in my car. We took a variety of photographs in the stairwell. As we left, I warmly thanked Brandy for telling me the truth. It might make all the difference for Annette. But I also knew that if only Brandy had told the truth to Annette and Jimmy the night of the fall, it might have made all the difference for Shania. As I drove home that night, thoughts about having my own child tumbled around in my head as they so often did now. Was I prepared, not only for the cares and concerns of having an infant, but also for the more complex issues a thirteen-year-old presented?

Two days later, at the unpleasant hour of 7:30, I was sitting in the office of Herbert Bannerman, M.D., a slender and surprisingly dapper man with an air of wary competence. As I asked him question after question about his findings, he was forthcoming, smart, and easy to understand. A formidable witness if he were against me, I imagined. Did I dare tell him what I had discovered? If I did, would he try to explain away the findings and then coach the prosecution on how to undercut them, also? I had had that experience with a pathologist before — one who saw his job as helping the prosecution — and I was leery of making the same mistake.

Dr. Bannerman looked at me shrewdly. He could tell I was holding back. I decided to chance it. First, I told him about Annette's confession and retraction and the reason for it. He interrupted me to comment that a mother might say anything to go to her child's funeral. I started to feel on firmer ground.

Then I took out the photographs. I had paid extra to have them developed speedily at Walgreen's. I told him about Shania's fall while he looked and nodded. Then he stood up. "Come on, let's go."

"What?" I asked, startled.

"Take me to the building. I want to see for myself." I could hardly believe he was serious. Despite what we see on television, I had never know anyone in the Medical Examiner's Office — and a doctor to boot — who would actually leave his lab to investigate.

"Yes, sir," I said, grabbing my things. "Do you mind riding in a Volkswagen?"

We went to Annette and Jimmy's building. Dr. Bannerman poked around, produced a tape measure from his pocket, took a few measurements, and then sat on a bottom step. He studied the autopsy photos and a copy of his findings, which he had brought with him. I told him how long it had taken Annette and Jimmy to find a place to treat Shania, about the wait in the emergency room, and the nurse who had seen CPR administered incorrectly. He just kept nodding. Finally he spoke.

"Between the fall and the incorrect application of CPR, which could have exacerbated the tear, the injuries are explained."

I tried not to jump up and down with excitement. Then I sobered quickly. Surely the prosecution would pressure him. How would the forensic scientist react to that? When we arrived back at Dr. Bannerman's office, he turned to me and asked, "Do you have the prosecutor's name and number?" I watched in speechless wonder as the pathologist called the DA's office. I listened as he told the prosecutor that if he were called to testify in this case, and the defense asked him if the child's fall, coupled with the CPR mistake, could have caused her death, his answer would be yes. Well, my faith in at least *this* scientist was restored.

I still had to try the case. Despite Dr. Bannerman's independent stand, the state refused to drop the charges. At a bench trial, we presented our evidence and the pathologist's opinion that the manner of death was accidental. The judge acquitted.

As Annette and Jimmy thanked me before leaving the courthouse at the trial's end, Annette promised to stay in touch. I knew she meant it when she said it. She had come to trust and even like me, and I had come to respect and like her, too. But I understood that I would be forever associated with a time in her life that was terribly painful. So I told her I looked forward to that, yet I never expected to hear a word. Later, when I made the commitment to myself that, one way or another, I would be a mother someday, I thought fleetingly of Annette. If she had still been my client, I would have told her.

More than a year later, I got a page at the office that I had visitors at the front desk. My friend Peggy was the only desk worker who ever said who the visitors were. The rest of the time, I had to trust that if it were an angry client, an unsatisfied relative, or a victim's aggrieved loved one, the metal detector at the building entrance would protect me from the worst.

As I approached the lobby area, I recognized Annette from the back. Then she turned, and I saw that she was holding a baby in her arms. She had come to introduce me to her new daughter. She and Jimmy had married, and she was working as a receptionist. They had named their little girl Andrea.

CHAPTER 8

The Pregnant Woman Defense

JUST WHEN I had firmed my resolve to adopt a baby to raise by myself, I met Gavin. The Chicago fireman was tall, muscular, and fine-looking. He was African-American, with a musical walk and a smile that dazzled. Those qualities alone might have been enough to attract my initial interest. But he was also intellectually compelling. Before Gavin, I had never known anyone — had certainly never dated anyone — who loved poetry as much as I did. We reveled in the Uptown Poetry Slams at the Green Mill Jazz Club and spent hours browsing at Barbara's Bookstore on South Halsted. This self-educated man read insatiably, and possessed a keen, if cynical, astuteness about America's place in the world.

I fell intensely in love. Over time, "Why don't you keep a key to my apartment?" became "Why don't you just move in with me?" My family welcomed him at holiday gatherings. After we had been together from more than a year, with the understanding that marriage was likely in our future, we decided to stop using birth control. Or, maybe I decided. Gavin and I discussed this step together, but I was the one who keenly desired a baby by that time.

Seven months later, at the age of thirty-six, I was pregnant. Gavin said he was happy. My family, after a little time to adjust to the idea of their unmarried daughter having a baby, was pleased. And I was thrilled to be pregnant. In the months of trying, however, my certainty about Gavin had eroded. A pattern of lying had surfaced, punctuated by the occasional, unexpectedly cruel barb. I put aside my doubts, though, because I wanted a child, and I still wanted Gavin.

If I suffered insecurity in my home life, in my professional life, I was finally finding rock-solid validation. When the chief public defender, my old chess partner James Doherty, stepped down in 1986, Paul Biebel was appointed acting chief. Paul was a former prosecutor, assistant attorney general, and partner in a large conservative law firm. With a résumé like that, the man was bound to inspire suspicion in the ranks of the anti-elitist public defenders, myself included. We were wrong. Paul brought order to our disorder, got computers for us at last, recruited women and minorities, and plucked some good lawyers out of obscurity and made them managers. I was one of them. After years of fighting to be accepted, followed by years of garnering respect without adequate pay or position, I became deputy chief and then chief of the Homicide Task Force. The "girl" was now in charge. Paul later became the presiding judge of the Criminal Division of the Cook County Court.

As chief, I assigned cases to lawyers, resolved turf battles, and ran interference with angry judges. (Thanks to one particularly frisky member of Task Force, I became a reluctant expert on contempt of court.) I also continued to carry a case load, the first task force chief to do so. Although the number was tiny compared to my load as a worker bee, the cases I took were generally the worst of the bunch.

Despite that, while I was pregnant, I was invincible. Even before my pregnancy began to show, I couldn't lose. In every case I tried during those nine months, my clients either were acquitted or avoided a death sentence. Two in particular stand out.

Early in my pregnancy, I defended William Ortiz. He was facing the death penalty on a murder and conspiracy case, but there were also charges for an attempted escape and aggravated battery. Ortiz had allegedly attacked a guard on the elevator that carries prisoners from the courthouse down to the tunnels that lead to the jails. We were expecting to try the murder and conspiracy case first, but at the last minute the prosecution elected to start with the less serious charges. Most likely, they assumed they could get a conviction on the lesser offenses. This would limit our options in the murder trial. The rule allowing a witness's prior record to be revealed in order to permit the jury to assess his credibility applies equally if the witness is the defendant. If Ortiz had a conviction for attempted escape and battery when he came up on the murder charge, we would think twice before putting him on the stand, and the prosecution knew that.

I had just two weeks to prepare the case on the lesser charges. A quick investigation turned up contradicting stories among the deputies who had witnessed the alleged escape attempt. Were the charges a smokescreen to hide the fact that Ortiz wasn't handcuffed when he should have been, or a way to explain the beating he took in the elevator? I was unlikely ever to find out what really happened.

Unfortunately, I could easily imagine my client having said or done something to provoke a deputy. Of all the accused criminals I have represented over the years, William Ortiz was among the few I have actively disliked. He was a racist, a sexist, a liar, and, sad to say, a former police officer. The murder charge was for a contract kill. I viewed the escape and battery trial as the opening act of the capital trial that would come later.

My cross-examination of the deputy who had filed the battery complaint was going to be crucial. Despite Hollywood's fondness for dramatic cross-examinations during which the witness suddenly tells all and the case is neatly sewn up, the cross is not where you win the case. It is, however, where you get what you need to win the case in the closing. A good cross conveys information to the jury. With a series of leading questions, you move to the brink of the conclusion you want the jury to reach. You shouldn't actually pose the concluding question to a prosecution witness, though. It's not likely he'll agree, and why give him the chance to deny it? Confrontation is occasionally the right tack to take, but those cases are the exceptions. I had learned that juries did not like my shouting at or overwhelming the witness with my physical presence. In a battle between a witness and a defense lawyer, just assume the jury likes the witness more. My goal in the Ortiz case was to lead the deputy in a matter-of-fact, nonconfrontational manner to confirm several pieces of information. I would make the conclusion — that the deputy's account was a lie — in my closing.

The problem was that regularly throughout my cross-examination of the deputy, I needed to throw up. Still in my first trimester, I hadn't yet told anyone at work about the pregnancy. But I felt sick almost constantly. I knew I'd never make it to the public washroom down the hall, so I had to ask Judge Truman for a brief recess and permission to use the bathroom in her chambers. In between breaks, in my nauseated, hormonal state, I ruthlessly drilled the testifying deputy.

"One of the procedures you are required to follow is" — I paused to pull out the sheriff's employee manual I had subpoenaed — "'the security of the prisoner must be maintained at all times,'" I read. "Correct?"

"I think that's what it says."

I was determined to make it clear that I was quoting accurately. "Your Honor, I am marking for purposes of identification, as defense exhibit one, the *Procedures Manual of the Sherriff of Cook County*. May I approach the witness?" The judge nodded her permission.

"Showing you what has been marked as defense exhibit number one for identification, I direct your attention to the section marked 'Transportation of prisoners to and from court.' Do you see that?"

I could tell he didn't like my being so close. "Yes, ma'am."

"Now look down to line five. It says 'the security of the prisoner must be maintained at all times.' Correct?"

"Yes, it does."

I moved back to the podium. "And the manual says any prisoner traveling alone with a single deputy must be handcuffed, correct?"

"Yes."

"That isn't a *should*, is it?"

"Ma'am?" he responded.

"The language doesn't say the prisoner *should* be handcuffed, does it?" He cleared his throat to answer, but I rolled over him: "It doesn't say *should*, it says *must*, right?"

"Yes."

"It doesn't say it might be a nice idea, either?"

"No."

"It doesn't say if you feel like it, either?"

"No, ma'am."

"It says 'must,' correct?"

He shifted in the witness chair and looked over at the prosecutor. I walked to stand between them. "It says *must*," I repeated.

He nodded. "Yes."

And on it went like that, for another hour, relieved only by my requests for breaks to be sick.

During the third break, Judge Truman confronted me in her chambers. "Miss Lyon," she asked bluntly, "are you pregnant?"

"Is it that obvious?" I answered forlornly.

"Well, it's not food poisoning." She smiled. "It's early, right?"

"Yes. Only about six weeks, and I haven't said anything to anyone because..." I found myself unable to go on, suddenly emotional.

The judge finished the sentence for me, "Because you're not sure yet if the baby will make it." I realized in that moment how much this baby meant to me, no matter how uncertain I might feel about the baby's father. The judge continued, "But, Miss Lyon, I have to ask you not to take out your feelings on the poor deputy." She didn't seem angry. She was, in fact, generously advising me that I was coming on too strong, and I appreciated that. Judge Truman was older than I was and had been a prosecutor before getting on the bench, which likely meant that she had faced even more misogyny than I had. She once told me that she felt more discriminated against as a woman in the legal profession than she did as an African-American.

I nodded. "I will keep that in mind, Your Honor."

"And I will tell the courtroom that we will be taking regular breaks." She smiled mischievously. "They'll think it's because I smoke."

So that's what we did throughout the trial. I relaxed, backed off on the deputy, and made the points I needed to make. In my closing, I carefully reviewed all the contradictions in the prosecution's evidence. Because Ortiz had obviously been in custody at the time of the incident, the jury knew that he must be facing other, more serious charges, and the fact that they knew this worried me. As I wound up the closing, I let my eyes make contact with every jury member.

"Each one of you can promise, right here and now," I said, "never, ever to violate any law. Never to commit any crime. And each and everyone one of you can *keep* that promise." I paused. "But what you cannot promise is that you will never be *accused* of one." That was sufficient, I think, to make them hesitate before letting the existence of another charge sway them in their verdict on this one. The jury acquitted.

Much later, Ortiz was convicted of the capital murder charges. I still despised the man, but that didn't prevent me from wanting to save his life. I simply had to find a way to "know" my client independent of the client himself, just as I had with the mentally ill Lonnie Fields. Luckily for Ortiz, he had a loyal and loving child just as Fields had. Ortiz's sweet twelve-year-old son became my, and the jury's, guide to the humanity of William Ortiz. The jury opted for life in prison.

EVENTUALLY, I BEGAN to tell people at work that I was pregnant. I had long ago erected a firewall between my personal and professional lives. I did it for self-protection, after fielding too many questions from my nosy male co-workers. *Why wasn't I married? Who was my boyfriend?* And when I wouldn't produce a boyfriend, even if I had one at the time: *Was I a lesbian?* With such a gossipy workplace, I preferred keeping the two spheres of my life distinct. The effort occasionally felt a little like a multiple personality disorder, but I could live with that. When I had begun to hope that I had a future with Gavin, I had slightly relaxed my internal security system, even though the fact that Gavin was black had provided more material than usual for the wagging tongues.

Keeping my pregnancy to myself was not an option, but when the news began to ripple widely throughout the courthouse world, I wished for the firewall all the more. Being a stubbornly honest person, I refused to spin the story by referring to any "fiancé." Although the people I trusted the most were supportive, others either disapproved or enjoyed the information as salacious entertainment. Being single and pregnant and not planning either an abortion or a wedding was still outside the norm for a professional middle-class white woman in 1989. This was three years before the fictional Murphy

Brown sparked a battle in the culture wars by choosing to become a single mother on the popular television series — and there was no interracial plotline in her story.

People felt entitled to say the most outrageous things. I was stunned by one comment in a setting where I least expected it: during a jury instructions conference. The judge's instructions tell the jury what the relevant law is in a particular case, so they can decide the case based on the facts as they find them and the applicable law. The prosecution and defense confer with the judge in chambers to determine what instructions will be given. For this case, I asked the judge to instruct on an evidence matter. I had pulled the language for the instruction from an Illinois Supreme Court case. I told the judge that I wasn't married to that particular language; if the judge had a suggestion for a better way to phrase the instruction, I would be fine with that. The prosecutor leaned over to his partner and commented, loudly enough for all to hear, "She's not married to any *man* either, but that hasn't stopped her from getting knocked up." I smiled sweetly at my offensive opposition. "Too bad you said that, Sean," I said. "I'll have to make you pay for it now." I did, winning an acquittal in the case.

In another instance, when I requested an alternate date for a hearing because I had a scheduled doctor's appointment, the prosecutor muttered under his breath something about my needing to make sure the "half-breed" was all right. I managed to hold back my tears until I got home. I didn't tell Gavin about any of these incidents. Given his increasingly angry response to everything, I worried that he would head to court and start a fight or two.

Despite the harassment, my winning ways continued. Five months after the Ortiz victory, visibly pregnant and awash in hormones, I had to battle for the life of a drug addict who had killed three members of his family while hallucinating on angel dust.

Milton Johnson was a young man who lived on the margins. He hadn't quite made it through high school. At twenty-five, he still lived at home with his parents, his sister, and his developmentally disabled aunt. He held down a part-time job in a video store, but never tried to find full-time work. He was too occupied with getting high. Milton went to work, went home or to a friend's house, and smoked marijuana. Every day. He didn't drive while under the influence or fight or bother anyone. After smoking, he was given to sitting in a corner and smiling. Milton was a quiet, inoffensive guy who drifted through life. His sister, Oletha, was more ambitious; she had graduated from high school and was in a secretarial program downtown. Their mother was a cashier at a grocery store, and their father had worked at the post office for more than thirty years.

One night in January, a hysterical Milton Johnson ran into an ER waiting room screaming that a monster was in his house killing everyone. Security had to tie him to a bed and inject him with a sedative. A doctor diagnosed him with phencyclidine-induced psychosis. The marijuana Milton had smoked earlier in the evening had been laced with PCP, or what was known on the street as angel dust.

The hospital notified the police, who went to Milton's home. What they found there looked like a scene from a slasher movie. Blood was everywhere. A large kitchen knife lay on the floor. Milton's mother, father, and aunt were dead. His sister was unconscious but alive. Milton was right that a monster had been in the house, but the monster turned out to be Milton.

Phencyclidine was originally marketed as a horse tranquilizer, and its effect on humans who ingest it is immediate. PCP blocks the normal activity of the body's neurons, causing spikes in the brain's electrical activity. Under its influence, a person may hallucinate, exhibit unusual strength, and feel little or no pain. Police officers have told me about people hopped up on angel dust who violently attacked them, were shot several times, and, "not realizing they were dead," continued to fight.

When the police arrested Milton, he denied the crime. He was convinced that someone had broken into the house — maybe not a monster, as he had said at the hospital, but someone. Anyone, anyone but him. He was in deep denial.

When I took on Milton's case, I found not only a horrific crime and an uphill battle to save my client from the death sentence demanded by the prosecution, but the additional problem of publicity. To everyone's joy, Milton's sister, Oletha, had recovered. Now she was making the rounds of talk shows. She was speaking out in support of victims' rights, and in favor of her brother's death. I didn't blame her. How could I? Nevertheless, his sister's desire to see him executed gave momentum to the quest for a death sentence.

Indeed, the extended Johnson family split into two camps over the question. The maternal grandparents, for instance, felt that Milton hadn't "been himself" when this happened and that executing him served no purpose. But the grandparents on his father's side felt he deserved a punishment that "fit" the crime — and that was death. One day I walked into their midst, needing to collect material for mitigating evidence should Milton be convicted. When I tried to talk to Milton's paternal grandparents, they showed me the door, his grandfather's mouth tight and angry, his grandmother looking regretful, but standing by her husband. Families of defendants in general are uncomfortable sharing sensitive information. The family of this defendant was simultaneously the grieving family of the victims.

Before we ever got to the need for mitigation in a sentencing phase, however, I had to defend Milton against a triple murder charge. There was no plea offer on the table. I knew all about insanity defenses, but

Milton was not mentally ill. I needed something like a temporary insanity defense, in this case, a drug-induced one. But even if such a defense existed, would a jury care? After all, Milton had voluntarily ingested the marijuana, although he claimed to have no idea it contained PCP.

Illinois, I discovered, did recognize a voluntary intoxication defense. It required that the intoxicant had rendered the defendant unable to conform his behavior to the law. This defense would not exonerate Milton completely, but it would reduce the crimes from first- to second-degree murders. This seemed fair to me, and I thought this approach was more likely to work with a jury. Instead of asking them to acquit Milton based on insanity, I would urge them to convict him of a lesser offense.

An acquittal is not always the goal. A defense attorney should aim for the fairest possible outcome, considering the circumstances and the mitigating factors. That's the ideal, anyway. In one of my saddest cases, a seventeen-year-old client was being tried as an adult on a first-degree murder charge. He was not the trigger man, but he was looking at a minimum sentence of twenty years. Because the trigger man was only thirteen, he was being tried as a juvenile and would be released when he turned twenty-one. In spite of this obvious imbalance, the prosecution refused to let my client plea to second-degree murder. In an attempt to put pressure on them, I filed an unusual motion, based on the lack of equal protection, to let my client be tried as a juvenile or dismiss the case. Still, the state refused to negotiate. Their stubbornness angered the judge, so he dismissed the charge. My client walked free. Four months later, he was picked up for a quadruple homicide. Many people think tragedies like this are common. In fact, they are extremely rare. And they are every conscientious defender's nightmare. When I was called to represent this young man for the multiple murders, I asked to be replaced. I told the court I could not give him the zealous representation to which he was entitled.

But I believed in the intoxication defense I had planned for Milton Johnson.

"Milton, I've brought you the lab reports, so you can see for yourself," I told him one day when we met. He had wanted me to "prove" to him that there had not been anyone else in their home that night. He simply could not allow himself to believe he had slaughtered people he loved. So here I was, trying once more to prove to him that there had been no one else.

I sat down at the Formica table in the visiting room and pushed the lab reports toward him. "Look at the highlighted sections, Milton. I highlighted the fingerprint stuff in yellow."

I sat quietly and let him read. All of the fingerprints belonged to his family, although there were some "unusable" prints that were too small or too smudged to be analyzed. Of course, he fastened on those.

"But, look here, Miss Lyon," he said excitedly. "These here prints, they ain't from none of us."

"No, Milton, those prints are just too smudged to analyze. There was no one in the kitchen that night but you and your family."

"You don't know that. Not for sure. It could be someone else." Milton's eyes darted back and forth, as they did whenever I tried to get him to accept what he had done.

"Milton, no, it couldn't." My tone was gentle. "You need to accept this, and you have to understand that I cannot try this case except on the intoxication defense."

"I know, you said that. But I didn't do this. I didn't kill Mama. I didn't." His eyes were moving even more rapidly now.

"It wasn't you, Milton — not the *real* you — but it was you physically." He got up and began to pace. I continued: "Milton, you have to be able to sit through my saying this. We're going to try your case soon, and you're going to hear this, and worse, many times before it's over.

"But them prints — " he interrupted.

"It was you, Milton."

"I…" He stopped pacing, sat down, and looked at the floor.

"Milton, can you allow that it might be possible? Just that it might be possible?"

After a while, he nodded miserably. This was as good as it was going to get. He would let me present the defense that the facts dictated. And actually, I worried that if he ever fully let the truth in, he might try to end his life. I changed the subject to more procedural matters.

By the time Milton's case came to trial, I was seven months pregnant. The nausea long behind me, I felt myself again, although my ankles swelled and I made sure I knew where all the bathrooms were on any route I walked.

At the same time, the happy family life that had once seemed within my grasp was slipping farther and farther away. Gavin now disappeared for days at a time without calling. When he was home, the piercing wit I had loved was too often turned on me. If I had not been pregnant, I would have broken off the relationship. But my body was instructing me to nest, so I decorated a beautiful room for my baby, basked in my mother's thrill over the coming of her first grandchild, and told myself that everything would be okay.

And through many hours of the day, I could practically forget that I was pregnant, single, and caught in an increasingly unhealthy relationship. After all, I was supervising twenty-two attorneys and trying murder cases at the same time. This all-consuming work was what I knew how to do. I knew how to do it well. And my clients needed me.

I prepared a voluntary intoxication/second-degree murder defense for Milton's trial. This approach, I was convinced, provided his best possible hope for avoiding a first-degree murder conviction. But, realistically? I knew the chances were slim that even this defense would succeed with a jury. The beauty of this approach was that even though the jury would likely convict him, this defense would lay the foundation for a successful mitigation argument in the sentencing phase. I knew this case was most likely going to come to that: life or death for Milton Johnson.

Judge Ellen Maddocks was hearing the case. The perfectly coiffed judge, whose black robe was always impeccably accessorized, had a middling reputation from a defense perspective. The prosecution's opening statement at the trial was graphic and horrifying. They painted a vivid picture of the deaths, of their deliberateness and cruelty. They told the jury that the evidence would show the defendant's fingerprints all over the bloody knife. A person is duty bound to know the natural consequences of his actions, the prosecutor stated, and Milton knew what he was doing when he stabbed his mother twenty times, his father and aunt a dozen times each, and his sister five times.

In my opening, I spoke of the tragedy of the case, of the unspeakable sights Oletha had seen, and her own horrific injuries. I told the jury about Milton's intoxication by the PCP-laced marijuana. I said that a doctor would tell them that Milton had been actively psychotic, to the point of hallucinating, when he came into the hospital screaming for help that night. I told them that, for these reasons, I would be asking them to convict my client of the lesser offense of second-degree murder.

The trial unfolded predictably. The prosecution called Milton's sister, and her testimony was as chilling and emotionally evocative as any I had ever heard. I cross-examined the hospital nurse about

Milton's condition that night and the need to restrain him. In addition, I called the doctor who had diagnosed his drug-induced psychosis. The testimony had distressed Milton at first, but he had maintained control and eventually lapsed into numbness.

Then came time for the jury instructions conference in Judge Maddocks's chambers. Each side submits the instructions it wants to be given to the jury, most of which come from the Illinois Pattern Instruction Book. Although the pattern instructions cover most situations, I am rarely satisfied with these one-size-fits-all directions. When have I ever been happy with one-size-fits-all? Attorneys may request instructions drawn from other sources, although judges don't have to grant those requests.

In the conference with Judge Maddocks, I asked for the instruction on second-degree murder, straight out of the pattern book, and for the voluntary intoxication instruction, which was not in the pattern book, but found in case law. The State objected. The Illinois Supreme Court cases I was citing were old, they said. The prosecution also claimed that I had not met the burden required under the case law to get the instruction.

I told Judge Maddocks the prosecution was mistaken. I argued that the law requires that if there is evidence to support the giving of a valid instruction, the instruction *must* be given. The evidence that PCP had caused my client to be psychotic was not contradicted; therefore, refusing to give the relevant instruction would be unwarranted.

Judge Maddocks looked at me for a moment and then announced that she would not give the instruction.

"Can you please explain your reasoning, Your Honor?" I asked.

"Your request is denied, Counselor," was all she would say.

I walked back into the courtroom and tried to marshal my thoughts. What could I do? I had pledged to the jury that I would present evidence of Milton's psychotic intoxication, and I had kept that promise. But without the instruction that would allow them to choose voluntary intoxication as a legitimate basis for second-degree murder, what could I ask the jury to do? They would be given the choice of either first-degree murder or acquittal. How could I ask for an acquittal? Besides the fact that there was no legal basis for it, Milton was looking more and more ragged each day at trial. If I asked the jury simply to free this fragile man who had slaughtered three members of his family, first of all, they would never do it, and second, I would lose their respect. And then, what would they do to Milton at sentencing? Would they ignore our sound arguments for mitigation and choose to execute him because they no longer trusted me? What could I say to this jury?

That night I drove home frightened, discouraged, and not knowing whether to hope that Gavin would be there or not. If he were, I couldn't count on him to be supportive. But he didn't show up that night. I lay in bed, yearning to turn on to my stomach, wishing I had been more persuasive to Judge Maddocks regarding the instruction, hoping to save Milton's life, and worried about my baby's future—and my own.

The following morning began with the prosecutor's closing argument, which was essentially a reprise of the opening. He spoke to the evidence of the murders and the lack of doubt as to the identity of the killer. He ended with his major theme: Milton was responsible for his actions.

Judge Maddocks turned to me. "Counsel for the defense?" she asked.

I stood and nodded politely to the judge and the prosecution. Then I faced the jury and spoke. "In light of Your Honor's ruling on jury instructions, Mr. Johnson will make no argument to the jury." Then I sat down to a shocked silence. No one had anticipated this.

They probably expected me to make an argument on his mental state. Something. Anything. No one ever gave up a closing argument. But I knew this phase of the war was over. Only one battle remained to be fought now, and that was the one for Milton's life. I could wage that fight successfully only with a jury that trusted me. A closing argument that didn't make sense risked alienating them.

The jury retired to deliberate and returned soon after with a guilty verdict. They looked at me with puzzlement, but I perceived it as a friendly curiosity. They had an idea that something had gone wrong at the trial, even if they didn't know what.

The sentencing hearing started immediately. Milton had only petty offenses in his background, so the prosecution's case for aggravating factors didn't take long. Despite the presence of family members who had said they wanted Milton sentenced to death, none of them testified. I presented psychological evidence, recalled the doctor from the hospital, and called a pharmacologist to explain the effects of PCP. For personal mitigating testimony, I called on Milton's great-aunt and cousin. His minister spoke about praying with Milton for his dead parents and aunt. While no one could say Milton was remorseful — he was still in denial — everyone agreed that he was ordinarily a gentle, nonviolent man.

Just as in the guilt-or-innocence part of the trial, the sentencing phase ends with closing arguments. Many judges give time limits to attorneys for closings. The more serious the case, the more time they'll allow. Judge Maddocks asked the State how much total time they needed for their opening close and their rebuttal close. They said an hour. Then she asked me how long I needed.

Ever since I had used the flip chart for Lonnie Fields's closing, I knew that taking my time was worthwhile. For Milton's case, I needed to talk about the evils of drugs and the tragedies they engendered. I needed to talk about Milton's divided family. I had to help the jury see that if Milton were executed, the loved ones separated now in their grief and anger would never find a way back to one another. I needed to take that jury with me until they were able to see the humanity and sorrow in Milton Johnson.

I told Judge Maddocks that I needed "a while."

"What exactly does that mean?" she asked, her tone hostile. She had not liked my waiving closing arguments at the guilt-or-innocence part of the trial. Perhaps she believed that my choice strengthened the appellate record in regard to her decision on the jury instructions. No judge likes to be overturned.

I tried to keep my voice neutral. "I mean that I need to speak with this jury for as long as it takes to save my client's life, and I can't quantify it for you."

"Well, I can quantify it for you. I'll give you an hour," she said, as if that ended the conversation.

Now I was angry, too. "Your Honor, this is the man's life we're talking about. I will argue for as long as is needed, or until you order me to stop."

"Miss Lyon," Judge Maddocks replied, "I will allow you more than an hour, but," she continued firmly, "no breaks. If you stop, you're done. If you take your seat, you're done. Is that clear?"

It was. She knew how pregnant I was, that it would be difficult for me to talk for long without sitting or using the washroom. But I could do it, I thought, because I had to.

After the prosecutor finished his opening close, I got to my feet, not knowing how long it would be before I could sit down again. I reviewed all the evidence about the havoc PCP causes in people's lives. I told the jury stories about Milton's childhood and growing-up years, attempting to paint not a sanitized picture of the young man, but a fully realized human portrait complete with flaws. Then I commiserated with Milton's family.

"There is nothing I can say that can come close to addressing the pain this family is in. I cannot pretend to understand what it would be like to lose your loved ones in this horrible way. But I do know one thing; more death will not assuage their grief. Another death will pin them to the pain and anger they feel right now; it will not allow them to heal, to feel any relief from the misery."

I turned from the jury to look at the family members sitting on the two sides of the gallery. "Nor will it allow the deep divisions between them to mend. Perhaps, just perhaps, allowing Milton to live will allow this family to reunite, to help the living, to feel just a little better." I nodded at both sides of the room, turned to the jury once again, and continued my argument.

After talking for two hours, I was very, very tired. I needed to get off my feet, I needed the washroom, I needed water. But more than that, I needed this jury.

My voice began to break as I neared the end of my plea for Milton's life. I had moved closer to the jury than I usually did. I am keenly aware that my size can sometimes make people feel their personal space is being invaded, but perhaps exhaustion led me to the railing in front of the jurors. Without realizing it, I rested my hand on the railing. Then, while I continued to speak, I felt a hand cover mine. I saw that the elderly juror in front of me had reached out. She patted my hand and then looked behind her at other jurors, who were nodding. She tilted her head at my seat, smiled at me, and nodded again. I paused to gain my composure, got out a brief conclusion, and walked over to sink into my chair.

The jury returned a verdict of life in prison without parole. My practically catatonic client was led out of the courtroom. When I spoke with the jury members afterward, the woman who had patted my hand told me that I had helped them to feel the human side of this case and this defendant. And now they hoped I would go home and get some rest.

My obstetrician soon echoed the woman's words, ordering me to end my winning streak and not try any more cases until after I gave birth. Apparently, my blood pressure was soaring, and that wasn't good for the baby. "Life is precious, dear," the doctor told me, and he patted my hand.

Yes, it is. On a sticky August day in 1989, my beautiful Samantha was born. I was besotted with her from the first moment. Gavin held her tenderly in his arms and then, a few weeks later, disappeared from both our lives. A long time passed before I regained my emotional bearings. Still, like most people whose children are the product of destructive relationships, I am not sorry to have known or loved him. If Samantha did not exist, that would be a tragedy I cannot contemplate.

CHAPTER 9

Life and Redemption

The fat file was labeled "Bauman."

"This is a bad one, Andrea," said John Lanahan, a fine lawyer on the task force, shaking his head. "The defendant was on parole for one murder, picked up some federal weapons charges, and this is a double." A double homicide, he meant.

"So, it's a real death case," I mused. Some crimes "technically" qualify for the death penalty, but you know they'll never get as far as a death hearing. The "real" ones have the marks of a case that will go the distance. This one, darkened by the shadow of three bodies, had that ring.

I was sitting in John's office in the spring of 1988. John was leaving Chicago to take a job at the federal defender's office in San Diego. I was going to miss the exuberance he brought to the task force. An actor in a previous life, he had a song for every occasion. ("There's a plea for us / somewhere a plea for us…" was an office favorite.) But a sober mood prevailed now as the two of us reviewed the twenty or so cases John had been carrying. As chief, I was going to have to distribute his load among the rest of the attorneys in the office, and I wanted to know which were the worst cases.

He continued describing the Bauman case. "He's in a gang, and this was a turf battle. At least, that's what the State says. The vics were rival gang members."

"Did he confess?" I asked.

"No."

"Well, that's something."

"On guilt-innocence, the case isn't so bad. It's two eyeballs. That's all."

"Right, one too many." John laughed with me. We talked in defense attorney code. A "single finger" identification case is far more easily tried than a "two eyeballs" case. A jury is likely to believe two witnesses making the same identification even if the testimony is riddled with problems. Of course, John explained, a complete investigation hadn't been done. It would be tough, though; the shooting had happened some three years ago in a depressed, volatile neighborhood on the South Side.

"Then again," John said and he looked away from me, "this client is really interesting. And there are some good motions to file." Only a lawyer would try to entice someone with the prospect of filing motions. But, hey, I'm a lawyer. I bit.

"Are you working on me?" I asked archly.

John laughed. "Andrea, this guy looks terrible from the outside, and the case is an uphill battle. I'm worried that if someone good doesn't take it, he'll end up on the row."

I reached for the file. "I got it. When can you take me to meet him?"

Before I had gone to John's office that day, I had decided that I would take the worst case from his caseload. I wanted to spare the people who worked for me. But I also intended to show them that their boss was willing to take on a case no one else wanted. Maybe they would become more willing to accept advice on their own cases. Supervising trial lawyers is a daunting task. Imagine an office filled with independent, competitive, often oppositional — well, imagine an office filled with people like me. Yet, my early political activism and my unconventional Antioch training had fostered in me a willingness to collaborate that was often lacking in other lawyers. Time, and the institution of weekly bagel-and-brainstorming sessions, eventually made most of the task force attorneys eager to share both their toughest questions and their winning strategies.

Of course, volunteering for John's formidable case would hardly encourage my staff if I took a beating.

The following week, John and I walked up the well-worn steps to the entrance of Division One. This old jail didn't have visiting rooms per se. You could meet with your client in the law library, which was generally crowded with other lawyers talking with inmates. Or you could go onto the tier where your client's cell was. They'd let your client come down to the guard post, where you could talk to him through the bars, assuming the catcalls from the other inmates allowed for conversation. Inmates frequently hollered out anatomically unlikely suggestions. I enjoyed responding to the ones offered in Spanish, knowing the speaker never dreamed he was making his lewd proposal to someone who actually *understood* it. I ventured onto the tier only if I was in a hurry and merely had to get a paper signed. Otherwise, I asked for Post 78, which is where we headed that day.

John had told me that he had written all of his clients that he was leaving his job. Mr. Bauman might arrive angry. "He's deeply suspicious of public defenders," John told me as we walked. "He thinks we're scared to fight, that we give in too easily, that we're always looking to cop everyone out."

"That hardly distinguishes him from most clients," I replied dryly.

"Yeah, I know. You have to meet him to understand."

We knew this was likely to be a difficult encounter. A man facing the death penalty was being abandoned by the lawyer whom he had been working with for a year and was being handed off to someone, a woman, he had never seen before. I was prepared for resistance.

On the positive side, I had read the police reports, and they did not reflect a particularly strong case against Bauman. When the two men had been shot on the street in 1985, the cops in the area knew Bauman. They had shown his photograph around, and two witnesses had picked him out. One was a woman who had been looking out her apartment window across the alley from where the crime occurred — not a great vantage point — and the other was a woman across the street who had heard the shots and seen the shooter run past her. There was no physical evidence: no weapon, no prints, nothing. The police had been eager to pick up Bauman at the time, but they couldn't find him. Not long after, he was nabbed in Tennessee for transporting weapons across state lines. When an investigator questioned him about the Chicago murders, all he said was, "Do I look stupid to you, motherfucker?" I had to admit, I admired the statement.

On the other hand, Bauman's history was less reassuring. At the age of fifteen, in the mid-1960s, he had been charged with the murder of another young man, tried as an adult, and sentenced to twenty years. When the double murder took place, Bauman had been out on parole. His rank in the street gang was "enforcer." No, not good.

Post 78 was tucked away in a dungeon-like basement. John and I ducked under exposed pipes, our eyes adjusting to the greenish cast in the air. A desk guard took our information and nodded us down the passageway to a large cinderblock room, Post 78. A waist-to-ceiling window in the room, its glass long gone, opened onto the corridor. Inside, two plastic chairs flanked a metal table. In the corner, inexplicably, was a school desk with an attached arm. I sat there, behind the pockmarked desktop, trying not to imagine the sights and sounds that had once dominated this room. Post 78 was the old execution chamber, erstwhile home to Cook County's electric chair.

Before long, we heard a hearty laugh, accompanied by a softer one, and then approaching footsteps. The loud laugh came from Bauman, the softer one from the guard. Richard Bauman was thirty-nine years old, about six foot one, and of medium build. His face was pleasantly ordinary, except for a set of piercing eyes. He walked in the door, looked at me, and then turned to John.

"Is this the replacement?" he asked loudly. I later learned that a hearing loss, perhaps incurred from years of living in noisy prisons, caused him to speak abnormally loudly.

I stood and offered my hand. "Hello, Mr. Bauman. I'm Andrea Lyon. And yes, I am the replacement." Ignoring my hand, he walked — or, more accurately, sidled — around me, moving his eyes up and down. The gaze didn't feel sexual, but he was clearly assessing me.

"Yeah," he said finally. "And who exactly are you?"

John said that I was his boss, actually, and that he had specifically asked that I take over the case for him. He added a few flattering comments about what a good lawyer I was. While John talked, Bauman returned to his evaluative posture, his head tilted practically sideways as he continued to stare fixedly at me. I had had enough of what I had now decided was an attempt to intimidate me.

"What's the problem, Mr. Bauman? You don't like women? You don't think we're smart enough or tough enough?" I wasn't at all sure that my gender was prompting the scrutiny, but I couldn't remain passive.

Now Bauman relaxed and chuckled. "Lady, if you were in my shoes…you know what I mean? You would be asking yourself, who is this here woman, and do she know what she doing? You know what I mean?" He spoke without hostility.

"Sure, I understand that, Mr. Bauman. It's very disconcerting to change counsel after all this time, and to meet someone new."

We had moved past the first stage of antagonism, but Richard Bauman was not a man to accept things without question. "What I want to know," he pursued, "is how far you is willing to go to defend a case like this. I mean, will you use what you got to help me?"

I didn't want to give him any facile reassurances. "What does that mean?" I asked.

"Well, in them ancient times, there was this woman, see, and she didn't like the fact her man, all the men, was at war all the time. There wasn't no work being done in them fields, and the children never would see their daddies." He leaned forward. "You get the picture?"

I nodded. He continued: "So this woman, she talked to all the other women, and they agreed they needed to do something. But they didn't know how to stop them men. They didn't have no weapons, no ships or nothing, to stop the emperor from taking they men. So they decided to use what they had. They told them men, ain't nobody getting no more loving until this war foolishness stop. And they cut 'em off. And them women brought those men to they *knees*."

I looked at Bauman and then over at John. John was smiling, just a little. The bastard hadn't told me why he found this client so interesting. This gangbanging convicted murderer was telling me the story of Aristophanes' *Lysistrata*. I was too astounded and amused to be offended at the question of whether *I* was willing to "use what I got" as the Greek women had.

I couldn't help asking, "Do you know where that story comes from?"

"Yeah," Bauman said, "but they only got short versions of that kinda stuff in they library here." He didn't say it in so many words, but this man was telling me that he was hungry for the real books, for the full story.

The rest of the meeting went smoothly. The three of us discussed the case, reviewing potential motions. The delay in bringing him to trial might constitute a basis for dismissing the case. Bauman had been in custody in Tennessee for the gun charges when the police first talked to him about the murders. That was nearly three years earlier. He had been brought to Cook County and charged with the double homicide before being transferred to the federal detention center in Chicago to face the weapons charges. He had not been brought back to begin the process of trying him for the murders for another six months. An effective investigation would be nearly impossible on a case that was so stale.

Bauman nodded throughout my explanation. Despite the delay, I told him that my investigator and I would track down the State's witnesses and see whom else we could dig up. I would report back to him in a couple of weeks with any news.

Now that I was task force chief, I relied more frequently on the professional investigators who were part of the Public Defender's Office. Many of these positions ended up as patronage jobs for former police officers. For the most part, they didn't much like the task force's clients or its work or, for that matter, the attorneys. There were, however, a few exceptions, and I loved working with those excellent investigators. One of them, the brilliant Mort Smith, collaborates with me still. I think of Mort as an African-American Steven Seagal; he even had the ponytail. Smart, wisecracking Mort has a degree in criminal justice. What makes him so valuable, though, is his understanding of how to put together and take apart a case, and the fact that he cares what happens to the clients.

To kick off the Bauman investigation, Mort and I, with student intern Erin in tow, went to talk to one of the eyewitnesses, the woman who had claimed to see the shooter from the street. Her address hadn't changed in the three years since the murders: it was still a street corner, from which she conducted her "oldest profession." We caught up with Rose on a warm summer day on that corner near the liquor store, kitty-corner from the site of the shooting. Although it was nearly ninety degrees, Rose was wearing a long-sleeve blouse, long pants, and a scarf. Later, I asked Erin if she had noticed anything unusual about Rose.

"She seemed inappropriately dressed for the heat," Erin replied.

"Good," I said. "Now why do you think that is?"

Erin looked blank. "I don't know."

"Track marks, Erin. Lots of them."

"Oh," she said, chagrined. I told her not to worry; it takes a while to pick up those sorts of clues.

Our interview of Rose was instructive. She had seen the shooting, she told us, but had been high at the time. When the police arrived at the scene, they had questioned her. "They sure don't like that man, what's-his-name, Bow Man," Rose reflected.

"What makes you say that?" Mort asked her, in the calm, listening way he has.

"Aw, child," Rose said, sighing, seeming to enjoy our attention. "They let me know 'fore they even showed me them photos who they believed did it. Everybody know that man ain't nobody to mess wit'."

We knew this already. To be feared by reputation alone is part of the job description for "enforcer."

"Had you ever seen the man who did the shooting before that night?" Mort continued.

"Nah. I ain't really seen it that clearly, but the dude did favor Bow

Man, so I said what them police wanted me to. Signed whatever. I needed to get home, you know?"

This was good news. The prosecution would still call Rose to repeat her identification on the stand, but we could lessen its impact by getting her to admit to her drugged state at the time, not to mention the tainted way in which the police had obtained her ID. But I didn't think I was leaping to any conclusions to assume she would not make a great impression on a jury.

When I met with Richard and began to tell him about Rose, he stopped me.

"Look here. I know we gotta talk about the case an' shit. And all that death penalty shit, too." He swallowed. "But I wanna talk about other shit, too — stuff that ain't got nothin' to do with my case."

Uh-oh. Had that look he had given me at our first meeting been sexual after all? Certainly, over the years, some of my clients had initiated inappropriate come-ons. Early in my career, when working less serious cases, I had learned to put them down fast and hard: *Do you want a girlfriend or do you want to get out of jail? If you want to get out of jail, we have to drop this crap and get down to business.* Homicides, especially death penalty cases, in which my goal was a close relationship with my client, required a more delicate response. I stayed silent and waited with trepidation for Richard to continue.

"I want to read them books — the real ones. The ancient Greeks, to start. An' then maybe some of that stuff by that guy Plato, an' I heard about a dude named Franz Fanon. I wanta read him, too." The words were tumbling out of his mouth faster and faster, and in his usual loud volume. "Can you loan me them books or something? An' maybe we could talk, you know, about 'em some of the time?" He paused and looked down, not wanting me to see how much this mattered to him. "I ain't got no one to talk to about this stuff in here."

My God, I thought. This man wants to go to school. He wants to read and talk about what he is reading. He wants to wake up to everything that eluded him in his first four decades of life.

I didn't want him to see how much his request moved me, either, and I answered in a measured way. "We can do that. I'll send a book over to you every couple of weeks. We can talk about the book for half of each visit. And then, in the second half of each visit, we can talk about your case and your *life*." I looked at Richard meaningfully while I emphasized the last word. "Is that a deal?"

He knew that I was reminding him that we had to prepare for a death hearing. "I know they wanna kill me, Miss Lyon." He was still not looking at me directly. "I get it."

"I know you do. Do we have a deal?" We were talking about more than the books. (I would get them.) And more than whether I would discuss them with him. (I would do that, too, even though it meant reading each book again or perhaps for the first time.) We were, in fact, negotiating whether Richard would help me to save his life. In exchange for the books and the conversation — or perhaps made possible by the books and the conversation — Richard would let me in. He would allow me to pass beyond what I already knew about him and penetrate the brittle shell he had constructed. And he would tell the people close to him to give me access to their knowledge of him as well.

He looked up. "Yeah, we do," he said.

The process of getting to know Richard Bauman began with the official record, and it was not encouraging. When Richard was fifteen, firmly entrenched in a gang by that time, he had handed a gun to another boy and encouraged him to shoot at a rival gang member. The boy did, and the rival died. Richard and his cohort were both charged with murder, and convicted as adults. Richard was sentenced to twenty years. He served nineteen of those, which, at that time — when you could earn an extra day off your sentence for every "good" day you passed in prison — is stunning. A person has to work hard at being bad to lose that much good time. And Richard did. He had more than a hundred "tickets" (prison violations) on his record. Some amounted to nothing more than taking an extra roll at dinner, but there were also fights. He cut another inmate once, and hit a guard, too. All of this was grist for "aggravating factors" if we got to a death penalty phase.

In sharp contrast to that side of Richard were his family relationships. I met his sister, Evelyn, and her two sons. One son was a sergeant in the Marines; the other worked at the University of Illinois at Chicago while he finished a master's in fine arts. As far back as these two young men could remember, their uncle Richard had encouraged them to be different men than he was. He warned them to avoid gangs, guns, drugs, and jail. I also spent time with Richard's girlfriend, Kendra, and their five-year-old daughter, Lila. Kendra was sweet and faithfully took the apple-cheeked Lila to visit Richard in prison, but she was considerably younger than Richard and possessed none of his curiosity or insight. My instincts told me that Evelyn and her sons would be the key to revealing Richard's humanity.

In the meantime, Richard and I studied. That is the only word for what we did. Prison rules decree that books sent to inmates have to come directly from a bookseller. I ordered books from Barnes and Noble and had them shipped to him. When I visited, we discussed what we had read. He especially savored books with political content, such as those by Fanon. To my delight, he also appreciated poetry. I introduced him to Wanda Coleman. "She be tellin' it true" was Richard's assessment of the Watts-born poet. Charles Bukowski, he decided, was "nuts, but in a good way."

The months passed, with our visits half book club, half attorney-client meeting. People not entrenched in the criminal justice system often want a simple answer to the question "Was he guilty?" I never knew, and I don't know now, if Richard killed those two men. We hardly talked about it. I asked him if he had an alibi for that night; he said he did not. When a client confesses, such as Charlotte Lyman did in the stabbing of her husband, or there's a weight of physical evidence, as with Milton Johnson, I need to know exactly what happened in order to defend my client. In this case, there was little I could learn from Richard pertaining to the murders that would help. I would give him the best defense possible. That was my job and that was what he deserved, whether he was guilty or innocent. When I am asked the classic question "How can you defend those people?" I answer that I am representing an ideal as well as a person. The ideal is justice, the principle that every accused person has a right to a vigorous defense. The State should be able to convict someone only with solid proof. Otherwise, we have no democracy.

As for Richard, I suspected that he had not done these killings. I thought this not because he wasn't capable of murder, but because there were witnesses. If Richard had done the job, no one would have seen it go down. Given that this was not a jury-friendly theory, I kept it to myself.

By this time, we had located the prosecution's second eyewitness. Charlene had told the police she had seen everything from her apartment window. One afternoon, Mort and my co-counsel on the case, Jerry Katz, went to interview her. The two of them came back to the office happy. Charlene had completely recanted her identification of Richard as the shooter, writing out the whole story by hand on several sheets of yellow legal pad. She not only recanted, but explained in the statement that the police had pressured her into an identification, that she really hadn't been able to see all that well.

This encouraged us to look for other witnesses, people who had seen the murders but were not identified in the police reports. They might be unaccounted for because they'd never talked to the police, or because their accounts didn't match the official theory. Finding them was a challenge, though. The neighborhood where the murders had taken place was highly transient, and nearly four years had passed since the crime. Finally, after considerable footwork and a stroke of luck, we found someone who knew someone who knew someone who had heard that a certain Robert Smithson had seen everything. We located Smithson and received the proverbial good news and bad news. The good news was that Smithson had been sitting in a car just a few feet away from the shootings, getting ready to pull out into the street after having bought a six-pack of beer from a nearby store. He had a good view of the shooter. Smithson studied Richard's photograph and told me that the shooter was much stockier than Richard, and darker in complexion, too. He was certain it wasn't Richard. The bad news was that Smithson was critically ill. He had had a heart attack, his kidneys had failed, he was on dialysis, and his blood pressure was dangerously high.

This might not have mattered to the case if we had been able to move quickly. By this time I had been working on the case for a year. I had scheduled Richard's trial to immediately follow Milton Johnson's. But then my doctor had ordered me not to try another case until I had had my baby. Richard had wanted to wait until I was available, so at the pretrial hearing, we had requested a continuance. The judge had tried to persuade Richard into moving ahead with another lawyer from the task force, but Richard had been adamant. The judge had reluctantly agreed to postpone the trial until I returned from maternity leave, some five months from then. In the meantime, we discovered Smithson. And it was not a given that Smithson would live that long.

One option was to depose Smithson. A deposition is sworn testimony taken outside of a courtroom that can later be presented in court as if the witness were present. Normally, depositions are permitted only in civil cases. At that time, in Illinois, the one exception that allowed a deposition in a criminal case was to preserve the testimony of an essential witness who was ill. Surely, I thought, this situation would qualify. I was wrong. The judge ruled that the only way I could use this witness was to have him appear in court. Smithson died before the trial began.

Then we learned that Charlene, the witness who had disavowed her original identification of Richard, had flipped back to the prosecution side. She would testify that she had seen Richard shoot the victims, despite her pages of statements to the contrary. The outcome was becoming increasingly evident. Whether Richard was guilty or innocent, he would be convicted. There was no physical evidence tying him to the crime, but Charlene and Rose would both point to him. His status as a gang enforcer with a murder in his past would do the rest. Without Smithson — and maybe even if we had had him — this was going to come down to whether or not I could save Richard's life. And the only way to do that was to learn about that life.

We were discussing Platonic love during one prison visit. I could practically see Richard's mind attempting to wrap itself around the concepts of ideal beauty and wisdom. He told me he wanted to think about it some more and talk about it again when I next came. "Sure," I said. "It's time to get down to business, anyway. I need to ask you some questions about your father."

Richard nodded, but I suspected this would be tough territory.

He could declaim enthusiastically and at length about Antigone's decision to bury her brother against the king's decree, but found it difficult to form the words when speaking about his own history. Nevertheless, I needed to uncover what had driven an intelligent young man from a two-parent home into a street gang. Richard's sister Evelyn had described their father as abusive, but I needed to hear Richard's perspective.

"You joined the gang when you were twelve years old, is that right?"

"Yeah."

"Why?"

I could see Richard considering what to tell me. His first instinct had always been to conceal. I hoped that by now, after the months of our meeting, talking about literature and working on his case, he would be willing to fight that urge toward self-protection. I wasn't sure what I would do if he weren't.

Finally, he spoke. "I couldn't be home no more." I didn't move or make a sound. I sensed an opening up, and I wanted to give him plenty of space.

"My dad, he would get drunk or whatever and hit my mother. Not all the time, but it kept getting worse." I nodded. "And see, I was a small guy. I didn't grow, really, till I was damn near twenty. I couldn't do nothin' to protect her." I thought of Charlotte Lyman's son, and all the sons and daughters I had heard from, who couldn't stop the violence in their homes.

"Then it stopped bein' just hitting. It got worse." Richard swallowed. "One day, they was arguing in the kitchen, and he grabbed a knife. He opened her up."

The implication was horrifying, but I had to make sure I understood. "What do you mean?" I asked quietly.

"He cut open her stomach and pulled some of it out. Onto the table."

We sat together in a long and heavy silence. Then I gently resumed prodding him. Somehow his mother had survived the attack. It seemed, though, that Richard had never recovered. The twelve-year-old had simply stopped coming home. He couldn't restrain his father, and he couldn't bear standing by. The gang out in the neighborhood welcomed him. They made him feel both tough and protected.

Richard talked at length, and I think he felt listened to, maybe for the first time. Eventually, he ran out of story. When I began to pack up my papers, subdued and thoughtful, he surprised me with a sudden exclamation.

"God damn you, anyway."

"What?" I didn't understand. Was he sorry he had opened up? Had I not responded the way he wanted me to?

Richard turned his back to me. "I had gotten to the place — you know what I mean — that I had written this whole damn thing off. I was sure ain't no one anywhere in this system worth a goddamn. And then you come along. Damn you."

"I still don't understand, Richard."

"I ain't want to feel no hope about nothin' no more. Damn you." Then he swung back around to look at me. Unexpectedly, his face broke out in a smile, tired but genuine. He could try to resist it, he could attempt to push it away, but hope insisted on breaking through. We shook hands, and I left without our saying another word.

I had to justify that breakthrough. I am opposed to the death penalty in all cases. Punishment may be necessary, even, in some cases, lifelong incarceration. I do not believe, however, that execution serves anyone. Redemption is always possible, even for the unrepentant, but death puts an end to all possibilities. In Richard's case, my determination to keep him from a death sentence went beyond my basic belief that every person is worth saving. Richard had gifts. Despite whatever he had done in the past, and the need for him to take responsibility for those deeds, he had wisdom and intelligence to offer in the future. I could not stand the thought of that keen spirit condemned to a slow rot on death row, or extinguished by a brutish end.

Piece by piece, through mounds of documents and personal interviews, I was constructing a life story that made sense. Richard's prison behavior still rankled, though, until the day I found an intake form and doctor's notes from the hospital arm of the jail. Normally, even if a minor is tried and convicted as an adult, he serves time in a juvenile detention center until he turns twenty-one and is transferred to an adult facility to finish out his term. For a reason that I was never able to determine, this didn't happen to Richard. At 15 years old, 5'9", and 127 pounds, he was sent to live among violent, imprisoned adult men. According to the documents I found, other inmates raped him, day after day. Finally, too weak to stand, he was found lying over the drain in his cell, bleeding into it. After recovering in the hospital, Richard was sent back to the general population. But now he was a different person. Now he didn't wait for anyone to attack him first.

Those are the discoveries that build a mitigation case. Now I knew why he had joined the gang, and I knew why he had fought so frequently in prison. I could explain his past, but the jury needed a reason to let him live into the future. Richard's sister and nephews could provide much of that. To close the deal, I would try to make the jury see what I saw: a man with a code of honor who consistently looked out for others, usually younger inmates without protection, and who possessed intellectual curiosity and abilities, along with an abiding love for his family.

By the time Samantha was born, I felt we were ready for trial. Trying Richard's case would be the first thing I would do when I returned from maternity leave. Then, a month and a half into my leave, my co-counsel, Jerry, called. The judge had an unexpected opening in his court calendar and was moving the trial date up by two weeks. He told Jerry that either I showed up or Jerry would have to try the case without me.

I was furious. Gavin had recently left. I was slowly admitting to myself that he had emotionally abused me and that I had let him. This humiliating realization, however, did not prevent me from grieving his loss as a partner for me and a father to our daughter. On top of that, I had an infant to take care of. This was also my redemption. I loved being a mother more than I could have imagined. Samantha amazed me. In my years of work, I had spent so much time mired in life's pain and degradation. Now I spent every waking hour with this gorgeous, innocent creature for whom every piece of the world was a revelation. When Samantha was a little older, I told a friend that I had always thought the most beautiful words in the English language were "We the jury, find the defendant not guilty," but I was wrong. Samantha reaching her arms up to me and saying, "Mama," had that beat all to hell.

A judge arbitrarily demanding that I choose between serving my client and being with my baby infuriated me. Ultimately, I knew I couldn't let Richard's trial go forward without me. There are miles of difference between being a first and a second chair on a defense team. Leaving this trial to Jerry would not have been fair to Jerry or, more important, to Richard, who had come to trust me and to believe that I could help him. Samantha and I would have a lifetime together; this might be Richard's only shot at having a future. So I arranged childcare with an astute and smiling baby-sitter named Maude, went to the Goodwill store to buy Richard the usual dress pants, button-down shirt, and sweater, and got ready for trial.

Returning to work early resulted in a few mishaps. I was still nursing, and there hadn't been enough time to decrease my milk production. During jury selection, a baby in the courtroom started to cry, and I began to lactate. I ruined some of my best blouses during that trial. On another day, one of the jurors inquired if I had recently had a baby. I said yes, but was curious why she had asked. She pointed to my jacketed left shoulder: baby vomit. Damn, I had meant to wipe that off before coming to court.

The trial was a travesty. That we didn't have Smithson to contradict the prosecution's two eyewitnesses was bad enough, but we were also hit with an unpleasant surprise right out of the gate. Charlene, the witness who had changed her story twice, took the stand and said that she had recanted her original statement to the police because my investigator, Mort, and my partner, Jerry, had threatened to shoot her. I wanted to scream. Well, actually, I wanted to smack the prosecutors. Besides the fact that this testimony was flat-out perjury, they obviously had known what Charlene was going to say and were entirely out of line not to have informed us about it before trial. But the judge allowed it. Now we had to scramble to contradict her story. Jerry had to withdraw as my co-counsel, so that I could put both Mort and him on the stand to tell what had really happened during Charlene's interview. That left me to try the case alone, which is an arduous experience anytime, much less during my scheduled maternity leave. Richard took lots of notes and tried to help as much as a non-attorney could.

Bad surprises kept on coming. The trial was filled with testimony that didn't match the police reports. Rose, the junkie prostitute, for example, had told the police at the time of the murders — and Mort and me when we interviewed her — that she had been standing in front of the liquor store kitty-corner from the shootings. Now, on the witness stand, she claimed to have been on the same side of the street, just yards from the crime. Inconsistencies like this are not unusual, but normally, you can "impeach" the witness with his prior statement. If the witness won't admit the prior statement, you can bring in the person, usually a police officer, to whom he made the statement. Cops don't particularly like testifying for the defense, but if something is in their report, they will "stick to their paper" and confirm it. Except in this trial. Time after time, when I called a police officer to confirm what the witness had originally said, the officer denied it. They must have hated Richard and wanted badly to bring him down. After the third officer in a row claimed that he must have made a mistake in writing his report, we took a break. I went to the lockup to talk to Richard and found him seething. "God damn it," he said, pacing in the small space. "These motherfuckers come in here and they be wolves walking around in sheep suits. Damn, I might be a wolf, but I wear a damned wolf suit!"

I was almost surprised when the jury took as long as five hours to return a conviction. Richard was prepared for that outcome and took it stoically, even though he knew his future had now been narrowed to two choices: execution or life in prison.

During the sentencing phase, the prosecution focused their arguments, naturally, on all the mistakes of Richard's life: the gang membership, prior murder, prison fights, and gun charges. Sadly, there was little in the way of a victims' impact argument. The two men who had been gunned down that night had faded almost into irrelevance. No family members of either man ever sat in the gallery.

When my turn came, I told the jury about Richard's family life, and how he had become involved in the gang. I reminded them that he had not been the actual shooter in the first murder, and that some uncertainty of his guilt on the more recent murders persisted. Juries convict based on guilt beyond a "reasonable" doubt; they are allowed to harbor some doubt and still find the defendant guilty. Any level of doubt, however, may be taken into consideration when deciding whether to impose a death sentence.

After my opening, both of Richard's nephews testified: the Marine sergeant in his dress whites and the college student in an ill-fitting suit and a skinny tie. They each talked about the beneficial influence their uncle Richard had exerted in their lives: his loving attention to them over the years, his lectures on staying off the streets and making something of themselves. I noted appraising looks at Richard from the jury box. My internal jury meter told me we might be pulling ahead.

Then I put his sister, Evelyn, on the stand. Evelyn's hard life showed in her eyes and in her prematurely lined face. She and I had sat in her living room and carefully prepared her testimony. She was supposed to focus on what a caring brother Richard was, even from jail. We agreed that she would talk about what he meant to her and what his death would mean, as well. But sometimes a person has an overwhelming need to say what has been eating at them. What Evelyn really wanted to talk about, she told me, was the racism in the system. She believed Richard had been harshly mistreated, in particular by his prison placement with adults when he was a juvenile. She was convinced this wouldn't have happened if he had been white. I didn't disagree with her point, but it wasn't strictly relevant. This life-and-death discussion had to be about Richard, and not about race. Evelyn said she understood.

On the stand, however, despite my guided questioning, suddenly she was talking about race and how Richard had been discriminated against. The State jumped up to object, the judge sustained the objection, and then turned to loudly and harshly berate Evelyn. She began to cry.

I heard a chair scrape behind me. Richard was on his feet. I had deliberately chosen not to put him on the stand. His hearing loss caused him to speak unpleasantly loudly, and every other word was a swear word, to boot. He had behaved impeccably throughout his trial, but now a judge was making his little sister cry.

"Evelyn," Richard shouted, "fuck these honky motherfuckers! Don't you beg for my life."

My mind raced wildly. How could I turn this potentially devastating moment into a positive? And then Evelyn did it for me. Still crying, she turned directly to the jury and said, "See? He would rather die than see me hurt."

The atmosphere immediately changed. In that brief contretemps among Evelyn, the judge, and Richard, the jury had seen some of what I had come to know in my client: not the intellect, maybe, but the humanity. I could feel it, and so could the prosecution. There was shouting on their part, and objections sustained by the judge. I didn't get a single jury instruction I asked for.

Nevertheless, those twelve men and women swiftly returned a life verdict. Evelyn wept and the nephews breathed large sighs of relief. Richard simply nodded at me and, I think, stood a little taller.

AFTER RICHARD'S TRIAL and another death case I tried less than a week later (at which we also won a life sentence), I was depleted. I conceded to myself that the demands of an effective and caring public defender were incompatible with the demands of an effective and caring single mother. In January 1990, after fourteen years on the job, I left the Public Defender's Office. The Homicide Task Force was in many ways different from the operation with which I had been so intrigued when I first visited Bill Murphy. The office was noticeably more diverse. By the time I left, for example, there were half a dozen women on the staff. (Since then, women have become the majority.) Both the atmosphere and the lawyering had changed, too. Teamwork was commonplace. The importance of developing mitigation was now taken for granted, and it had paid off. When I came on, the task force was losing most of its death penalty phases; when I left, we were winning a large majority of them.

With everything I had learned, and a Selectric typewriter set up in my spare bedroom, I founded the Illinois Capital Resource Center. Funding from the state allowed me to represent people whose cases had been lost both at trial and on direct appeal. That essentially encompassed all of the 160 death row inmates in Illinois. While this kind of quasi-appellate work was demanding, I could control my schedule to a greater degree, and much of the research and writing could be accomplished at home.

As I began working on these cases, I learned how poorly some of these men, and a few women, had been represented. I became dismayed at the amount of evidence that had been hidden from them. And I discovered, to my rage and despair, how many innocent people — more than even I had imagined — were living on the row. Sometimes, those realities weighed me down in a cloud of depression.

Fortunately, there was someone to whom I could always turn for reassurance that my work had value and that the lives of those on death row were worth fighting for. There was Richard Bauman. Unlike almost every other former client, Richard has remained a part of my life. We still correspond. I still send him books.

❖

CHAPTER 10

Supreme Judgments

ONE DAY I'M WRITING a brief to be read by the United States Supreme Court. The next day I'm on my hands and knees marking off the sidewalk with a tape measure to evaluate whether an eyewitness could actually have seen what he said he saw. Or I'm treating an eight-year-old to a Happy Meal while he tells me what games his daddy used to play with him. It's all part of the job.

I spent years fighting to keep my clients off death row. Then, when I founded the Illinois Capital Resource Center in 1990, that's precisely where all my new clients were. Illinois had not executed anyone in decades, but its death row population had been growing steadily since capital punishment was reinstated in 1977. By 1990, some 160 inmates had been condemned to die. Within a year after the center started up, a man named Charles Walker was put to death, the first in Illinois since 1962. If there had been any doubt that the State was willing to execute, it was dispelled then.

I had been recruiting lawyers to represent condemned prisoners for two years when I added Anthony Baker to my own caseload.

While driving the two and a half hours from Chicago to the Pontiac Correctional Center to meet him, I reviewed what I knew of the case. He had been sentenced to die for a gang hit. The direct appeals, based on what had happened at his original trial, were not yet exhausted. A petition to the U.S. Supreme Court was pending, but the chances of the Court hearing it were small. So, in the meantime, I was starting work on a post-conviction petition, for the purpose of addressing constitutional issues. For example, had the police or prosecution withheld exculpatory evidence? Had Anthony Baker received effective assistance of counsel? Were there juror "investigations" outside of what happened in the courtroom? Sometimes jurors will visit the crime scene on their own or "investigate" on the Internet. This is illegal — jurors are supposed to decide the case based on the evidence adduced at trial. If any of these things were true, they would be violations of constitutional rights. But to find out if such violations occurred, a new investigation into the case was needed.

Despite the fact that I was no longer a newcomer to death row, my visits to Pontiac and Menard prisons, the two facilities in the state where condemned men were housed, were always discomfiting. Inmate and visitor alike were continually reminded that a sentence of death hung between them. After registering and clearing security, I knew to pass through the regular visiting room into another area out of the line of sight of the friends and family members who sat chatting with inmates. Once in that chamber, I faced a set of heavy metal doors. Above them, a sign read, "Condemned Unit." With surveillance cameras trained on my every movement, I was admitted through the doors and into the death row visiting room. One guard sat at a check-in desk; two more paced the room, around which several tables were set up for visiting or meeting. You were never more than a few feet from a guard.

Anthony Baker was brought shuffling in, with both his wrists and ankles shackled. The wrist chains were attached to a belt around his waist. The first time I had visited a death row client, I had naïvely asked a guard to unlock my client's handcuffs so he could sign a legal document. The guard merely shook his head. They will not unshackle a death row prisoner outside his cell even for a moment. I became used to seeing my clients struggle to produce a signature with their wrists locked together.

Another client of mine once spoke in an interview of his time on the Condemned Unit: "Living on death row is like a living hell. The lights stay on twenty-four hours a day. Anytime they bring you out of the cell, you have to be handcuffed and shackled and walked like a dog, even to the shower. You actually smell death on death row, because that's the common theme, death."

"Mr. Baker?" I stood up as the guard brought him to the table where I had been sitting. I did my best to inject warmth into my eyes and voice when I met a new client here. It was challenging to establish a quick rapport with someone with whom it was physically impossible to shake hands.

"Yes?" Anthony looked at me curiously. He was a dark-skinned, average-size man with a square scar impressed on his forehead.

"Didn't Mr. Young tell you I'd be coming? My name is Andrea Lyon and I'm an attorney from the Illinois Capital Resource Center. I wanted to meet you so we can get started on your post-conviction petition."

We both sat. Anthony shifted in his chair, trying to find a comfortable way to accommodate the chains. "I thought Mr. Young was still my lawyer."

"He is, but we can't count on the Supreme Court taking your case. I wanted to get a jump on starting a new investigation, so we won't have lost time if they don't."

Anthony nodded, but I wasn't sure he understood. I spent a few minutes explaining the differences between the appeals process and post-conviction. I had brought a simple chart with me that named the various steps. As I pointed at each step, Anthony nodded. He thanked me when I gave him the chart, but I noticed that he laid it in front of himself upside down. I wondered if he could read.

"Mr. Baker," I said, "we need to look at your whole case all over again."

"Why?"

"To see if there's evidence that might help you with another trial if we get one, or with your sentence, something that might show, for instance, that this wasn't a 'hit' like they say, or — "

"It weren't," he interrupted. "Half that stuff they say ain't right, either."

It was my turn to nod. "That's just it. I need to go over the police reports with you, talk over your life history, get permission from you to get records, and... well, just start digging."

A slow smile spread across Anthony's face. "You gonna look at this, for real?"

An hour later, I left the Condemned Unit with signed permission slips to obtain his personal records. My client had confirmed that he couldn't read or write, except to sign his name.

In the original trial, two public defenders, both African-American, had represented Anthony in front of my old nemesis, Judge Novak, aka Judge Misogyny. Women weren't the only category of lawyers His Honor didn't like. During the trial, he referred to the public defenders as "laughing boy" and "smiling boy." Once, after a conference in chambers, he said he would have to "fumigate" after they left the room.

The trial had been a mess. Even before the first argument, one potential juror said that she felt death would be the only appropriate punishment—and she was seated anyway, because there were no peremptory challenges left and the judge denied the request to excuse her for cause. Judge Novak had interrupted the defense attorneys during cross-examinations, imposed time limits on them, and did not give the jury any of the instructions to which the defense was entitled. Anthony was convicted and sentenced to death. The Illinois Supreme Court affirmed those decisions.

Despite the debacle, the trial lawyers did something that later made all the difference. When I was the chief of the Homicide Task Force, I pushed people hard to "dog a record." I had never forgotten the lesson I learned in my first job in the Appeals Division of the Public Defender's Office: bring up every possible issue during the original trial, because those are the only ones that can be addressed on appeal. I pushed the lawyers on my staff to do just that, even on issues they feared were hopeless, especially on death penalty cases.

One of the areas I pushed was jury selection. Thanks to *Witherspoon v. United States*, the prosecution has the right to find out which potential jurors would *never* be able to impose the death penalty, and to eliminate those jurors "for cause." This means the State doesn't have to use up their limited number of peremptory challenges on those jurors.

Lawyers defending capital cases figured that if *Witherspoon* gave the prosecution the right to find out who would *never* be able to impose the death penalty and to eliminate them for cause, then the defenders should be able to find out who would *always* choose the death penalty for a capital offense—and eliminate *them* for cause. For years, lawyers filed motions asking for the right to "reverse *Witherspoon*" capital juries. Trial judges repeatedly denied these motions, and the Illinois Supreme Court repeatedly affirmed those denials. Nevertheless, because you never knew when there would be a breakthrough,

I made it task force policy that the attorneys in any death case must file a motion asking to "reverse-*Witherspoon*" the potential jurors. Anthony's lawyers had done this.

And because they had done this, we were able to appeal to the U.S. Supreme Court to overturn the decision rejecting the reverse *Witherspoon*. And, while I was preparing the post-conviction petition, to everyone's surprise, the Supreme Court took the case.

Anthony's appellate attorney, Gerald Young, asked me to file a supporting brief. I had never before written anything for the U.S. Supreme Court, and I took to the task with relish. My job was to examine the social science data on death-qualified jurors, particularly those who said they would automatically vote for death if the defendant were convicted of a capital offense.

"Recent studies reveal," I wrote in the introduction, "that individuals who would automatically impose the death penalty represent a significant and identifiable portion of the potential juror pool." Near the end of the brief, I concluded, "Since jurors who will automatically impose death upon conviction will not consider mitigating evidence and, thus, not follow the law, they must be excluded."

Young, as Anthony's lawyer for direct appeals, then traveled to Washington to present the arguments, with me cheering him on from Chicago. In June 1992, the Court released their response, agreeing with our position. In the majority opinion, written by Justice Byron White, the Court held that the defense has the right to question potential jurors regarding pro-capital punishment views, primarily the unwillingness or inability to consider mitigating evidence and vote for a sentence other than death.

Since then, defenders in capital cases routinely "life-qualify" potential jurors, and those who will not consider mitigating evidence are disqualified for cause. If the trial lawyers representing Anthony

Baker had not requested to reverse-*Witherspoon* his jury, if they had not been willing to hear the word *denied* one more time, then this right would not exist.

That was the importance of the ruling in the long run. For Anthony Baker, the Supreme Court's decision meant that he could leave death row, for the time being, and get another sentencing hearing. The nine justices paved the way, but wrapping up the case called for a top-to-bottom investigation.

The sentencing hearing would begin with a new chance to combat the notion that Anthony's crime was death penalty eligible. The prosecution maintained that this was a death case because the killing had been a gang hit, a contract murder. Anthony vehemently denied this. If I could defeat this "aggravating factor," then Anthony would be subject only to a prison sentence. Because he had a criminal record, the probable sentence would be life without parole.

The only direct evidence that the killing had been a hit came from a jailhouse snitch. These guys are a fact of life in prisons and jails. If a convict is looking at ten years on a robbery, he can become a key witness on a more serious case — a potential death penalty case, for instance — and then he has enough bargaining leverage to play Let's Make a Deal. In Anthony's case, the informant had testified that he and Anthony had been in adjoining cells in an Indiana jail when Anthony was first arrested. The snitch said that he was in cell 1 and Anthony was in cell 2, on Tier B, and that they talked to each other. What Anthony had said, so the snitch reported, was that he was in jail for "following orders — you know, got to do what the generals say do." These words did not amount to a confession per se, but they nevertheless provided the crucial basis for the prosecution's claim of murder for hire.

Mort and I set off for the Indiana jail. We weren't sure what we were looking for, but we agreed that we needed to see the place in which these fatal words had allegedly been spoken. We found the jail tucked inconspicuously next to a strip mall. Although small by Cook County standards, the building was big enough to hold several tiers. We followed a friendly guard through a series of convoluted hallways and up flights of stairs until we arrived on Tier B. The guard led us to cells 1 and 2, where Mort and I looked around in initial confusion. The two cells were, indeed, next to each other. But the doors of the even-numbered cells let out onto one hallway, and the doors of the odd-numbered cells led onto another hallway on the opposite side. In between cells 1 and 2 was a floor-to-ceiling, two-foot-thick steel wall. In order for Anthony and the snitch to have had the conversation the snitch reported, the men would have had to talk through a two-foot-thick steel wall. That wall was going to make all the difference. Mort and I whooped with pleased laughter until the guard insisted on knowing why we were so elated. When I explained, the guard laughed, too. He declared the snitch's testimony "bullshit" and asked if we wanted him to be a witness. Did we ever!

Based on the lack of evidence that the murder had been a hit for hire, the judge decided that Anthony was not death-eligible. He was sentenced to life without parole. For some clients, the prospect of serving a sentence with no end in sight looms worse than a death sentence — at first. Most of the time, however, these clients eventually become grateful for the chance to remain connected to family and to try to do something productive, even under the circumscribed conditions of prison life. Anthony was happy to leave the dehumanizing atmosphere of death row, and he looked forward to learning how to read.

I spent five years running the Death Penalty Center. Early on, I moved the operation out of my spare bedroom and into a real office, but the job continued to allow me a relatively flexible lifestyle. I worked a hard day, but at the end of eight hours, I could pick up Samantha from Maude's on time because I wasn't stuck in court. After dinner or on the weekends, Samantha and I would watch Disney movies. I can still recite by heart the dialogue from *Beauty and the Beast*. Sure, the life of a single working parent is challenging — even going to the grocery store required advance planning — but being a mom to Samantha satisfied me, body and soul. I may not have been good at picking men, but I had taken to this mothering stuff pretty darn well. Of course, Samantha made it easy. She was bright, eager to discover the world, and ready to take it on. She started talking at seven months. Before I knew it, she had grown into, and remains to this day, a person of strong opinions — for which no one gives me the least sympathy.

Despite my forgiving schedule, soon the stress of being responsible for the representation of all the death row inmates in Illinois, following eleven years of homicide work, began to wear on me. I had witnessed lawyer burnout in the past: attorneys who drank too much, slid into dangerous depression, or simply stopped trying. I wasn't there yet, but I could feel the warning signs.

Casework had been my first love. But teaching courses at the National Criminal Defense College in Georgia and giving continuing legal education sessions all over the country had made me realize that communicating what I knew about this work also gave me profound satisfaction. My ideal job, I decided, would combine teaching with working on a limited number of cases. If I could pass on to others what I had learned, I could, essentially, replace myself. You can't stay on the front lines forever. To my delight, in 1995 the University of Michigan Law School hired me to teach in their clinical program. I enjoyed the small student-to-teacher ratio of the clinic, where my students worked on actual cases with me. Although I remained on the advisory board of the center, my second in command took over the day-to-day operations.

While teaching in Ann Arbor, I took on a death penalty case, which is surprising, since Michigan has not had a death penalty since 1847. But the federal government does have a death penalty, and Uncle Sam is everywhere. The Federal Defender of Detroit contacted me to ask if I would accept a capital case. It turns out I was the only lawyer in the state who had ever defended against the death penalty.

The client was Thomas Sewell, a black man charged with two murders and multiple drug conspiracies in a federal indictment. When I looked at the file, I was reminded of a former task force colleague who had developed his own lettering code to describe cases. The worst designation was BC-ND, which meant "Bad Case, No Defense." That was Thomas Sewell: BC-ND. As the alleged kingpin of a crack cocaine operation, Thomas had lived a brutal life. He had supposedly hired a man to kill the head of a rival faction, Thomas's own half-brother. Then he was alleged to have killed the killer in order to keep him quiet. There were two additional murders — including a dismemberment after death — to be introduced as part of the criminal conspiracy. Not a pretty picture.

The case encompassed 923 potential witnesses and thousands of pages of reports. By the time we were scheduling a trial date, all of the 19 co-defendants had turned on Thomas. Each of them had had his charges reduced or dropped in exchange for testifying against my client.

Despite the horrific case, I was in a kind of lawyer's heaven. I have a lot to say about bad judges and prosecutors, but I'm also happy to talk about the good ones. In this case, I was in front of the brilliant, intellectually curious Judge Arthur Tarnow. Over the years I worked on this case, Judge Tarnow became a mentor to me. Instead of being annoyed with my complicated motions, he was fascinated by them and enjoyed discussing them with me. Once, he even suggested I research some nineteenth-century cases that might be relevant.

And if that weren't enough, I was trying the case opposite Michael Leibsen and second chair Kathryn McCarthy. Those two made up one of the smartest, most ethical prosecution teams I have ever known.

During the course of working on this case, the Department of Justice published a statistical report showing that 73 percent of the federal prosecutions asking for the death penalty were against African-American men. Mike and Kathryn were sincerely distressed over these findings, but I was ready to use them. With the general data in hand, I filed a motion requesting access to more specific information detailing how the federal government decided whom to seek a death penalty against. I was looking, of course, to show that my client was being discriminated against based on race. If this had been an employment discrimination case, for example, the lopsided statistics would have shifted the burden of proof to the prosecution, who would then have had to demonstrate that the discrepancy was actually caused by something other than race.

It doesn't work that way in criminal law, though; the courts are reluctant to interfere with prosecutorial decision-making. In order to get my hands on the information that would show the biases in how they determined who was worthy of the death penalty, I was required to demonstrate not just a discriminatory effect, but a discriminatory intent. But how do you show the intent to discriminate without knowing how the decisions are made? Anyone thinking "Catch-22"?

Mike, personally, agreed with my motion, although that was not his office's position. "The facts are what they are, Andrea," he said. "I say, let's open the damn thing up, and whatever they show, they show."

"Too bad the Department of Justice doesn't see it the same way," I answered.

"I think that the policy guys in Washington don't know they can trust us," Mike insisted. "I bet once you look at that data, you'll see race has nothing to do with it."

"Maybe not in Detroit, Mike," I replied, "but what will the data in Texas or Virginia look like?"

"No comment," was all he said. That's why I liked Mike.

I convinced Judge Tarnow that there was justification for giving us access to the national data, and he accepted my motion. The Department of Justice, however, refused to comply. In response, Judge Tarnow barred them from asking for the death penalty in this case. The feds took it to the U.S. Court of Appeals for the Sixth Circuit, where we won again. Then the Department of Justice decided to appeal to the United States Supreme Court.

My Michigan colleague Sam Gross and I wrote a brief opposing the government's request for the case to be heard. Instead of deciding to hear or not hear the case, the U.S. Supreme Court, in June 2002, simply reversed the lower court's decision to allow us access to the data. The opinion made it clear that without evidence of intentional racial discrimination on the part of the prosecutor in a specific case, the decision-making process would be off limits, whether for the purpose of making a point in one defendant's case or for analyzing the system as a whole. The opinion gave me the impression that the Supreme Court simply didn't care if there was racial bias in our country's implementation of capital punishment.

The federal government was allowed to proceed with their death penalty quest against Thomas Sewell. There would be no changes in the law to help me out this time.

After five years at Michigan, I had returned to Chicago in 2000 to join the faculty at DePaul University Law School, but I continued working on Thomas's case. When the time came for the trial, I rented a furnished apartment in Detroit, where my DePaul colleague Emily Hughes, investigator Mort Smith, and I bunked together. For five weeks our lives revolved exclusively around the case. The trial caused a local sensation. In 150 years, only one other death penalty case had been tried in Michigan. Judges came to watch the trial, and the press closely followed the proceedings. While the air of significance was inspiring, the case remained extraordinarily tough and its context painful.

We had the reverse-*Witherspoon* decision, at least. I dismissed for cause some fifteen potential jurors based on their unwillingness to give any punishment other than death if they convicted.

I used other tools as well to eliminate jurors for cause, including a written survey that prospective jurors completed prior to being questioned. People may be willing to reveal certain beliefs and opinions in writing that they would not bring up in open court. What the attorney must do is design questions that will make it safe to disclose biases.

One member of the jury pool for the trial had indicated in her questionnaire that her relatives were prejudiced against black people. When I questioned her in court, I asked her to explain what she had written. Her husband had been a policeman during the race riots of the 1960s, she said. Her father-in-law, who had also been a policeman, had once killed a black man in the line of duty and had been known to brag about it. The whole family, she said, expressed dislike for African-Americans. "I really can't say that I am prejudiced," she said, "but I've heard these things."

"It sounds to me," I said, "that you're worried that you've been affected by this yourself."

"Yes," the woman replied.

"And you're a little bit ashamed of that."

"Yes," she answered quietly. She went on to reveal what she had not written on the questionnaire: that her teenage granddaughter was dating a young black man. The potential juror admitted her discomfort with the interracial relationship.

Gently, I persisted: "You have to forgive me. Obviously, you can see I'm sitting next to Mr. Sewell here, who is an African-American man. I know this is difficult, but would you think that this might not be the best case for you to be a juror on, because of the things we've been talking about?"

"I think that would be a true statement," the woman said. "Yes."

Because I showed respect, listened carefully, and gave this woman the opportunity to recognize her own biases, she essentially removed herself from the jury. Judge Tarnow thanked her and dismissed her.

In selecting this jury panel, I had my eye focused squarely on the penalty phase. I had no illusions that we would win the guilt-or-innocence part of the trial, and indeed, Thomas was convicted.

As awful as the crimes in this case were, the mitigation was also compelling. We decided to introduce the story of Thomas's life using a videotape of interviews with relatives and friends of the family. Lawyers commonly present videos in court now, but at the time, I had never heard of anyone doing it. The initial reason we turned to taped interviews to supplement courtroom testimony was the problem of Thomas's mother. She wanted to help her son. She was willing to admit how her own actions, including killing her live-in boyfriend in front of her children, had subjected Thomas to terror, privation, and the need to turn to crime to feed his younger siblings. The problem was that she was an addict. If I called her as a witness, I couldn't be sure she'd be in any shape to testify. In order to talk coherently, she needed to be not too high, but just high enough. If we taped her, we could keep trying until we got what we needed. And eventually, we did get what we needed, and more. We ended up taping a dozen different people. The finished video was a raw and moving testament to the way deplorable circumstances can push an innocent child into criminal activity — and how, in spite of that, he can be deeply loved by the family he never stops taking care of.

After I showed the tape, Thomas's sister and aunt testified in person, as did a psychologist. To counter the prosecution's assertion that Thomas would be a continuing danger in prison, I called four prison officials, who asserted that Thomas was not just a good prisoner but a peacemaker among inmates.

The prosecution's closing arguments began with Mike Leibsen talking about Thomas's "decade-long series of violent acts, including assaults, torture, and murder." He didn't contest that Thomas had grown up under appalling conditions, but he told a story about another person with a difficult history. This man had suffered many deprivations, he explained: early years in poverty, limited education, the murder of his grandfather, childhood head injury, the death of his mother when he was young, gang associations. "He had so little respect for his father that he would not visit him as he was dying or attend his funeral. Now, according to the information presented by the defense, this person would seem to have a considerable chance of coming to no good. In fact, that describes Abraham Lincoln." Great argument, especially to a death-qualified jury.

For my closing, I determined once more to take my time. I reviewed all the horrifying elements of Thomas Sewell's life. "It doesn't relieve him of responsibility," I conceded. "You have already assigned him responsibility. The question is, what's the right punishment?"

I countered Mike's Lincoln story. "A person with an extraordinary intelligence, who reads well and excels in school, who receives positive attention from sources outside the family, may be able to overcome terrible difficulties. But Thomas Sewell didn't have those things. Thomas Sewell was not operating with the same tools that many of us use to overcome obstacles."

I reminded them of the psychologist's testimony regarding the impact that Thomas's execution could have on his children. "You have evidence that his execution may cause his children to believe that they are worthless; that their father is so vile, that we must kill him; that they, therefore, must be equally vile. And that is something you may consider as mitigation."

Of course, the jury knew that the men Thomas had killed had had children of their own. "When I speak about the effect of an execution," I said, "I hope you understand that I'm only trying to tell you about the effect on Thomas Sewell's family, and not in any way deprecating the seriousness of the offense you've convicted him of or the loss of life that was incurred. No one deserved to be murdered. Life is precious."

I reminded them that a verdict for death must be unanimous. "Some of you may feel death is appropriate. Some of you may feel a life in prison is enough. If you wish to, you can agree to disagree. Any one of you, all alone, has the awesome capacity to save Thomas Sewell's life."

I told a story that illustrated that point. "It used to be, when the State electrocuted condemned people, that four guards were assigned to the execution. And these four guards would each place a finger over a black button. The warden would give the signal, and all four of them would push the buttons. But they all knew that one of the buttons was a blank, unconnected to the electrical current. Do you know why that was, ladies and gentlemen? That was so when each guard would go home that night and wake up sweating in the bed next to his wife, remembering the smell of burning flesh, the sound of the condemned man's heart exploding in his chest, reliving the awful moments of the execution, he could take comfort and say to himself, maybe I didn't do it. Maybe I had the blank.

"There are no blanks here, ladies and gentlemen. One of you has to lift your finger off that button. And if you do, Thomas Sewell lives.

"Either way, your verdict will guarantee that Thomas Sewell will not leave prison except in a pine box. The question is, will it be in God's time or yours?

"I've talked to you about the law. I've talked to you about the facts. I've talked to you about this overwhelmingly hard life Thomas Sewell has lived. I've talked with you about the love his family feels for him. All of that is important. But when it comes down to it, I'm just a person, just a person asking twelve individual persons — please, don't kill him."

Finally, with nothing left to say, I stood silently. I glanced over at the prosecution table to signal that I was finished. It was their turn to rebut. Kathryn was wiping tears from her face. Mike stood and said: "Your Honor, everything that needs to be said has been said."

The jury sentenced Thomas to life. An unusual atmosphere of relief and satisfaction pervaded the crowd. I sensed in the Michigan courtroom a general feeling of joy that a man's life had been spared. Four of the "death-qualified" jury members later said that the experience had shaken their long-held convictions. In the sometimes-bitter national battle over the death penalty, these four had switched sides.

CHAPTER 11

Whose Case Is It, Anyway?

I WASN'T PREPARED for the stunning woman the guard led into the room. Her beauty leapt out from the drab surroundings of the Dwight Correctional Center. Juliette Vega was tall and slender, with an aristocratic neck, high cheekbones, and full lips. Her dark eyes were framed by thick, softly curling brown hair. She had the carriage and exotic air of a runway model. Instead of couture, though, she wore a prison jumpsuit. Its blue color and the shackles that bound both her wrists and ankles were the signs that distinguished Juliette as a prisoner sentenced to die. Once she sat down, though, the guard unlocked and removed the wrist chains, a courtesy granted to female residents of death row. The private attorney's room we met in was also a luxury not available when I met with my condemned male clients.

The Illinois Capital Resource Center took on Juliette Vega's case in the spring of 1995. At the request of the lawyer responsible for her first appeal, I had agreed to handle her case myself. At that time, four other women were residing on Illinois's death row; Juliette was the only one who became my client.

She had been sentenced to die three years earlier for the murder of her husband. The aggravating factor that made her crime death-eligible was that it was Juliette's second murder conviction. As an eighteen-year-old unmarried mother, she had smothered her eleven-month-old daughter. The child's death had been attributed to Sudden Infant Death Syndrome; for a while, Juliette had literally gotten away with murder. But she couldn't live with what she had done. Almost four years after her daughter's death, she walked into a police station and confessed. She pled guilty in exchange for twenty years. Now those convicted of murder must serve 100 percent of their sentences, but at that time, one could still earn good time even on a murder charge. So Juliette, who was a model prisoner, was out in ten years. While in jail, she married Dominic Vega, a man on the outside who was almost twice her age. Some five months after leaving prison, she shot him to death with a .357 magnum.

When the Resource Center got involved in her case, Juliette's most recent attorney warned me that getting the prisoner to participate in her appeal would be difficult. Juliette was withdrawn, depressed, and feeling hopeless. I decided to delay seeing her until I had finished a basic investigation and a review of her file. I was sure that nothing approaching the complete story had been told at trial, and I hoped that if I got closer to that story, she would be more willing to help us work for her.

There was nothing in Juliette's file or in the trial transcripts about Dominic Vega's background, but when a woman kills her husband, that's the first thing to look at. Sure enough, Mort and I quickly turned up a history of violence. Vega had no convictions, but several arrests: all batteries, all against women.

Another intriguing find was a statement in the file on Juliette's first murder conviction. The police report that contained the young woman's confession to suffocating her baby daughter quoted her as saying, "I sent Jenny to heaven to protect her." Protect her from what? Hadn't anyone asked?

While driving the sixty miles to the all-female Dwight Correctional Center for our first meeting, I had fumed over what seemed like the blatant mishandling of both of Juliette's cases. If Juliette or her daughter had been threatened somehow, couldn't that have reduced the level of the offense? And if there had been no actual danger, might it not mean that Juliette suffered from mental illness? And how could her second trial lawyer have missed Vega's arrest record? There was nothing in the files to indicate that any of these possibilities had been looked at.

Sitting with Juliette in the attorney's room at Dwight, I was immediately reassured by her responsiveness. She didn't appear to feel hopeless. She was impressed that Mort and I had dug up Vega's arrest record, including the names and addresses of the women who had pressed charges against him. I explained to her that if the State withheld that evidence, or if her lawyer had failed to find it when it would have been reasonable for him to do so, we had grounds for a good constitutional claim.

"So, you saying that I could maybe win?" she asked. God, I hated that question. Clients want odds or, worse, assurance that you can win for them.

"I wish I could say that, Ms. Vega." I lifted my shoulders in a little shrug. "But I can't. I can tell you from my first look at your case that we have some good facts to work with. I also have to tell you that whenever you're trying to undo something that is done — in this case, your conviction and sentence — you're rolling a big stone up a very steep hill." I explained the legal presumptions that were against us, such as that the trial court was correct and that the lawyer knew what he was doing. "We have to overcome those to win."

She thought about this. And then, she smiled. "I'll be damned. You ain't lying to me."

The thirty-six-year-old woman in the blue prison jumpsuit seemed almost energized now. Telling her the truth — that it would be an uphill battle — motivated her to fight her conviction and sentencing. She was ready to work with me.

Then I said what I had said in similar circumstances so many times before: "In order to help you, Juliette," I explained, "I'm going to need to know everything. I'm going to need to know all about your life and how you ended up here."

Her almost-black eyes clouded for an instant. But she nodded her head, looked down at her hands with their long fingers intertwined, and began to talk. Now, I am in the business of hearing life stories that are the stuff of nightmares. But what Juliette told me that day, supplemented by records I later dug up, constituted the most horrifying biography I had ever heard.

Juliette was raised by the Reynauds, a man and woman she believed were her parents but who were actually her grandparents. Her biological mother, in the presence of the fourteen-month-old Juliette, had jumped out of an apartment window to her death. Juliette's father reportedly abandoned the toddler to the care of her mother's parents. Juliette grew up in a household with boys and young men she thought were her brothers, who were actually her uncles. This family specialized in secrets.

When she was six years old, the eldest uncle, Maurice, began to rape her, anesthetizing her pain and resistance with shots of whiskey. The sexual predation continued for years. When Juliette was eleven, her grandmother walked into the room while Maurice was assaulting the girl. Mrs. Reynaud said nothing and did nothing. Juliette grew prettier and prettier, and less and less functional. She became addicted to the whiskey her uncle provided. Her school records report that she was bright but inattentive and unmotivated.

When she reached adolescence, Maurice passed her to the next brother to sexually exploit. About this time, her grandmother, whom Juliette called Mama, explained their true relationship. Mama dismissed Juliette's mother's suicide as the mark of a weak woman. Juliette never met the man who her family said was her father. I have always wondered if Juliette was not, in fact, a child of incest.

The brutalities continued. At sixteen, she was sold by her family in marriage to a green-card–seeking immigrant. The two lived together for a while and then divorced. At seventeen, she became pregnant by another man. After Jenny was born, Juliette turned tricks and worked as a stripper to support her baby. Using her body in the crudest way possible was all she knew how to do. Her grandmother told Juliette that she wasn't fit to be a mother — just like Juliette's own mother. Mrs. Reynaud threatened to report the girl to Family Services and get custody of Jenny herself. Rather than see her daughter taken into that household, Juliette asphyxiated the baby with a pillow.

After confessing, Juliette went to prison. She was relieved in many ways by the order and predictability of the days there. Sometimes her grandmother came to see her, although not as often as promised. Juliette looked forward to those visits, she told me, even if they meant being yelled at. I cannot fathom their relationship, but ties of dependency can survive cruelty and neglect.

Eventually, Dominic Vega found Juliette through a pen pal organization for prisoners and began to write her. Most of these groups cater to women looking for men behind bars, women who hope, perhaps, that being supportive of a man who's locked up will lead to a real relationship later. Guards derisively refer to these women as "outmates." But men sometimes find women behind bars, too.

Vega claimed he had been "with" Juliette when she was a prostitute, although she didn't remember him. She looked forward to his letters and visits. He put money into her commissary account, flattered her, and eventually pressed her to marry him. He promised love, money, stability, and a house without her uncles in it. I don't know if Juliette felt anything for Vega other than gratitude, although she claimed to have loved him at one time. She said yes, and they married at the prison. When she was paroled, he picked her up and took her to his home in the suburbs west of Chicago.

Vega made decent money working for an airline; he even gave Juliette a car. Life was good — for a few weeks. Vega liked to drink, and after ten sober years, Juliette joined him in this. The anger started initially because, he said, the house was messy. Soon he was accusing her of meeting other men; then, of sleeping with women. (After all, he had heard what went on in women's prisons.) Then he started hitting her.

Juliette felt trapped and resigned until the night he broke a beer bottle and used it to cut her vagina. He was marking his territory, he told her. When the bleeding wouldn't stop, he took her to an emergency room. Vega refused to leave her side as she recited to the doctors and nurses a patently ridiculous story about a shaving accident. I don't know why no one at the hospital called the police. After treatment, Juliette left the hospital with her husband.

I stopped Juliette at this point in her narrative. She had been talking for a long time. I was overwhelmed, myself. We could leave the discussion of the night of the murder until my next visit. I wanted to get records to support what she was telling me and investigate further before we talked again.

I drove Highway 55 back to Chicago with Juliette's strange and terrible tale rolling over in my mind. I couldn't help but think of my own life in comparison. I had endured heartbreak, and bad treatment from a man, but right now, compared with Juliette's life, mine was a fairy tale. Or a 1950s sitcom, at worst.

Gavin had been gone almost five years. I had made a few feeble attempts at dating, but with my broken heart, a child I adored, financial pressures, and the responsibility for 160 death row inmates' cases, my physical and emotional resources were really stretched. How could I also think about where to meet someone, how to dress, who would pay, and — oh my God, what would happen at the end of the evening?

Nevertheless, one day I had been reflecting on men and my choices. In the past, I had invariably ended up with the guy who looked good getting on a motorcycle, not the guy who looked good with a baby in his lap. Why was I so capable of selecting smart, supportive, and sensitive women to be my friends and so bad at picking men? I decided that if I was ever going to get into another romantic relationship, it would have to be with a man I might select as a friend if he were a woman.

Almost magically, once I shifted my perspective, I met Arnold Glass. He was — there's no other way to put it — square. In my wilder days, I would not have given him a second look. But he was also intelligent and politically aware, respectful of and interested in my work. And he was six four. Arnie was divorced with two children: a grown daughter and nine-year-old Will. The "sounds-Jewish" Arnie Glass was, in fact, black, and his children, like Samantha, were biracial. Arnie had met their Finnish mother while in the army and stationed in Germany.

One evening, during our courtship (his word), my friend Colleen came to my house with her baby to meet Arnie. Will had brought his trombone that evening, and we all sat in the living room while he played for us. Five-year-old Samantha was perched on Arnie's knee in wide-eyed attention to the music. Samantha liked Arnie, but she worshipped Will. I couldn't help laughing at the scene. How far I had come from uninhibited nights spent in downtown blues clubs.

When Colleen had to leave, I walked outside with her to help load the baby into the car, and to smoke out her appraisal of Arnie. Without prompting, she said, "He's really nice, Andrea."

"I think so, too," I replied. "But I don't know. I don't know if this is love." Part of me was still wondering if I should be seeking a grand passion instead of listening to a third-grader play "Hot Cross Buns."

Colleen gripped my arm with some frustration and fiercely asked me, "Andrea, what exactly do you think love *is*?"

Like a well-crafted question in a cross-examination, Colleen had opened my eyes. I hugged her instead of answering and returned to the noisy, toy-filled living room where my future lay wrestling on the floor with the kids. Colleen had given me permission to acknowledge what I already knew: my gentle Arnie and I were meant to be together.

Sadly, women such as Juliette never get to know that feeling. Juliette never had a chance. This became clear when I went to talk with her grandmother. My intern and I found "Mama" Reynaud in a classic U-shaped apartment building in northwest Chicago. Although the older woman seemed to be alone in the large unit, the amount of clothing and possessions scattered about and glimpsed through doorways made me think that many people lived there.

Mrs. Reynaud let us in, not exactly friendly, but willing. I sat across from her at a kitchen table covered by a dirty vinyl cloth. My intern sat behind me. Juliette's dark-haired "Mama" looked surprisingly young to be grandmother to a thirty-six-year-old. They have babies young in this family, I surmised. Gingerly, I began to feel my way toward getting information.

In response to my questions, the woman confirmed some of the basics of Juliette's story: her mother's suicide and father's abandonment, and the birth of Juliette's own child. At that point, Mrs. Reynaud pursed her lips and shook her head in disgust. "I told her and I told her, 'You are not fit to raise no child. You just like your mother.' I told her I gonna have to do just like what I done with her mother. 'I have to take that baby and raise it up, just like I took you in.'" She expelled a breath in disdain.

I looked down at the tablecloth, noting the years of grime that outlined the pattern of vines and flowers. I struggled to find a way to phrase my next question.

"Mrs. Reynaud, I'm sure you're aware that Juliette has claimed she was abused while she was growing up."

The woman's dark eyes revealed nothing. She shrugged and said flatly, "You don't live here." That could be interpreted several ways, I thought, but just as I was preparing to ask her to explain, the door to the hallway opened behind me. I turned to see a man in his fifties, dressed in work clothes. He walked in and skewered me with his gaze. No one said a word, no one made introductions, but I felt sure that this was Uncle Maurice. I was suddenly glad that my tall male intern was sitting just a few feet away. I turned back to Mrs. Reynaud. Fear had replaced the detached indifference on her face.

"You go now," she said.

"Sure," I answered. "Thank you for your time." While I got out a card to leave with the woman, her son hovered silently in the background. I would make damn sure the next time I talked with Mrs. Reynaud that Uncle Maurice was far away. I assumed there would be a next time.

By now, I felt hopeful that we could get Juliette off death row. There was so much to work with, going all the way back to the killing of her baby. As far as I was concerned, Juliette should never have pled guilty to first-degree murder in that case. Given her statement to the police about protecting her daughter, her attorney should have pursued a mental health defense. Perhaps he had tried to get her to plead not guilty on insanity grounds and she had refused. A client has the absolute right to choose her plea. But I didn't think so. More likely, it was an easy disposition. Most judges and lawyers want to get rid of cases — the quicker, the better. That's understandable with large caseloads, but bad calls often result. Pleading a client guilty may be the right choice for the client's sake, but it shouldn't happen in the absence of full information.

Then there was the trial in front of a judge for Vega's murder. Juliette had told the police that Vega and she had quarreled. He had turned the gun toward her and started to transfer it to his other hand. She took it from him, there was a struggle, and the gun went off, killing him. The prosecution presented a different story, of course. They said that Juliette had intended to kill Vega in order to claim his insurance money. If Juliette's attorney had investigated the relationship between the husband and wife and the victim's record for violence, the charges might have ended up as second-degree murder or manslaughter. The case might even have ended in acquittal if the judge had believed that Juliette's actions were in self-defense, accidental, or both. If the lawyer had done his job, Juliette would not have been subject to the death penalty. I didn't entirely blame the defense, though. Surely the prosecution knew Vega's history. How could they have countenanced asking for Juliette's death?

But even if one accepts the inevitability of everything that happened up to that point, how did she end up with a death sentence? Did her lawyer just assume — a potentially fatal assumption — that a judge would not order a woman to be executed? Making conclusions about gender and the death penalty is a tricky business. A much smaller percentage of women convicted of murder are sentenced to die than men convicted of murder, and far fewer women commit murder in the first place. But while the courts rarely give the death penalty to men who kill family members, roughly half the women on death row are there for murdering husbands, lovers, or children. And when a woman shocks society's notion of femininity with a particularly bloody or brutal crime, the probability of a capital sentence increases even more.

Whatever his assumptions, Juliette's attorney had presented none of the compelling mitigating evidence we had turned up after just a few weeks of work. The judge was told nothing about the deplorable circumstances that precipitated Juliette's killing her daughter and none of the mitigating evidence related to Vega's death. All he saw was a woman who had smothered her baby and then, ten years later, shot her husband to death. He likely thought Juliette was some kind of serial killer or "black widow." He had little else to go on, and he sentenced her to die.

By the time I made my second visit to Juliette, I was raring to go. I was not expecting the angry woman who waited silently for the guard to unlock her wrist shackles before she tore into me.

"What is this shit?" Juliette demanded as soon as the guard had left the room.

"What do you mean?" I asked.

Her husky voice barely suppressed her rage; I could hear the desire to scream behind her clenched teeth.

"I never told you that you could talk to my family."

"Juliette, we agreed that I would fight your case. Your *whole* case." I responded as mildly as I could, not wanting to start a fight with her. I would never be able to salvage the conversation if I mirrored her manner. And I wanted so much to move the case forward. I had come prepared to spend hours with her, bringing with me ten pages of typed questions.

"You didn't tell me you were going to Mama's."

"Of course I was going there. How am I supposed to learn about you without talking to your family?" My speech remained even in volume and tone.

She looked away and something changed in her face. When she spoke again, she sounded more tired than wrathful.

"Look, I don't want to live here the rest of my life," she said. "If there's nothing you can do to get me out of here, then fuck it, let's go."

"Go?" I didn't understand.

"Let them give me the chair or the needle or whatever. I got no reason to live no way."

Okay. This reaction was not unusual in death row inmates. I just had to lay out for her the reasons she did have to live. I would talk to her about the positive impact she could have on other inmates, about her importance to her family, about how important it was that the public see her as she truly was, not as an evil caricature. I licked my lips.

"Juliette, I will try to get the murder conviction overturned, so you don't have to live here forever. But just in case, we have to deal with the mitigation aspect, too."

She looked at me and shook her head. Once she started shaking it back and forth, she didn't seem able to stop. She was looking wildly around the room, as though listening to something I couldn't hear. I got the impression that this was how this woman wept.

"Juliette," I started.

"No, Andrea," she interrupted. And now she looked straight at me. "I want to give up my appeals. I don't want nobody going to Mama's house no more. Don't want nobody to do this no more." She slumped down in the chair. "I'm done. Let's just get it over with."

For more than an hour, I talked to her. I tried to show her that I was only doing what should have been done a long time ago. Now we had a chance to save her life and maybe even overturn the conviction. There was no reason to give up now. But the more I talked, the more entrenched she became. Finally, I stopped, asked her to keep thinking about it, and promised to return in a week. "In the meantime," I told her, "I'll look for more records in your case." It was the best I could do. Maybe she wouldn't help me, but maybe she would let me continue to work.

Capital defenders regularly run up against the thorny phenomenon of death penalty "volunteers." These are clients driven by depression, fear, despair, guilt, or sometimes just exhaustion. They want to die, and they want the State to do it for them. Some are pushed to that point simply by the experience of living on death row. They are locked up twenty-three hours a day, alone, in cells that are maybe ten feet by six feet. Visits and phone privileges are severely limited. They get a shower twice a week, if the staff remembers. The unique pressures of that lonely consignment, coupled with the continuous specter of death, could drive even a person with substantial personal resources into a tailspin. The effects can be devastating on our clients, who are unstable to begin with. The wish to die under those circumstances is easy to understand, but a defense attorney's job is not to help deliver the poison. While it's unfair to encourage unrealistic expectations, a death row client still needs hope.

A week later, I returned to Dwight, nurturing my hope that Juliette would be in a different frame of mind. Glancing at her visitor sign-in log as I entered, I saw her grandmother's and uncle's names. This didn't bode well. I was right; the elapsed week had only solidified her resolve. She admitted that the Reynauds had been to see her and she told me of their ultimatum: "If that lawyer doesn't take her nose out of our business, this will be our last visit." What terrible power emotional dependency exerts: Juliette was literally willing to die in order to hold on to a little bit of attention and approval from the people who had repeatedly abased her. She told me that if I wanted to help her, I should file a motion to withdraw all appeals and let her die. This time, when we parted, I was the one agreeing to think about it.

Deciding what to do about Juliette Vega was the toughest ethical dilemma I'd ever confronted. I was not bound legally to do what she wanted, but what about morally? On the one hand, she wanted the appeals to stop, and any court would have considered her competent to make that decision. My belief that we could win her case made no difference. That her wretched family had put her up to this was also irrelevant. It was her case and her life. Shouldn't she have control over them both? On the other hand, didn't I have some obligation to tell the court about her life so that it could make the appropriate legal decision? In addition, I could not countenance the deliberate use of our criminal justice system to commit suicide. Lastly, I simply didn't want her to die, and I didn't believe she really wanted to. What was driving her was fear of being abandoned by the only family she had ever known.

I thought about it, discussed it with colleagues, and puzzled over it some more. Once again, I drove to Dwight. "Juliette," I said, "I refuse to help the State murder you."

So she fired me. She found a lawyer who was willing to assist in her execution, and the case went on without me.

THAT SUMMER, SAMANTHA, Arnie, Will, and I moved to Ann Arbor, where I joined the law school faculty at the University of Michigan. More than once, I found myself discussing with my students the issue of client autonomy. I told them that they must be willing to tell a client no — not just in the common case of a client who wants to commit perjury, but also in the larger context of knowing what lines you will not cross.

Months passed. The courts determined that Juliette could allow her own execution. Her death from lethal injection was scheduled for Wednesday, January 17, at 12:30 a.m. A week before that, the parole board met to review her death sentence. Its job is to make a private recommendation to the governor, who ultimately decides whether to permit the execution to go forward. Then-governor Jim Edgar, in his five years in the Illinois Statehouse, had never granted clemency. The previous year alone, he had allowed five executions. A group from Amnesty International appeared at the parole board hearing; they were campaigning to save Juliette's life. Juliette's attorney submitted an audiotape she had recorded in her cell, in which she addressed the group directly: "Stay out of my case; stay out of my life."

On the Friday before the scheduled execution, Governor Edgar announced that he would ponder the matter at his country cabin over the weekend.

The pending execution of a woman — which would be only the second in the United States since the reinstatement of the death penalty — was featured prominently in Chicago news. There was less coverage in the national press, however. Busy with teaching and my new blended family, I had lost track of where the case stood. On a snowy Sunday afternoon in January, my husband called me to the phone. Someone was pulling his leg, he guessed, but the woman on the line said she was Bianca Jagger. I took the call, and it was, indeed, the human rights activist and former wife of the Rolling Stone. She was leading the Amnesty International drive to save Juliette, had come across my name, and thought I might be able to supply the governor with information that would make a difference. As Juliette was scheduled to die in just days, she asked if I would write a letter to Governor Edgar immediately.

Perhaps I should have agonized over that decision, too; perhaps I should have hesitated to interfere. But I didn't. I said yes, hung up the phone, and immediately wrote a letter that I faxed to the governor's office later that night. In it, I laid out Juliette's shocking family history. I reflected on the almost inevitable results, "When [she] began to drink at age 13, it was no surprise. When she was 'dancing' in a disreputable place at age 15, it was no surprise, and when she was hooking thereafter, it was no surprise. At least not to any of the mental health professionals I spoke about this case with. Her behavior is all too typical of abused children: no self-esteem, self-destructive behavior, sexual promiscuity." I went on to explain that the sentencing judge did not know of Juliette's past. "Nor did he know that she had reason to be afraid of her husband because, while he was painted as a 60-year-old frail man...the opposite was true. He was physically abusive...and although she was certainly guilty of shooting him, had the jury heard the whole story, it is likely she would have been convicted of second-degree murder rather than first-degree."

All Monday, I went about my teaching duties with thoughts of Juliette and the governor constantly in the back of my mind, but by bedtime, there was no word. On Tuesday morning, Arnie called my office and told me to turn on the news. At ten o'clock in the morning, fourteen hours before the planned execution, Governor Edgar commuted Juliette Vega's sentence to life in prison without parole. "Horrible as was her crime," his statement read, "it is an offense comparable to those that judges and jurors have determined over and over again should not be punishable by death."

Even though Juliette had not been my client for many months,

I still felt responsible for her. Relief and joy lifted me. This was the closest I had ever come to losing one of "mine" to the death penalty.

Despite my satisfaction, I knew Juliette might be angry with me for thwarting her. I wrote to her, telling her that I believed her life had purpose and meaning. With time, I said, I hoped she would forgive me. And I hoped she would see that I was right: that her life had significance and value, even behind bars.

More than a decade has passed. Not long ago, Juliette completed her associate's degree through a prison education program. She devotes much of her days to showing her young fellow inmates how to transform their lives. They credit her with inspiring them to pursue their schooling, their goals, and their dreams. Juliette wrote me to share the news of her graduation. She signed the letter and then, as an afterthought, scribbled a note: "You knew. Thank you."

CHAPTER 12

Injustice Is My Business

TRY IGNORING A personal letter from a nun. No matter what one's opinions are with regard to religion, a beautifully handwritten appeal from a vow-abiding woman exerts a kind of primitive force. Sister Ruth's letter introduced her as director of a faith-based prison project at the Scott Correctional Institute for Women in Wayne County, Michigan. She wrote: "I want to assure you that we are concerned with the spiritual well-being of the women incarcerated here and rarely discuss cases. But in Deirdre's case, dear professor, it has become obvious to us all that a grave injustice has been done, and that an innocent woman is in prison, serving life without parole."

Uh-oh, I thought. I had been teaching at the University of Michigan for about a year when I received Sister Ruth's letter. In the law school clinic there, I had set up a criminal concentration program in which my students could gain real-life experience defending misdemeanor cases under my supervision. In addition, students assisted me with a death penalty case I had brought from Illinois. Despite almost daily letters requesting our help, I had no intention of taking on another big case. I didn't have time. Besides, how do you choose whom to help? Nevertheless, I read on:

"I was mentioning this to my dear friend Sister Miriam Wilson, and she said that a friend of hers was now teaching in Michigan. She was very sad when you left Chicago because of the enormous good you did there."

Uh-huh. This sister was dangling in front of me not just an innocent woman but also a powerful personal connection. Sister Miriam in Chicago was my valued friend and associate, someone who advocated tirelessly for prisoners and against the death penalty.

"And Sister Miriam," the letter went on, "told me I should write you, because perhaps God has sent you to Michigan to help this poor woman."

Even worse.

"Sister Miriam said if there was anyone who could perform the sort of legal miracle this woman needs, it is you. I hope you can find it in your heart to at least come meet her."

Oh, well. It wouldn't hurt to visit the woman…right?

To prepare for the meeting, I read the appellate opinion. Deirdre Jennings had been convicted in a bench trial of first-degree murder and arson. Her boyfriend, Pete Tomas, had been stabbed to death in his bed in October 1991. The killer had then set a fire, presumably in an attempt to hide the crime. There were no signs of forced entry. Deirdre had a house key and garage door opener, so she quickly became a suspect. The evidence against her was entirely circumstantial, however. Six months after the murder, a neighbor, Elizabeth Ann Snell, came forward at the behest of the victim's family. She told police that she had seen a woman with hair, coat, and a car similar to Deirdre's driving out of the subdivision early in the morning on the day of Pete's death. It was raining and still dark when the two cars had passed each other. Nevertheless, Mrs. Snell picked out Deirdre's picture from a photo lineup.

The only physical evidence the prosecution had was an artificial fingernail the police had found in Deirdre's trash. They asserted that a tiny chip in the nail had occurred during the crime. The only motive the State produced was Pete's mother's testimony that she had told her son that she didn't like Deirdre. Pete must have subsequently refused to marry her, the prosecution maintained, and Deirdre had killed him in anger.

A thin case against her, it seemed to me. On the other hand, she had been placed near the scene at the right time, and she did have access to Pete's house.

What was appalling, however, was the defense in Deirdre's original trial. Her attorney filed no motions and called no witnesses. Apparently, he believed the weakness of the prosecution's case would be entirely persuasive to the judge — the judge who then found her guilty of first-degree murder and arson and sentenced her to life in prison without parole.

What happened in Deirdre's direct appeal would later turn out to be crucial. A defendant has a right to a lawyer for his trial and for one appeal. At that "direct" appeal, the lawyer is limited to talking about what happened in court during the original trial: Was the judge correct when he admitted or refused to admit certain evidence? Were exhibits admitted that should not have been? Or a motion denied that should have been granted?

Deirdre's appellate lawyer, a different attorney from her trial lawyer, conducted the direct appeal as the law requires. Since Deirdre's first lawyer had brought up little to nothing for the judge to respond to during the original trial, there was little or nothing to appeal. The appellate lawyer did not reinvestigate the case, because no law or statute required her to do so. Believing that Deirdre's trial lawyer had been clearly ineffective, the appellate attorney also three times requested the special hearing that Michigan requires to present that issue. The request was denied every time without explanation. Deirdre's appeal failed, as most do.

If the direct appeal is unsuccessful, the defendant may file post-conviction appeals, or habeas corpus petitions, based on constitutional issues. Those issues could include ineffective assistance of counsel and the withholding of evidence by the prosecution. The defendant has no right to representation by a lawyer for these subsequent actions. That's why so many prison inmates draft their own habeas petitions, most of which fail. And that's why law school clinics are besieged with requests for free legal assistance.

On a dreary morning in December 1996, I drove from Ann Arbor to Scott Correctional Institution, one of two Michigan prisons at that time that housed women. On Five Mile Road, outside of Plymouth, some thirty miles west of Detroit, the archetypal brick-and-barbed-wire structure came into view. After moving through the usual registration, search, and stamping procedure, and through a metal detector and locked doors, I entered a large carpeted visiting room. Seats arranged in conversational groups and snack-filled vending machines provided a semblance of hospitality. In this room, wives laughed and cried with their husbands, and mothers raised their children in increments of a couple of hours weekly, sometimes for years on end. At the back of the visiting room, two small offices provided privacy for inmates and their attorneys. A guard directed me to one of these rooms, and I sat down to wait.

The woman who came in to meet me that day, of all the people I had met in courthouse lockups or prison visiting rooms, seemed the most like me, at least on the outside. The divorced mother of two boys was just my age at the time, forty-two, and white. A pretty woman, she was of average height, with a trim figure and blue-gray eyes. The sides of her medium-length brown hair were swept up and held back with a rubber band. Beyond these prison walls, you wouldn't have noticed her. She looked like the mother sitting next to you at a PTA meeting or the woman who works in your dentist's office, which, in fact, was what she had been doing before her life dropped into this incomprehensible parallel reality.

"Ms. Jennings?" I stood and extended my hand to her. "I'm Andrea Lyon."

She looked slightly disoriented. Later, she would tell me that she was surprised that I had stood to shake her hand. None of her previous attorneys had ever done that. Also, I was simply bigger than she imagined Sister Ruth's miracle worker would be.

But she recovered quickly, shook my hand graciously, and said, "The nuns told me they had written you."

I grinned. "It's hard to say no to them, even if I am Jewish."

"I didn't ask them to write," she insisted, "but I am so..." The pale woman searched for words. I could fill them in for her: depressed, downhearted, desperate. I waited, letting her find her own way. Glancing out the window into the courtyard, I saw a few white plastic picnic tables with attached seats for families to use in good weather. Maybe it was the drizzly winter sky, but the patio furniture seemed even sadder than the visiting room itself.

I glanced back to Deirdre, who had given up looking for words and was waiting for me to commandeer the conversation. If I had seen this woman walk out of a courthouse lockup on 26th Street, I would have bet my paycheck that the prosecution would have been waving a signed confession. She looked like a woman who couldn't hold a glass of water, let alone keep a secret. If she had committed this crime, I thought, she would have been on the phone to the police a minute later, crying and telling them, "I just stabbed my boyfriend." Then again, who knows?

"So, let's talk about your case, Ms. Jennings."

She swallowed, nodded, and clasped and unclasped her hands. "I don't know where to start," she said.

"Well, I've read the appellate opinion. I know the evidence against you was circumstantial. I know there was some problem with your attorney."

"He did nothing. Absolutely nothing. I asked him to investigate things, but I didn't know, really, what to ask for. I didn't know anything about this system. I thought..." her voice trailed off again.

"What?"

"I thought if you were innocent, you would be found innocent." She looked at me with moist and questioning eyes, but her voice was calm. "Stupid, huh?"

"Maybe. But I don't think believing in something is stupid," I answered. "I believe in justice, even though I know it's an ideal to aspire to, not a state one can achieve." I don't normally jump into philosophical concepts with a client at the first meeting, if ever, but Deirdre's manner drew me in.

For the first time, she smiled. Despite three years in prison, her smile was warm and unforced. "Ms. Lyon, I didn't do this. I'm sure everyone says that, and it must be hard to believe, but I didn't."

"Ms. Jennings, I'm not here to pass judgment on you. I'm here to try to figure out if you have a case, if my students and I can help you, and if it's a good idea for us to do so."

I was trying valiantly to pretend to myself that I hadn't already succumbed. There were so many reasons not to take her case. It had already been lost twice; the inertia of defeat is difficult to overcome.

And a thorough post-conviction investigation can take hundreds of hours of time.

She considered my words and made her pitch. "Well, don't you want to represent someone who is innocent? I mean, wouldn't that be what you would want for your students?"

"Actually, no," I answered. "The burden of representing an innocent person is enormous. Most of the time, you lose. And once the ball has started rolling, or, as in your case, when it's rolled pretty darn far, it's hard to undo the damage."

Deirdre nodded sadly. She seemed to understand. And maybe it was that touching comprehension that pushed me over the edge. I knew then that I was committed to taking her case. I had no idea yet if there were procedural moves I could make; I had no idea if any could be won. I knew only that it felt like the right thing to do.

"So," I said as I picked up my pen, "tell me what you know, and let's see if I can roll that ball back up the hill."

For the next two hours, we talked. Deirdre told me about the night of Pete's death. They had been together at his house that evening. Their relationship had run through rocky patches, particularly over Pete's drinking, but things felt solid at that point. She had left his house about 11:00 p.m., and called him once after she got home. She went to bed, woke up her two boys at the usual time, and by 7:30 a.m., was in the younger boy's junior high school counselor's office for a scheduled appointment. Later that morning, at work, she got the call that Pete was dead.

Deirdre also told me, with evident discomfort, about Detective Zelinski, the lead police investigator in the case, who had retired since then. She had unknowingly put herself in a hazardous position from the start. Before Zelinski interviewed her, Deirdre's brother-in-law, a police officer in a neighboring town, had told her details about Pete's murder. When she revealed her awareness of these facts when talking with the detective, Zelinski became convinced that her knowledge was guilty knowledge, even after she explained how she'd come upon the information. Over many months, he followed her, showed up at her job, cornered her children for questioning, and flat out told Deirdre he was going to get her. What he didn't do was pursue other leads.

Back in Ann Arbor, I told my students about the convicted woman, and they responded, some with naïve enthusiasm and some with skepticism. We began to investigate the case as it should have been investigated in the first place. We obtained the trial transcripts, the former attorney's files, and the police reports. When launching work of this kind, you have to mentally juggle two opposing suppositions. You must assume that everything the prosecution says is true, and ask yourself what it means, in legal and factual terms. Simultaneously, you must assume that everything they say is a lie…and ask, how can I prove it false?

On balance, the case against Deirdre still appeared to me surprisingly weak. I kept thinking I would find the one thing that had convicted her. But I couldn't see it. The strongest element seemed to be Mrs. Snell, the neighbor who identified Deirdre as the woman she had seen driving out of the subdivision that morning. But her testimony was inherently unbelievable. She claimed to be able to identify a driver in a car passing by in the dark and rain and, according to her, driving fast. No matter how many times I pictured this, it made no sense. When I later found out that Detective Zelinski had spent hours with Mrs. Snell looking at beauty magazines, in order to help her identify the suspect's hairstyle, and then showed her a photo lineup in which Deirdre's informal Polaroid stood out among the police mug shots — well, that explained a lot.

My students and I began to walk Pete's neighborhood, chatting up the residents, looking for anyone who might have seen something. One neighbor said her son might have information. Accompanied by Nicole, a bright, tough young law student who intended to be a prosecutor, I caught up with the son at a car dealership, where he was the service manager. He told us that "everyone" knew that Pete dealt drugs. He had been home from college around the time of Pete's death, he said. While Rollerblading around the subdivision at night, he would see people coming and going from Pete's garage, averting their faces in the dim light. This opened up a world of alternate scenarios and suspects, supported by our discovery that Pete was on methadone maintenance for a heroin habit.

Drug cronies were just one category of "persons of interest" we turned up, though. Deirdre's access to Pete's house was a strong strike against her. But she wasn't the only one with a garage door opener. Pete's former housemate, who was a known drug user, had one, too. Detective Zelinski had interviewed the ex-housemate by phone but had never brought him in for questioning.

Neither had the officer followed up with Pete's former wife and her new husband, who had been Pete's next-door neighbor when he began an affair with Pete's wife. Not surprisingly, the divorce had been rancorous. Deirdre reported to me that the ex-wife and her husband had once left a hateful, threatening voice mail message on Pete's phone.

Most suspicious, in my opinion, was Deirdre's former boyfriend, Jeff Reed. Despite Deirdre's feet-on-the-ground demeanor, she had made some poor choices in men, perhaps one reason I so quickly felt a kinship with her. Reed was a police officer wannabe, a washout from a local police department's reserve officer program. Deirdre had broken up with him when she discovered that he was not, in fact, a police officer on disability, as he had said, or dying from a brain tumor, as he had also claimed. Reed had not taken the breakup well, and had continued to pester her in person and on the telephone. In the course of investigating Reed, we found a letter written to him by the chief of the local police department warning him to stop wearing a uniform, since he was not an officer, and threatening to criminally charge him if he did so again.

This bizarre piece of information took on added importance when we interviewed an elderly man who had been delivering newspapers in the neighborhood early on the morning of the murder. He had seen a man in a uniform — he wasn't sure if it had been a police or fireman's uniform — walking near Pete's house. When the paper deliverer had inquired if anything was wrong, the uniformed man had told him there had been a "little fire." This was an hour or two before the fire at Pete's house was reported. I interviewed Reed, who denied having been in the neighborhood and told me that he had passed a polygraph test the police had given him. I had seen no polygraph paperwork, so I figured he was lying.

The intrigue didn't end with interesting suspects. Using a Freedom of Information Act petition, we obtained the complete police file. Deirdre's original attorney had taken a court order to the police station to get the reports. In the attorney's files was a signed receipt for 650 pages of reports. But when I presented the FOIA petition, I was given 1,187 pages. Her attorney had been missing more than 500 pages. This was no Xerox machine error. I was convinced that the omission was deliberate, especially when I saw what the reports contained.

Among the pages lurked exculpatory lab results: the fact that Deirdre's car, clothing, and shoes had tested negative for blood had been known at her trial; that a lab test concluded that the gouge on Deirdre's artificial fingernail was a manufacturer's defect rather than damage done to it during the stabbing, as the prosecution had inferred, had been hidden from the defense.

Another piece of evidence not turned over was a postcard sent to Pete from his ex-wife and her husband. "We're married," it said. "Thought you'd want to know." Police found it on the kitchen counter next to the block of knives from which the murder weapon had come.

What was *not* among those pages was also telling. We had interviewed the school guidance counselor Deirdre had met with just a few hours after Pete had been stabbed. The counselor told us that Detective Zelinski had taken a statement from her in which she said that Deirdre had not behaved at all unusually. But that statement was never recorded.

We later discovered an even more damaging omission. Deirdre's ex-boyfriend, Jeff Reed, had been right about having taken a police polygraph test. But the record showed that, in fact, he *failed* the part in which he was asked if he had killed Pete. The officer who gave him the test promptly Mirandized him and tried to get a confession, but Detective Zelinski released him. This occurred just a few days before Deirdre's arrest, but the defense never knew.

The elements of a perfect storm of injustice had converged: a naïve woman, a bad lawyer, and an obsessed detective who was willing to cheat to get his conviction. By the time we had gathered all this evidence, even my future prosecutor student Nicole was convinced that Deirdre was innocent. If only that were all that mattered.

Through the long months of investigation, I got to know Deirdre well, along with her parents and eight siblings. On a regular basis, the Jennings family — Mom, Dad, several brothers and sisters, miscellaneous nieces and nephews, and Deirdre's two sons — would assemble in a law school conference room to hear my update. Deirdre's sister Colleen, the family spokesperson, would kick things off by "thanking everyone for coming," and then wait patiently while they all made fun of her. The family was lovingly supportive and believed staunchly in Deirdre's innocence. They never missed a weekly visit with her for all the years she was incarcerated. I admired their loyalty and the way they coped with the tragedy that had disrupted their lives.

My visits with Deirdre left me inspired. Like meetings with my former client Richard Bauman, the time with Deirdre was only partially spent talking about the case. Instead of discussing classic literature, though, Deirdre and I talked about the other inmates. In a quiet way, my client's religious faith infused her life. She felt intense compassion for the other women at Scott, especially the younger ones. She told me about one seventeen-year-old. The girl had landed in prison, Deirdre said, due to "hormones and too many hours with no parents at home." Deirdre was trying to provide her with support and guidance. My client and I grew close, bound by a passionate belief in human redemption, even if we came at the concept from different directions.

One day after the investigation was nearly complete, and I had filled Deirdre in on all the exculpatory evidence we had discovered in the 500 missing pages of evidence accumulated by the state, I was taking leave of her when she said, "Oh, Andrea, I don't know how to thank you. This is all such good news, isn't it?" She was almost buoyant.

"Yes, it's great for the case. But it just makes me furious. Why weren't you *told* these things before..." My voice trailed off.

"It *is* good news, right?" Deirdre's voice had quieted.

"Sure," I conceded, obviously holding back.

"But, really, how can they deny us in the face of all this?" she asked.

"Look," I tried to explain, "if it were just a case of guilt versus innocence, you'd be right. But at this point in the process, we have procedural hurdles. Still, I'm...cautiously optimistic."

She smiled. "Okay, that's what I'll be, too. Cautiously optimistic."

I had no idea just how high those procedural hurdles would be.

If nothing else, this case demonstrates how far from guilt versus innocence the law can sometimes veer. A defendant can fall into a procedural hole from which it is nearly impossible to extricate her. We filed a state habeas petition for a new trial based on all the newly discovered evidence, but the state judge threw us out of court without a hearing, saying that Deirdre should have brought all these new facts to light during the direct appeal, even though no law required reinvestigating the case at that juncture. That was the point I emphasized on our subsequent appeals to the Michigan Court of Appeals and the Michigan Supreme Court. Both courts refused to hear the case.

Now, four years after I began work on this case, we had exhausted the state remedies. We filed a habeas corpus petition in the federal district court and drew Judge Raymond Ferrano to hear it. I was not pleased. Ferrano was a Reagan appointee, conservative and pro-prosecution. When I went to see Deirdre, I told her we had been assigned to a federal judge and began to explain why I wasn't happy with the choice.

Deirdre interrupted: "You always said our best chance would be in federal court."

"Yes," I agreed. That was true, because any state is loath to admit it was wrong.

"So this judge doesn't change that, does it?"

"Unfortunately," I said, "politics has everything to do with what happens in court. Once you enter the part of the process where the judge has 'discretion' — discretion to hold a hearing, discretion to look at the evidence — then the judge's view of the world becomes much more important."

"Okay. But doesn't it matter that I didn't do it? That I'm innocent? Isn't it conservatives who are always complaining about the 'technicalities' in the legal system?"

How could I explain what barely made sense to me to a woman who had spent her sons' teenage and college years behind bars for something she hadn't done? What could I do but try?

"You're right. Of course it matters, and that's exactly how we're framing the petition. If Judge Ferrano is a conservative — not a prosecution zealot, but a true conservative — who will call the balls and strikes fairly, we should do well. I just can't tell yet from researching him." I could hardly bear to add to her burden at this point, but I had no choice. "Deirdre, listen, there's something else we need to talk about."

I then broke the news to her that Arnie and the kids and I were returning to Chicago. I was joining the faculty of DePaul University College of Law. Many motivations were prompting the move back after five years in Michigan. My mother wasn't well. I missed the stimulating legal environment in Chicago. And I wanted to start a death penalty clinic. Michigan had not been interested, but DePaul was. Arnie had gone back to college to become a high-school history teacher, and he could finish up at DePaul.

Panic flashed in Deirdre's eyes.

"Don't worry," I hurried to say. "I'm staying on the case. I've asked a colleague here, Bridget McCormack, to assist, and she's very good." Deirdre brushed at her eyes and asked if I had told her family yet. I told her I was meeting with them later in the week. We hugged hard when we said goodbye. "No doom and gloom now," I said. "I'm cautiously optimistic about our chances."

In this case, my optimism was justified. Judge Ferrano was fair. He held a hearing and heard a lot of our evidence. The lawyer who represented Deirdre in her original trial admitted in open court that he had exerted almost no effort on her behalf because, he said, he was "cocky" and believed he couldn't lose such a weak case.

This time around, Deirdre took the stand. Emotional but calm, she looked each interrogator in the eye and answered each question simply but thoroughly. The room grew still with her presence. "I don't know who killed Pete," she said when asked. "I wish I did. Pete had his faults, but he was a good man. He didn't deserve this." You could feel the courtroom — with the exception of the bullying prosecutor, perhaps — believing her. Deirdre said later that she thought that if she had testified at her first trial, she might have been acquitted. I could only agree.

Judge Ferrano granted our petition for a new trial. He ruled not on the issue of what the prosecution had withheld, but on the issue of ineffective assistance of counsel. The state immediately announced it would appeal the case to the U.S. Court of Appeals for the Sixth Circuit, but we were able to get a bond set. One of Deirdre's sisters pledged her house as bond, and Deirdre was released pending the appeal. I joined her family at Scott to welcome her out. It was 2002; Deirdre had been in prison for nine years. She had missed both her sons' high-school graduations, her eldest son's graduation from college and his marriage, and the birth of her first grandchild. She had never used a cell phone. She didn't know anything about email. But she was free, at least for now.

On my birthday a few days later, Deirdre called me at home. She told me I was her hero. I was unexpectedly moved. Maybe I had felt heroic once or twice before, but no one had ever called me that. I threw myself into the work on the appeal and felt good about our chances of holding on to our win.

But, in fact, we lost. Two to one. There are some sixteen judges on the Sixth Circuit. Three are randomly drawn to consider each case. Of the three we drew, two were Republicans, one appointed by Reagan and one by George W. Bush. The third was a Democrat appointed by Clinton. The vote was clearly divided along ideological lines. The two judges who decided against us constructed a brand-new technicality. They held that we were procedurally defaulted because the appellate lawyer hadn't reinvestigated the case. That omission could have been addressed, they said, if I had claimed the appellate lawyer had been ineffective because she had failed to reinvestigate. But I had no reason to think there was any support for such a claim. There was no case or statute requiring an appellate lawyer to do an investigation outside the record if she was going to raise ineffective assistance of counsel on appeal. All she had to do was ask for a hearing, just as Deirdre's appellate lawyer had done. The Sixth Circuit judges were creating new case law, but expecting the appellate lawyer or me to have anticipated their change in advance. And because we hadn't, Deirdre would have to return to serve out her life sentence.

Putting aside my wrath as best I could, I pursued every possible action that would stop Deirdre from having to go back to prison. We petitioned for the entire Sixth Circuit to hear the case. We were turned down. We asked the U.S. Supreme Court to hear the case. They said no.

The U.S. Supreme Court is the end of the road. On a terrible day in September 2006, four years after our triumphant exit from Scott penitentiary, I walked Deirdre back through the same door. Within me, rage at the injustice battled with guilt. This was my fault. I could have raised the issue of ineffective assistance of appellate counsel, whether I believed there was support in the law or not. What would it have taken? A few more lines of ink? I could have cut off the technical exit that the cowards had taken. But I didn't, and now Deirdre Jennings would die in prison. How could I bear this? More important, how could she?

While out on bond, Deirdre had gotten a counseling degree and had been working in a homeless shelter for women. She'd chosen this work, she told me, because her faith compelled her. But she was also guided by the desire to help people as I did. She said she believed in the power of hope, in part, she said, because of me. I said that she was my shining symbol of what a person could accomplish even under the worst of circumstances. We two were a devoted mutual admiration society. And here I was, walking her back into prison.

We stood in the Scott lobby. "I don't know what to say," I said to her.

"Tell me you won't give up," Deirdre replied. "You never do, Andrea. And if these four years that I had on bond are all I'll get, well, I wouldn't have had them without you. I got to see one son married, to be there for the birth of my third grandchild. I got to finish college, and find a career I love. None of it would have happened without you. None of it." She stopped and looked at me. "I love you," she said.

I had been trying mightily not to cry. "I love you, too," I responded. "And I won't give up. We'll find a way."

She hugged me and walked the remainder of the way alone.

If criminal defense is your chosen profession, you're going to lose cases, sometimes cases you should win. All my clients, even the ones I may not like, matter to me, and I am pained when I lose on behalf of any of them. But I have always found a way to bounce back from those losses. I have always kept hopeful, and have continued to find ways to reach justice — at least, as close to justice as it is reasonable to expect.

This time, I didn't bounce back. At home, Arnie tiptoed around me, not knowing what to say. Will, at college locally, made dates to meet me frequently for lunch. Seventeen-year-old Samantha reiterated her resolve to be a scientist and work in a realm where objective answers could be found and where one's heart didn't get broken.

Deirdre's case spun endlessly through my mind. First, I would defend myself: How could I have known that we would draw the political panel that we did or that they would change the law? Then I would answer myself: I should have seen it coming. Then I would rail against the law: Why have our courts elevated form over substance? I acknowledge the need for rules. Cases must end at some point, and a defendant shouldn't be allowed to hold issues in his back pocket and continue to bring claim after claim. The rules, however, have become byzantine to the point of irrationality. Contrary to popular belief, there are no "technicalities" that free a guilty defendant — unless one thinks that disallowing a confession forced out of a suspect is a technicality — but there are many that imprison the innocent.

After cycling through all these arguments, mentally exhausted, I would seek refuge in Deirdre's simple point: her four years of freedom would never have happened if I hadn't taken up her cause.

Around this time, I wrote a letter to Richard Bauman, my former classics-loving client, who was serving a life sentence. I told him I felt like a failure. What would it have cost me to add that extra element to the petition, even if there was no support for it in the law? It was my fault, I said.

"Dear Andrea," he wrote. "You are a warrior. I know you don't think like that, but that is what you are, a fierce Amazon warrior. All warriors know defeat, and it only makes them stronger. A true warrior keeps her eyes on what matters, fights each battle like it will be her last, and knows that being a hero don't come from nobody but yourself. You will find a way to prevail. Because injustice matters to you, deep down. In your soul. Believe me, I know."

So I called my brothers. Not my actual brothers, or rather, not my brother, Jon, but the two men with whom I had worked, taught, and lived through so many changes over the years. Bill Moffitt and Raymond Brown were both amazing lawyers, from D.C. and New Jersey respectively, and both were leaders in the criminal defense bar and the African-American bar. We had a little fraternity called "Cappa-cappuccino."

I called Raymond, and he patched in Bill. We had discussed Deirdre's case before, but now I needed some perspective from the people whose judgment and dedication I could trust. Completely.

"The inertia of losing hurts," I said.

"But ultimately, the outcome comes down to politics," Raymond said. "You have to understand that these forces inexorably grind down the individual in favor of the system's survival."

"But," Bill said, "that doesn't mean you have to accept what rigid law-and-order judges decide. They refuse to contradict the prosecution even when their own damn common sense should tell them different." He paused. "That shit sent your client back to prison."

Raymond interjected: "If politics sent her back to prison, maybe a different kind of politics could free her."

He was on to something. We talked some more, with Bill encouraging me to find the right theme for a political solution and Raymond discussing the inherent logical contradiction in elevating form over substance. We talked about whom to approach for political support, and how to do it. When I got off the phone, I had a renewed sense of purpose. I set my sights on Jennifer Granholm, the governor of Michigan, the first woman to hold the job.

Governor Granholm couldn't grant Deirdre a new trial — her commutation power didn't include that — but she could commute her sentence to time served. Deirdre's family, my former colleagues in Michigan, and I began to mine every political connection we could think of. We collected letters of support from a U.S. senator, members of the clergy, and many people Deirdre had helped at the homeless shelter. My heart and soul was on every page of the clemency petition we filed with Governor Granholm.

Months passed before the Michigan Parole Board notified us that they would hold a hearing in order to make a recommendation to the governor. On an icy day in December 2007, more people than there were seats for jammed the parole board hearing room. The pastor who directed the homeless shelter Deirdre had worked at testified in her support. Her family, friends, and former clients spoke. Deirdre herself withstood a ninety-minute belligerent grilling from Michigan's assistant attorney general. Because any argument that Deirdre presented a potential danger to society was absurd, he attacked her on the basis of guilt. "Mr. Tomas wouldn't marry you," he bellowed, "so you killed him, didn't you?" He pressed on and on, finally just shouting that she was a liar. The more he yelled at her, I thought, the better she looked.

The hearing had gone well, but nevertheless, the decision was political. The governor was a Democrat, but she was also a former prosecutor. No one could predict what the panel would recommend or what the governor would decide. We might never hear another word.

Weeks, then months passed. Deirdre called from prison as often as she could. We would chat about her family or mine, the homeless shelter, politics, and then, inevitably, talk would turn to the case. Deirdre maintained an abiding faith that she would be released again someday. Even more remarkably, she believed that she must have been sent back to prison in order to fulfill a divine purpose. In the meantime, she remained interested in my analysis of the situation.

"So, what do you think this delay means?" she asked me.

I didn't know what it meant, and I said so. "I wish I felt she was paying attention," I said, referring to the governor. "I wish that this mattered to her more." In five years in office, Governor Granholm had commuted only twenty sentences out of the more than three thousand petitions she had received, and most of those twenty were for medical reasons.

"But…" Deirdre said, cueing the trademark response that had sustained us through more than a decade.

I hesitated just an instant before completing her thought: "I remain cautiously optimistic."

She laughed, and we said goodbye.

On a summer day in 2008, I picked up my office phone to hear the husky voice of Deirdre's sister Colleen. "She granted the petition." Neither of us spoke a word for a long time. We just sat holding our receivers, and cried.

Six weeks later, I once more walked Deirdre out of prison, nearly two years after having left her there. Someone took a photograph of her, Bridget McCormack, and me that now sits on my desk. In the picture, Deirdre is beaming with confident joy. I am grinning goofily. A long time passed before I shook the ever-present feeling in the back of my mind that there was something I needed to be doing to free Deirdre.

I HAVE BEEN at the business of criminal defense for a long time, and I hope to be at it a long time to come. It doesn't get any easier, and I expect it never will. I accept that. There are no shortcuts. The law grows ever more complex, and the political seesaw produces some progress, followed by crushing setbacks. Intractable human problems produce damaged people who then do violence to others. Somehow their actions must be addressed, and yet so often we fall short of doing so in a fair and compassionate way.

Despite all that, the passion for fighting injustice that I felt stir at the age of fifteen has only grown stronger. The world can be a cruel place, and I have witnessed much of its brutality at close range. But I remain cautiously optimistic.

EPILOGUE

ON JANUARY 10, 2003, media trucks with satellite dishes, cameras, microphones, and miles of cable invaded DePaul University College of Law in downtown Chicago. Illinois governor George Ryan, days before completing his term in office, was about to deliver the first of two announced speeches on the death penalty in Illinois. The second would be given the next day, at Northwestern University Law School. The Republican governor had made international news three years earlier when he imposed a moratorium on executions, pending a study of capital punishment in the state.

My connection with this highly anticipated speech had begun when I took on the case of Madison Hobley, an innocent man condemned to death for the arson murder of seven people, including his wife and young son. I started work on Madison's case in 1994, while I was running the Illinois Capital Resource Center. I took it with me when I taught at the University of Michigan, and I brought it back to Chicago when I founded the Center for Justice in Capital Cases at DePaul. The Illinois Supreme Court had granted Madison the right to a hearing on newly discovered evidence, but at the hearing, the judge denied us a new trial. We were working on an appeal of that ruling and, simultaneously, had petitioned Governor Ryan for a full pardon.

The governor, a lifelong supporter of capital punishment, had not informed any of us at DePaul what he was going to say that day in January. That he had chosen to give the speech at our center was a good sign, but I was anxious nonetheless. In addition to dealing with requests for seats and the needs of seventeen live news feeds, I had been talking to Madison on the phone every day. After sixteen years of imprisonment, including thirteen and a half years on death row, he was caught now in the tension between hope and the memory of previous disappointments.

After I introduced the governor to the crowd, the plainspoken former pharmacist began to summarize what he had learned since he had taken office:

"Three years ago, I was faced with startling information. We had exonerated not one, not two, but thirteen men from death row... The state nearly killed innocent people, nearly injected them with a cocktail of deadly poisons so that they could die in front of witnesses on a gurney in the state's death chamber."

He went on to describe those who remained sentenced to death:

"Thirty-three death row inmates were represented at trial by attorneys who had later been disbarred or at some point suspended from practicing law. Of the more than 160 death row inmates, 35 are African-American defendants who were convicted or condemned to die by all-white juries. More than two thirds of the inmates on death row are African-American. Forty-six inmates were convicted on the basis of testimony from jailhouse informants.

"I'm not a lawyer, but I don't think you need to be one to be appalled by those statistics. I have one question. How does that happen?"

The governor told Madison Hobley's story as an example of how it happens, one defendant at a time. Because Madison had survived the disastrous apartment fire in which his wife and son died, he became an immediate suspect. He was grilled by detectives who tied a typewriter cover over his head in an attempt to get a confession. The only written record they came away with was his denial. Nevertheless, a detective claimed that coffee had spilled on Madison's purported confession, and the wet document had been thrown away. The governor went on to recount the planted evidence, tainted eyewitness testimony, and jury intimidation.

"Madison Hobley was convicted on the basis of flawed evidence," he concluded. "He was convicted because the jury did not have the benefit of all existing evidence, which would have served to exonerate him. So Madison Hobley has sat on death row and waited, waited for justice."

I could only imagine this coming to one conclusion, but I didn't dare take my eyes off the podium. Finally, asserting that a "manifest injustice" had occurred, Governor Ryan announced the full pardon of Madison Hobley, as well as three other death row inmates wrongfully convicted.

Arnie and I drove to the prison in Pontiac to pick up Madison. We brought him to our home, where he stayed for a week. That first night, we cooked everything he loved: fried chicken, mashed potatoes, green beans, and chocolate cake. Former and current students, and others who had worked on his case, joined us. After dinner, Madison sat on our couch next to his mother, holding her hand. Seeing him there gave me as much satisfaction as I have known in my life.

The next day, at Northwestern, Governor Ryan commuted the sentences of all the remaining death row inmates in Illinois to life without parole.

In the whirlwind of publicity following these events, Madison and I appeared together on *The Oprah Winfrey Show*. During a break, Ms. Winfrey talked to us about her own visit to death row. She and her cameras had been given access to the row itself (even though Amnesty International and lawyers like me had only ever been allowed in the visiting room; she *is* Oprah, after all). She told us of her surprise at discovering that the inmates condemned to death were people like any others, that they encompassed strengths and weaknesses, dreams and frustrations, beyond the crimes for which they had been convicted. Her words took me aback. Winfrey is one of the savviest women in our country, someone acutely aware of the effects of child abuse and poverty on the human spirit — and this revelation had surprised her? She hadn't already understood the myriad forces that bring people to death row? On that day, I determined to write this book.

Because of Governor Ryan's courageous actions, many people believe that the death penalty has been abolished in Illinois. This is not the case. As of this book's publication, fourteen men have been sent to death row in the state since Ryan's commutations. Many face death penalty prosecutions still.

Nevertheless, some things have changed. Fewer juries are imposing death — not just here in Illinois, but nationwide. The public has become understandably wary of wrongful convictions. But I also believe that attorneys are doing a better job of defending capital cases. Defense lawyers receive specialized training at places such as the Darrow Death Penalty Defense College we run at DePaul. Law school clinics have begun to have an impact, too. They train law students and lawyers to see a case not just in terms of legal and technical issues, but from their clients' perspectives, with an understanding of their clients' lives. My students investigate, write motions, develop mitigating evidence, discuss the politics as well as the law behind court decisions, and learn with me about the humanity of the people we represent. The better we tell our clients' stories, the less likely juries are to decide that death is the answer.

The work is exhausting and often heartbreaking. It takes enormous effort to drag the courts, sometimes against staggering opposition, toward what is fair and humane. And to me, fair and humane is the definition of justice. We may never arrive at a state that perfectly balances these two concepts, but we affirm our own humanity in the attempt.

ACKNOWLEDGMENTS

I WANT TO THANK a lot of people who helped me with this book, but I want to start with my editor and friend Christine Intagliata—a fine writer in her own right—who helped me in too many ways to enumerate. I want to thank my agent, Regina Ryan, my attorney, Todd Musberger and all of the wonderful people at Kaplan Publishing who worked with me to make this happen—most especially my editor there, Shannon Berning.

I also want to acknowledge my colleagues and fellow teachers at the National Criminal Defense College who have encouraged me in so many ways, my present and former colleagues in the criminal defense bar, especially at the public defender's office, and my colleagues where I am privileged to teach, the DePaul University College of Law.

I want to also acknowledge my family—for their support in spite of their occasional misgivings of my chosen work. My daughter Samantha and my son Will, I thank you both for understanding the long hours and the worry and occasional obsessive behavior. And my husband Arnie, thanks for putting up with me typing away in the car when we were supposed to be on vacation, and for always listening and understanding that this is not just what I do, but who I am.

READER'S GUIDE

Discussion Questions for Book Groups

1. Andrea Lyon believes that, as a woman, she brought a different style to criminal defense. What characterized her style? Do you believe the differences were gender-based? Do you think gender-based differences still exist in professions such as law and medicine?

2. Andrea states that her physical size is a significant part of her identity. How do you think it affected her professional life? What are other ways in which you have seen a person's appearance affect his or her career?

3. In Chapter 2, Andrea struggles with her client's tolerance of her husband's abuse. If a battered woman continues to live with a man who harms her, do you believe she can be reasonably excused for later killing him?

4. In both Chapters 3 and 11, Andrea makes decisions counter to the wishes of her clients. Under what circumstances, if ever, is it valid for a defense attorney to override a client?

5. Imagine one of these cases, such as the Lincoln Freeman case in Chapter 4, told from the prosecution's perspective. How might it differ from Andrea's version?

6. Do you think Andrea's assessments of her clients are accurate? In Chapters 4, 6 and 12, for instance, she believes her clients are totally innocent of any crime. How do you think she came to those conclusions, and do you believe they are reliable?

7. Andrea consistently decries bigotry on the part of judges, but then, in Chapter 5, allows a judge's bias to work for the benefit of her client. Could she have made a different choice?

8. Imagine you are a family member of a victim in one of Andrea's cases. How would you feel about Jose Medrano eventually going free in Chapter 6? How would you react to Thomas Sewell's life sentence without parole in Chapter 10?

9. In Chapter 7, the police imply to the mother of a dead child that she could attend her daughter's funeral if she confesses to the murder. Under what circumstances do you believe police are justified in using physically and/or psychologically coercive techniques? Should police be allowed to lie, such as telling suspects that their fingerprints have been discovered at the scene of the crime?

10. Can you imagine defending people accused of terrible crimes? Are there particular crimes that would be most difficult for you, such as the alleged murder of a child in Chapter 7 or the murder of parents as in Chapter 8?

11. To what extent should mitigating factors affect a defendant's sentence? Should an abusive childhood, such as that suffered by Richard Bauman in Chapter 9 for instance, result in a lesser sentence for murder?

12. In Chapter 12, Andrea defends a woman who spends years in prison for a crime Andrea and many others believe she did not commit. Can you imagine finding yourself in Deirdre's situation? How do you think people stay sane under those circumstances?

13. Many unconscious biases seem to be embedded in people. Given that, how can we make our criminal justice system fair? What beliefs might make you a juror Andrea would want to excuse? What beliefs might make you a juror the prosecution would want to excuse?

14. Have you ever been involved in a criminal case or served on a jury? How was your experience similar to or different from Andrea's descriptions of the process?

15. Andrea believes that the state is never justified in taking a life, no matter what the crime. Do you believe a death penalty is sometimes warranted? Under what circumstances? And why do you think the United States, alone among developed countries, executes people?

ABOUT THE AUTHOR

ANDREA D. LYON is Director of the Center for Justice in Capital Cases and Clinical Professor of Law, Associate Dean for Clinical Programs, at DePaul University College of Law. She began her career at the Cook County Public Defenders' Office, working her way up to Chief of the Homicide Task Force, a 22-lawyer unit that represents people accused of homicide.

Lyon has tried more than 130 homicide cases, both within the public defender's office and elsewhere. She has defended more than 30 potential capital cases at the trial level. Of these, she has taken 19 through the penalty phase, and won them all. She lives in Chicago, Illinois.